THE ENGLISH KITCHEN

JELLIES & THEIR MOULDS

Frontispiece. Classic jellies of the Victorian period: (1) Mosaic of lemon jelly and custard, 1891; (2) Oranges à la Bellevue, 1855; (3) Timbale à la Versailles, 1891; (4) Ribbon jelly, 1855; (5) Macédoine jelly, 1855; (6) Bavaroise à la Impériale, 1891; (7) Jelly à l'Andalouse, c. 1900; (8) Rice à la Parisienne, 1888.

JELLIES
&
THEIR MOULDS

PETER BREARS

PROSPECT BOOKS

2010

First published in 2010 by Prospect Books,
Allaleigh House, Blackawton, Totnes, Devon TQ9 7DL.

British Library Cataloguing in Publication Data:
A catalogue entry for this book is available from the British Library.

ISBN 978-1-903018-76-7

Typeset by Tom Jaine.

Printed and bound in Malta by Gutenburg Press Ltd.

CONTENTS

List of illustrations   6

Acknowledgements   9

Introduction   11

CHAPTER ONE
Of Gelatin   17

CHAPTER TWO
Of Jellies, Gums & Starches   35

CHAPTER THREE
Medieval Jellies   53

CHAPTER FOUR
Tudor Jellies   63

CHAPTER FIVE
Stuart Jellies   71

CHAPTER SIX
Georgian Jellies   83

CHAPTER SEVEN
Victorian Jellies & their Moulds   117

CHAPTER EIGHT
The Twentieth Century & its Moulds   181

CHAPTER NINE
The Repertoire   221

Bibliography   239

General index   243

Recipe index   250

LIST OF ILLUSTRATIONS

Colour plates   between pp. 96 and 97
i.   A seventeenth-century laid tart or tart royal, filled with jellies.
ii   Mrs Raffald's jellies of the 1760s.
iii *Oranges en Rubans* or *à la Bellevue* were introduced in the Regency, but remained a Victorian favourite.
iv   Louis Ude published a recipe for this marbled cream in 1813
v   The Belgrave mould of 1850 introduced spiral columns of coloured creams into jelly.
vi   The Brunswick Star mould of 1864 (left) and the Alexandra Cross mould of 1863 both used inner liners to form internal star- and cross-shaped columns of white jelly.
vii Mrs A.B. Marshall's mosaic jelly of 1891 is lined with rings of set custard.
viii Some High Victorian jellies.

Drawings and reproductions
Frontispiece: Classic jellies of the Victorian period   2

1. Advertisements for 'patent' gelatines   18
2. Medieval jellies   54
3. Stuart jellies   72
4. Georgian jellies   84
5. Georgian leaches   88
6. Elizabeth Raffald's jellies, 1769   94
7. Wedgwood moulds   97
8. Georgian moulds   100
9. Regency jellies   105
10. Prints of mould-makers' factories   118
11, 12, 13. Minton jelly moulds   150–152

14. W.T. Copeland & Sons' catalogue of shapes   154
15, 16, 17. Copper jelly moulds, from the catalogue
    of Herbert Benham & Co.   156–158
18, 19. Copper jelly moulds, from the catalogue
    of A.F. Leale   160–161
20. Late nineteenth-century makers' and retailers' stamps
    found on copper jelly moulds   162
21. Specimen page from Mrs Marshall's *Book of Moulds*   163
22. Moulds for specific Victorian jellies   168
23. The rib mould   172
24. Moulds designed by Alexis Soyer before 1846   173
25. Tinplate moulds made by J.H. Hopkins & Son   175
26. Tinplate moulds made by Sellman & Hill   178
27. Tinplate moulds from Mrs Marshall's *Book of Moulds*   179
28. Stoneware and pottery moulds from Pearson & Co.,
    Joseph Bourne & Son, Pountney & Co., and Leeds   182
29. Moulds from the catalogue of C.T. Maling & Sons   197
30. Shelley moulds of 1922; new shapes introduced
    by Spode *c.* 1902–1910 and 2002   198
31. Earthenware moulds made by Burgess & Leigh
    and by Joseph Unwin & Co.   201
32. Tinned steel jelly moulds from E.T. Everton   202
33, 34, 35. Tinned steel jelly moulds from
    Treliving & Smith, ironmongers   204–206
36. White-enamelled steel moulds by Orme,
    Evans & Co., Macfarlane & Robinson, and
    J.A. Bratt & Sons   208
37. Aluminium jelly moulds, 1920s and 1930s   210
38. 'Diamond Aluminium Ware' moulds   211
39. Plastic moulds and aluminium moulds, 1930s–2010   213
40. Jellies in orange peels   217
41. Moulded rice dishes of around 1900   222

ACKNOWLEDGEMENTS

I would first like to thank the Gelatine Manufacturers of Europe, who, through Team Saatchi and its representative Beverley Wigg, asked me to organize the first British Jelly Festival in 1995, and to thank Chivers who asked me to lead the week-long events which culminated in Ireland's first National Jelly Day in 1996. These projects concentrated the mind on a previously neglected area of our culinary heritage to such a degree that my life appeared to be dominated by jelly for several years. The success of these events would not have been possible, however, without considerable practical help from my friends Marc and B. Meltonville, Richard Fitch and Robin Mitchener, and the cooperation of Diana Owen of the National Trust's Petworth House in Sussex, Terry Suthers, Director of Harewood House Trust in Yorkshire and Richard Pailthorpe, manager of the Duke of Northumberland's seat at Syon House, Middlesex. Chivers' in-house staff could not have been more helpful, nor the cooks at Dublin Zoo, who welcomed me into their kitchens. Particular thanks are also due Rosie Allan at The North of England Open Air Museum at Beamish for her great help when researching mould-manufacturers' catalogues and to Pam Woolescroft of Spode for access to the catalogues and other resources in their collections.

I would also like to extend my warmest thanks to Mrs Susan Houghton for contributing so much to this book, and my publisher Tom Jaine for the care he has taken in putting it into production. Finally, I must thank the late Peter Williams, one of the finest still-life and food photographers of his generation, for his work at the Jelly Festivals where we first met. His great skills in composition and lighting are self evident on the front cover and elsewhere in this volume.

Peter Brears,
Leeds 2010

INTRODUCTION

Today's jellies tend to fall into the cheap and cheerful category of food. You can buy a basic pack of soluble flavoured jelly squares for 9p in some supermarkets, and it only takes a couple of minutes to dissolve them in hot water, pour them into a bowl and leave them to set to provide a treat for the kids. This approach is economical, trouble-free and efficient, but it completely undervalues and underplays the true potential of probably our most versatile and exciting of foodstuffs.

Jellies are unique in their range of physical properties. Although they are virtually tasteless, they can instantly absorb any chosen flavour drawn from fruits and spices, as well as readily dissolving sugars, wines and spirits throughout their mass. Having no texture of their own, they can take on those of creams, cereals, fruit purées, ground nuts and many other things, or they can be whipped up into foams. They can also be used to embed fresh, preserved or candied fruits, or stiff custards and other jellies of contrasting flavour and colour. Being colourless at the outset, they immediately take on the widest variety of tones, tinctures and degrees of opacity as imparted by all manner of edible liquids and colourings. They have no shape of their own, but take on the shape of any mould or vessel into which they are poured. This list of attributes is already impressive, but has yet to include their final most important and unique characteristics. The first of these is perfect transparency. No other food is so capable of allowing light to pass through it, reflected and refracted by the facets of its outer surfaces. The second is dynamic movement, the wobble factor, always a delight to the eye. The third, just as important, is their capacity to slowly release their flavours and textures into the mouth, prolonging the pleasure and appreciation of ingredients which otherwise would be much more rapidly swallowed.

Over the last seven hundred years generations of cooks have laboured hard and long to convert the most unpromising of waste animal products into the finest luxurious, succulent, attractive and delicious high-status jellies. In the courts of medieval and Tudor England, they were only served at the tables of kings, queens, princes and nobles, so great was their prestige. Their use then slowly percolated to the gentry class below, before entering into general use with the introduction of prepared gelatins in the mid-nineteenth century.

My first detailed study of early jellies started in 1995 with a 'phone call from Beverley Wigg of Team Saatchi, who had been commissioned by the Gelatine Manufacturers of Europe to promote jelly-making in the home. The approach was to be historical, restoring the lost status of jellies by recreating the most impressive examples in the kitchens of great country houses. Unfortunately, it seemed no-one knew anything about early jellies, and no country-house owners were interested in the project. Having myself researched, trialled and published some initial studies of jellies, as well as being involved in the restoration of some large country-house kitchens, I was asked to meet the clients and see what could be done. The result was Britain's first Jelly Festival, which took place at Petworth House, Sussex, in the first week of August 1995.

Living and working in the original servants' quarters, we spent a few days recreating the most interesting jellies made between the 1390s and 1930s, only to discover that virtually none had set sufficiently to be turned out, since this was one of the hottest summers on record. Much re-melting and re-moulding with stronger gelatins followed, so that there were approaching a hundred jellies ranged along the great kitchen table and dressers on the first morning. As soon as the doors opened and members of the public began to flow through, it was obvious that it was going to be a great success. Everyone looked remarkably happy, grandparents seeing jellies which brought back memories of past events which had involved jellies, and children looking in wide-eyed wonder at the jelly lions or bunny-rabbits feasting on jelly grass and carrots. There was also great conversation between the generations, and lots of repartee between visitors and cooks. The message was clear, English people still love a good jelly. So do the press.

Both national and local media were 'All of a Quiver!' with these 'Jelly Japes', 'Shaking all over' as we were 'Breaking the Mould', explaining 'The Shape of Things to Come' in this 'Perfect Setting'. The festival was 'Jelly Good Fun' and we were all 'Jelly Good Fellows', going 'Great Shakes' and even 'Throwing a Wobbly!' Such raucous reportage was just what was needed. Jelly was back in the news. This event lasted a week, and was enjoyed by many hundreds of visitors, similar crowds coming to subsequent festivals at Harewood House near Leeds over Easter 1996, and at Syon House over Easter 1997. In the meantime *Country Life* informed me that I was now one of their 'Living National Treasures' as a 'Traditional English Jelly-maker', later, thankfully, modified to 'Food Historian'.

About this time, late one evening, someone with a deep and strong Northern Irish accent 'phoned to ask, 'Are you the jelly person?' This sent a shiver down my spine. In the mid-1970s I had stood in my museum and watched the minutes tick by the deadline for an IRA bomb threat, which the British security forces had informed me was probably real; did the man want 'jelly' or 'gelli'? On asking who was calling, I was told it was Chivers of Ireland: 'Could you do for the Irish jelly what you've done for the English jelly?' The result was one of the most enjoyable of all jelly experiences. It was arranged for me to do a week of historic jelly demonstrations in an elegant Georgian town-house hotel in Dublin in July 1996, with full media coverage. Just before departing, Chivers rang to confirm the arrangements, then announcing that the venue had been changed.

'Why?'

'The orang-utan!' Apparently this recently-born primate had been rejected by its parents and was being nurtured by the keepers. 'It's in bed with them, wearing nappies, feeding from the bottle, and loads of folk are going to see it, so we've cancelled your place at the hotel, and put you in the Zoo with the monkeys.'

Although unexpected, this was good promotional policy. Over the next week, the staff at Dublin Zoo's kitchens gave me a great welcome, a bench to myself, and full access to their fine refrigerated larder. It was hard work, but enormous fun; punctuated by demonstration sessions for the food-writers of Ireland and the nation's media, the most delightfully enthusiastic and intelligent of audiences. The long tables of jellies, both English and Irish, created much interest and conversation, 'Why had I adopted such an injellyectual approach?'

The television reporter from RTE couldn't understand why a foaming pint of Guinness stood amid the jellies.

'What's the black stuff doing there?'

'It's a jelly.'

'No it isn't – its the Black Stuff – I should know.'

'It's a jelly.'

'Prove it.'

At this point the glass was turned upside down, the Guinness and its foam remaining firmly in place.

'Dear God! The Englishman has jellified the Guinness! Why, on earth would anyone want to do a thing like that?'

Its potential for being consumed while lying helplessly horizontal at the end of a night of social inebriation was then explained, the point taken, the new product sampled, and pronounced good.

Surely no other foodstuff could ever create such careless happiness, frivolity and enjoyment. However, jelly has its serious side too. I published the first outline study of its seven-hundred year history as 'Transparent Pleasures – The Story of the Jelly' in *Petits Propos Culinaires,* volumes 53 and 54, in 1996–7. This went on to win the Oxford Symposium on Food and Food History's Sophie Coe Prize in 1997. The present book extends the story and provides greater detail. In order to be as practical as possible, the majority of the historic recipes have been re-written in modern form, but follow closely the working methods and proportions of ingredients in the original texts. Where gelatin was specified, the same proportions have been retained, although they may need to be adapted to meet the setting qualities of modern gelatin, or particular temperature conditions when serving. Where the earlier recipes start off with calf's feet, hart's horn, ivory dust or isinglass, however, their place has been taken by an appropriate quantity of gelatin as a workable alternative.

The recipes are arranged in approximate date order, convenient for those who wish to make jellies to form part of a recreated meal of any chosen period. The same approach is taken for the moulds. Reproductions of pages from manufacturers' and retailers' catalogues also offer a substantial amount of new information for all those who collect them as a hobby. Where moulds are known to have been made for the production of a particular jelly, the associated recipe is also given, thus uniting the frequently disparate worlds of the cook and the collector.

CHAPTER ONE

OF GELATIN

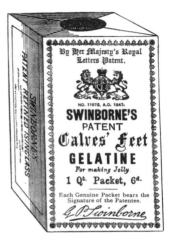

For a Cheaper Jelly

NELSON'S TABLET JELLIES,

Which are manufactured from the very finest ingredients, and are absolutely unsurpassable for brilliancy and delicacy of flavour.

Made in the following flavours :— **Calf's Foot, Lemon. Orange, Vanilla, Raspberry, Cherry and Pineapple.**

OR

NELSON'S GRANULATED JELLIES,

Lemon, Orange, Vanilla, Calf's Feet, Raspberry and Cherry

In Pint and Quart Packets.

Will be found perfectly pure and wholesome, and the flavours excellent, while their exceeding cheapness brings them within the reach of all classes.

NELSON'S SPECIALITIES

By Royal   Letters Patent.

For First-Class Jellies

NELSON'S OPAQUE, BRILLIANT,

OR POWDERED GELATINE

SHOULD ALWAYS BE USED.

Figure 1. Advertisements such as these promoted the use of improved 'patent' gelatines in the mid-nineteenth century.

The substance which is the basis of the jellies into which certain animal tissues (skin, tendons, ligaments, the matrix of bones, etc.) are converted when treated by hot water for some time. It is amorphous, brittle, without taste or smell, transparent, and of a faint yellow tint; and is composed of carbon, hydrogen, nitrogen, oxygen, and sulphur.

This definition provided by the *Oxford English Dictionary* covers all the essential characteristics of this remarkable substance.[1] It is based on collagen, a stiff fibrous protein found in all animal skin and connective tissue. Instead of being a single molecule it has three separate molecules twisted around each other like strands in a rope to form a triple helix structure, tough and almost inedible. Only by heating the collagen above some 70°C does the helix unwind, its separate strand-like molecules interacting with each other to form a random three-dimensional network. This holds the surrounding water in place, making it behave more like a solid than a liquid, in other words, a jelly. This process is closely governed by temperature, the molecules separating every time they exceed about 30°C, and re-connecting when they fall beneath about 15°C, phenomena we know as melting and setting.[2] If raw egg-whites, for instance, are mixed into the melted jelly and then heated, they form permanent molecular links with the gelatin strands and so form a jelly which cannot be re-melted. Similarly the addition of certain enzymes, such as those in fresh pineapple or kiwi fruit, can break down the links in the gelatin structure, causing it to become unsettable.

(1) *O.E.D. sv* Gelatin.
(2) Barham, 22–23.

Medieval cooks were certainly ignorant of the scientific explanation behind the formation of jelly, but this did not prevent them from developing considerable skill in its preparation. When any of their meats and fishes with a high collagen content had been boiled to tenderness and then allowed to cool, they could not fail to have noticed how they set to firmness, the fats rising to the surface and the sediment dropping to the bottom. Once tasted, they would appreciate the pleasure of feeling it melt on their tongues, the flavours it released and the satisfying glutinous smoothness it left in the mouth. From this stage it would take little ingenuity to start to make jelly not as a by-product, but as a dish in its own right.

Probably the earliest English recipe for 'jelly' comes from a manuscript written in the first quarter of the fourteenth century:[3]

> Gelee. Vihs isodeen in win & water & saffron & paudre of gynger & kanele, galingal, & beo idon in a vessel ywryen clanlicke; ye colour quyte.

Experience shows that this method of just cooking fish in white wine, saffron, ginger, cinnamon and galingal only produces a spicy fish stew, nothing remotely resembling anything we could ever describe as a jelly. A further recipe of about 1381 is similarly unpromising:[4]

> For to make mete gelee that it be wel chariaunt, tak wyte wyn & a perty of water & saffroun & gode spicis & flesh of piggys or of hennys, or fresch fisch, & boyle tham togedere; & after, wan yt ys boylyd & cold, dres yt in dischis & serve forthe.

This thick pork or chicken stew might just hold itself together in a serving dish, if the weather was cold, but again lacks sufficient gelatin to produce a good jelly. However, the same manuscript also contains the following:[5]

(3) Hieatt & Butler, I 26.
(4) ibid., II 36.
(5) ibid., I 56.

For to make a gely, tak hoggys fet other pyggys, other erys, other pertrichys, othere chiconys, & do hem togedere & seth hem in a pot; & do in hem flowre of canel and clowys hole or grounde. Do thereto vinegere, & tak & do the broth in a clere vessel of all thys, & tak the flesch & kerf yt in smale morselys & do yt therein. Tak powder of gelyngale & cast above & lat yt kele. Tak bronchys of ye lorere tre & styk over it, & kep yt al so longe as thou wilt & serve yt forth.

This is an excellent recipe, one which any traditional farmer's wife or pork butcher would immediately recognize as a stiff, jellied brawn. The feet and ears or porkers and suckling pigs were among the best sources of gelatin, giving a rich, glutinous stock. Proof of how successful this recipe would be is provided by the following version published almost six hundred years later in *The Farmer's Weekly*. It was sent in by Mrs H.M. Diamond of Worcestershire.[6]

2 pig's feet, 1lb of shoulder steak, ham scraps ... pepper, salt. Stew the ... pig's feet very slowly with the shoulder steak and ham scraps. Season with pepper and salt. When thoroughly cooked cut up the meat into small pieces, and pour with the liquor into a mould which has been well rinsed in cold water, then leave to set and turn out next day... This dish is economical and easily prepared – which is what we require in these days when, as farmers' wives, it is necessary to consider expenses and our time.

The first evidence of care being taken to ensure that jelly stock was being filtered and reduced separately to ensure good clarity and firmness comes from recipes such as the following of around 1390. After being well boiled with the meat or fish, the stock was to be passed:[7]

thurgh a cloth in to an erthen panne ... Lat it seeth [boil or simmer] & skym it wel. Whan it is ysode [boiled], dof

(6) Hargreaves, 244.
(7) Hieatt & Butler, IV 104.

the grees clene: cowche [the flesh or fish] on chargours
& cole the sewe thorow a cloth onoward & serve it forth
colde.

The jellies served at the earl of Derby's table were certainly
being clarified by careful filtration at this time, his accounts
for 1393 recording money spent:[8] 'ex prop iii vergis tele pro i
gelecloth xviii*d*.'

The late fourteenth century saw the first documented use
of calf's feet as a source of gelatin, this appearing in a recipe
in the *Forme of Curye* 'compiled of the chef Maister Cokes of
kyng Richard the Se[cu]nde ... the best and ryallest vyaund[er]
of alle cristen [K]ynges.'[9] By the fifteenth century calf's feet
were being used to create a clear firm-setting jelly stock which
was then used as a separate culinary medium in its own right.
In some recipes small chickens and the sides of sucking pigs
were poached in it, the stock then being re-warmed, flavoured,
coloured, skimmed, strained and eventually poured over the
jointed meat in a dish, and left to set. To check if the stock would
form a jelly, the cook was advised to 'put thin[e] hande ther-
on; & if thin[e] hand waxe clammy; it is a syne of godenesse.'[10]
In others, the jelly stock was mixed with almond milk, sugar
and colourings to create what was then called Vyaunde leche, a
'sliceable food',[11] and, in later centuries, blancmange.

Obviously calfs-foot jelly could not be consumed on fish days,
when the Church banned the eating of meat. These included
every Friday, (the day of the crucifixion), Saturday (dedicated
to the Virgin Mary) and Wednesday (when Judas accepted the
thirty pieces of silver). If jellies were to be served on these days,
they would have to be based on a strong fish stock. Instead of
calf's feet, barbell, conger eel, plaice or thornback were boiled
in fish stock until they would jellify. To test this, the cook was
to 'take up som thereof, & pour hit on the breed of a disch, &
let hit be cold; & ther thu shall se where it be chargeaunt; or
els take more fisch that woll gely, & put hit theryn.'[12] If it still

(8) *O.E.D. sv* Jelly.
(9) Hieatt & Butler,
    IV 105.
(10) Austin, 25, no.
    cix.
(11) ibid., 37, no. xvii.
(12) Hieatt, 74–5.

JELLIES & THEIR MOULDS

would not set, another contemporary recipe advised further simmering with 'Soundys of watteryd Stokkefysshe, or ellys Skynnys, or Plays.' The 'sounds' were swim-bladders, at this time those of the cod, which were already being used to mix fine paints and make glue for book-binding in the fourteenth and fifteenth centuries. They were ideal for making jellies too.[13]

By the end of the medieval period the techniques for making clear gelatinous stocks were thoroughly understood and practised in all major kitchens. The use of 'jelly' as a word to describe those versions containing pieces of cooked meat or fish was now rapidly falling out of common parlance. From now on it was to be restricted to the clarified, sweetened and flavoured varieties which we still recognize as jellies today. Most jellies remained relatively flaccid, however, lying dormant either in or on their dishes, even those cut in slices barely standing up by themselves, and being totally unable to maintain the shape given by a mould.

In the early 1500s a more effective gelling ingredient began to be imported from Europe. This was isinglass, the swim-bladder or 'sound' of the sturgeon, composed almost entirely of gelatin. It was subject to a high level of customs duty, at £1 13s. 4d. per 100 lb or 4d. the pound in 1545.[14] Most appears to have been employed in making glues and sizes, but it had certainly entered culinary use by the 1590s when Thomas Dawson instructed cooks to:[15]

Take a quart of newe milke, and three ounces weight of Isinglasse, halfe a pounde of beaten suger, and stirre them together, and let it boile half a quarter of an hower till it be thicke, stirring them al the while.

The interest in this recipe is twofold; firstly it assumes that the reader is already familiar with isinglass, suggesting that it had been used for jellymaking for some time, and secondly, it boils insinglass in milk for half an hour. In this, it exploits the

(13) *O.E.D. sv* Sound I.2.
(14) *O.E.D. sv* Isinglass 1.
(15) Dawson (1590), II 19.

great distinction between isinglass and other forms of gelatin; it can be boiled with milk without splitting it into curds and whey. This problem always occurs if a milk and gelatin solution is heated above around 70°C.

Both gelatin and isinglass continued to be the principal ingredients used for making jellies throughout the seventeenth and eighteenth centuries. The only piece of specialized equipment required for their preparation was the jelly-bag, an open-topped cone of cloth used for finely filtering the stock. They had already been made of woollen cloth, probably flannel, for centuries, the Durham Priory account roll for 1516-17 recording:[16] 'Pro una uln. Panni lanei pro le gelypoke 8*d*.'

Unless kept hot, the jelly set within them instead of dripping through. Patrick Lamb, Master Cook to Charles II, James II, William and Mary and Queen Anne, prepared his jelly bags by washing them in cold water, drying them away from any smoke, filling them with the stock, and then hanging them on a spit, apparently close to the fire, to keep their contents liquid.[17]

By the mid-eighteenth century, ladies who wished to display fine jellies on their dining tables were being offered a completely trouble-free way of acquiring them: they could buy them ready-made from a professional confectioner. In Manchester, for example, they could call at Mrs Elizabeth Raffald's at 12 Market Place for all their 'Creams, Jellies, Flummery ... which any lady may examine at pleasure ... daily, in my own shop'.[18] Her sister Mary Whitaker similarly offered 'Jellies, Creams, Flummery, Fish Ponds, Transparent Puddings' from her shop opposite the King's Head in Salford.[19] In fashionable Bath, the newspapers carried advertisements for:[20]

JOSEPH BICK, PASTRY COOK and Confectioner Remov'd from Broad-Street ... Jellies fresh every day 3*s*. per Doz. Blancmange and Jelly ornamented for Dishes, Compote, Creams ...

(16) *O.E.D. sv* Jelly.
(17) Lamb, 30–31.
(18) Raffald, xii–xiii.
(19) ibid., xv.
(20) Information from the Museum of Building, Bath.

Making a reliably clear, firm and successful jelly from basic ingredients remained a challenge for most everyday cooks and housewives. What they needed was a source of pre-prepared gelatin, one they could keep in their store cupboards and use at their convenience.

The isinglass or 'Muscovy Talc' imported from Russia most closely met these requirements. In Russia the 'nervous and mucilaginous parts of [sturgeon] were boiled to the consistency of a jelly, they spread it on a leaf of paper, and form it into cakes, in which state it is sent to us.'[21] This would form the basis of the 'Adams' prepared Isinglass' being made by John Adams of Cushion Court, Old Broad Street, London, in 1824.[22] In 1847 G.P. Swinborne took out patent no. 11975 for the purification of both isinglass and gelatin by 'the solvent power of water alone.'

In the patent, George Philbrick Swinborne, of Pimlico, stated that to date it had been the general practice to break down hides or skins with acids, alkalis and mechanical means, reducing them to pulp in a paper-grinding machine, and then clarify them with blood. In contrast, his new method took fresh hides or skins, free from hair, cut them into fine shavings, soaked them in water for five or six hours, then renewed the water two or three times each day until no smell remained. Having been drained, they were put into a vessel with hot, not boiling water, to extract the gelatin, which was then either run off as a clear solution, or strained through a linen cloth on to beds of slate to set. Next it was hung up in nets to dry and finally cut up for packaging.

For his isinglass, cod sounds or other gelatinous parts of fish were treated in the same manner.

To confirm the quality of their products, Swinborne's published a report commissioned from Professor W.T. Brande, F.R.S. and J.T. Cooper, the leading analytical chemists of the day. They stated that the 'Patent Refined Isinglass' was 'perfectly clear from colour, taste and smell; makes a clear solution in

(21) Rees sv Isinglass.
(22) BL 1801 d 2(5), quarto advertisement.

hot water, leaves no deposit [and] is stronger, firmer, and more durable than that prepared from the same proportions of Russian Isinglass.' As for the gelatin: 'though it is not so free from colour nor so powerful a gelatiniser, yet it can be produced at a much lower price, may become very generally useful, especially as if kept dry it will undergo no change in any climate ... there are many other Gelatines in the market, which we deem objectionable.'[23]

By reprinting this report as part of a strong advertising campaign which continued over the following half century or more, Swinborne's isinglass and gelatin became one of the leading brands supplied to the wholesale and retail trade. Their products came in elegantly printed and sealed packets, those for isinglass containing one ounce, and the gelatin, enough to set a quart of liquid. The housewives and cooks who bought them were virtually guaranteed good, trouble-free and attractive jellies, especially if they followed the recipes published on the packets and in booklets such as *The Pastry Cook & Confectioner* which went through fifteen editions between 1879 and 1911.

In mid-Victorian England there was an increasing unease about all manufactured products, for adulteration was rife. In 1855 one analyst decided to buy samples of isinglass from twenty-seven of the leading London grocers and Italian warehousemen, to see if they were genuine. Those of Fortnum & Mason of Picadilly passed the test, selling it for 1s 2d the ounce, so did:

VICKERS
GENUINE RUSSIAN ISINGLASS
FOR INVALIDS AND CULINARY USE

This article is guaranteed to be prepared from the pure Russian isinglass, as imported, and has not undergone any other process besides being passed through rollers and cut into shreds, for the purpose of making it soluble. Purchasers who are desirous of protecting themselves from the adulteration which is now extensively practised

(23) Howard, 1–2.

are recommended to ask for "VICKERS' GENUINE RUSSIAN ISINGLASS" in sealed packets (containing one ounce, two ounces, a quarter of a pound, or one pound), that being the surest guarantee for their always obtaining a really PURE AND UNADULTERATED ARTICLE.

FACTORY, 23 LITTLE BRITAIN, LONDON.

The results of the analysis confirmed the need for caution. More than a third of the suppliers fobbed off customers seeking isinglass with cheap gelatin which ought to have cost around 6*d*. the ounce, instead charging up to 1*s*. 4*d*. the ounce thus more than doubling their profits. Clearly it was worthwhile to buy a branded isinglass with an impeccable reputation, such as Swinborne's. However, when the chemist bought a sealed packet of 'SWINBORNE'S PATENT REFINED ISINGLASS' from Sidney, Manduell, & Wells of 8 Ludgate Hill, he found it contained nothing but ordinary gelatin. Swinborne's, however, carried on publishing the 1847 guarantee of purity, and promoting their gelatin 'isinglass'. Effective legislation to counteract such substitution was some years away from enactment.

In her *Book of Household Management* of 1861, Mrs Beeton continued to give directions for making calf's foot and cow-heel jellies, the latter requiring an eight-hour boil and at least forty-five minutes to clarify. Her recipe for isinglass or gelatin jellies still required their stocks to be boiled, have the scum removed and then be filtered through a jelly-bag, since most still varied so much in quality and strength:[24]

The best isinglass is brought from Russia, some of an inferior kind is brought from North and South America and the East Indies; the several varieties may be had from the wholesale dealers in isinglass in London. In choosing isinglass for domestic use, select that which is whitest, has no unpleasant odour, and which dissolves

(24) Beeton, 708–711.

most readily in water ... If the isinglass is adulterated with gelatin ... in boiling water the gelatine will not so completely dissolve as the isinglass; in cold water it becomes clear and jelly-like, and in vinegar it will harden.

Such problems could be avoided by buying either a pure, reliable brand, or a sealed bottle of ready-made and flavoured jelly. The latter had only to be uncorked, stood in a pan of hot water until completely dissolved, and poured into a freshly-rinsed mould.

From this period many companies made gelatins for domestic use, some of them being closely linked to the leather industry, the by-products of which provided the necessary raw ingredients. In Leeds, the centre of the British leather trade, William Oldroyd & Sons made the 'Finest Powdered Calf Gelatine, Quality Unequalled' at their massive Scott Hall Mills which they depicted in the frontispiece of their promotional recipe booklet.[25] Such products were now in widespread use, even though:[26]

It [was] within the memory of many persons that jelly was at one time only to be made from Calf's Feet by a slow, difficult, and expensive process. There is indeed a story told of the wife of a lawyer early in the [nineteenth] century having appropriated some valuable parchment deeds to make jelly when she could not procure Calf's Feet. But the secret that it could be so made was carefully guarded by the possessors of it.

The first company to promote the use of skin-based gelatins on a large scale was G. Nelson, Dale & Co. of Emscote Mills in Warwick. From 1881 it published a 124-page red cloth-covered hardback recipe book entitled *Nelson's Home Comforts* containing recipes for its products, as well as pages of advertisements for its:

(25) Oldroyd, 1–2.
(26) Nelson, 3–4.

BOTTLED CONCENTRATED JELLIES
Invaluable to Invalids, Made in the following flavours;
Calf's Foot, Lemon, Sherry, Port, Orange and Cherry.

Patent Opaque Gelatine ... sold in packets from 6d to
7/6d'

Powdered Gelatine ... dissolves readily in boiling water
... 1 lb. tins 3/3, ½ lb. 1/9, ¼ lb. 1/-

Leaf Gelatine, IN VARIOUS QUALITIES. For
all who have been in the habit of using Foreign Leaf
Gelatines this will be found in all respects superior and
of more uniform quality and strength. In 1 lb. and ½ lb.
Packets.

Patent Refined Isinglass. Sold in 1 oz packets price 1/-

Patent Isinglass. Sold in 1oz packets. Price 8*d.*

FAMILY JELLY Box. Contains sufficient materials for
making 12 Quarts of jelly. Price 7*s.* 6*d.* each

These give a good idea of the range of prepared gelatins
available throughout the Victorian and Edwardian periods.
In addition, flavoured packet jellies were being produced by a
number of major companies which had now developed many
other new and relatively instant foodstuffs. These were to
meet the demands of hard-pressed housewives who, through
the diverse effects of industrialization, frequently lacked the
time, money and domestic skills required to make dishes in
the traditional way. Bottled sauces, gravy brownings, custard
and blancmange powders all helped, as did pre-flavoured and
sweetened packet jellies. Many were manufactured by firms
which became household names from the late Victorian period,

through to the present time. They included Alfred Bird & Sons, Chivers, William P. Hartley, Pearce, Duff, Rowntree and W. Symington, among others. Slabs of concentrated jelly which had only to be dissolved in hot water before moulding had been introduced by the 1920s. In 1932 Rowntrees moulded them into cubes. Other makers followed their lead, jelly cubes rapidly becoming the standard form in which prepared jellies were sold to the public throughout the twentieth century.

Given all the technical advances of the last two hundred years, it might be thought that nothing could be easier than to buy a packet jelly, dissolve it in water, pour it into a mould, leave it to set, and then simply turn it out. However, those who attempt to do so are almost certain to face failure and disappointment. The main problem is that most cube jellies made up with the specified quantity of liquid are far too weak to stand up. If made with half the specified amount of liquid, they might just stand up at room temperature, but then have flavours which are unpleasantly concentrated. The only solution is to dissolve additional gelatin in a little of the cold liquid before making up the jelly cubes with the remaining hot liquid.

TO MAKE A MOULDED JELLY FROM CUBES

1 pack jelly cubes   *1 pt / 600 ml liquid*
1–3 tsp / 2–4 leaves gelatin

Sprinkle then stir the gelatin (or cut the leaves into pieces) into 5 tbs of the liquid in a glass or clear plastic measuring jug, and leave to soak for 10 minutes. Stir to break up any lumps, add the cubes and half the remaining liquid and microwave for some 2 minutes, or gently heat in a pan, until completely dissolved. On no account must the liquid boil. Stir in the remaining liquid thoroughly, then set aside until cool, but not set, and pour into a prepared mould.

TO MAKE A MOULDED JELLY FROM GELATIN

Follow the recipe above, using 5 level tsp gelatin or 8 leaves of gelatin for each 1 pt/600 ml of liquid.

Many historic recipes give the quantity of gelatin in ounces. For these 1 oz/25 g represents 10 level tsp, or 15 standard 4½ x 3 in./11 x 7.5 cm leaves, both sufficient to set 2 pt/1.2 l of jelly suitable for moulding.

N.B. There is no such thing as a correct amount of gelatin to liquid. The main considerations to be made include:

Serving temperature. Jellies to be served in a warm room or on a hot summer's day will require more gelatin. Similarly if they are to be served chilled, directly out of a refrigerator, less will be needed.

Size. Larger jellies need proportionately more gelatin.

Shape. Packet jellies will set in a dish, bowl or glasses without any additional gelatin. A greater quantity will be required if they are to be turned out as shallow mounds, but much more if from an almost vertical-sided mould.

Ingredients. Jellies including a large proportion of fruit purée or similar thickening additives will require less gelatin. Those including alcohol will require more.

If preparing jellies for a particular occasion it is always best to make one as a sample beforehand, and adjust the recipe accordingly.

TO MOULD A JELLY

Metal moulds such as those of copper, aluminium and tinplate require no preparation.

Moulds of glass, pottery and plastic tend to stick to the jelly, even if freshly-rinsed before use.

Their interiors should therefore be given the thinnest possible coating of vegetable or walnut oil, or of butter, just before being filled with the cold but unset jelly liquid. If this is still warm, it melts the oil or butter, and absorbs it, rather than leaving it in place as a separator.

TO LINE A MOULD

For a number of recipes, particularly those of the Victorian period, it is necessary to line metal moulds with a $\frac{1}{8}$ – $\frac{1}{4}$ in./3 –7 mm all-over layer of clear jelly. To do this, embed the mould in iced water, pour in about $\frac{1}{4}$ pt/150 ml jelly (made with at least 5 tsp/8 leaves of gelatin to the pint), when just about to set, then rotate the mould at an angle, to coat both the walls and the base. If the first coat is too thin, apply another in the same way.

TO UNMOULD A JELLY

1. If using a metal mould, dip it briefly into warm water, or rapidly revolve its exterior under the flow of warm water from a tap.
2. For every mould, hold it open-side up in one hand, using the other hand to wet both the flat surface of the jelly and also the plate it is to be turned out on.
3. Tilting the mould slightly to one side, use the fingers of the free hand to ease the edges of the jelly from the mould, all round.
4. Slowly rotate the mould while tilting it further towards the

horizontal, holding it in place with the free hand, until it has fully separated, and its full weight can be felt.

5. Tilt the mould until almost upside down, still holding the jelly in place. Put part of the rim of the mould onto the plate, and slide away the fingers of the free hand, leaving the jelly to fall free onto the plate.

6. Slide the jelly into position, holding it there if necessary for about one minute for it to absorb the water beneath it, and so set itself neatly in place.

7. Other methods, such as covering with a plate, inverting, and shaking vigorously, or blasting the exterior with the flame of a blowtorch, as seen practised on television by Michelin chefs, are not to be recommended.

8. Use a straw to suck up any surplus water or liquid jelly from around its base, leaving a clean line between the jelly and the plate.

When working with gelatin, the following points should always be considered:

1. Never sprinkle gelatin into hot water, or it will form lumps which are very difficult to dissolve.

2. Never pour hot, melted gelatin into cold liquid as it may form 'strings', always mix when tepid.

3. Never use fresh kiwi fruit, figs or pineapple in jellies, since their enzymes will prevent them from setting. There is no problem if they are in the form of tinned fruit or pasteurized juice.

4. Never heat gelatin in milk over around 70°C, or it will cause it to curdle.

5. Never bring gelatin to the boil, as this weakens its gelling properties.

6. Unmould jellies just before serving.

7. Never allow a moulded jelly to fall below the freezing point, since the long ice crystals slice through the jelly, causing it to break up and collapse.

8. Jellies are best stored in cool, relatively humid conditions and eaten within a day of unmoulding. Dry conditions or a draught can cause their surfaces to dry out and become tough. Jellies also provide an ideal environment for the growth of infectious cultures, and must always be kept in clean conditions. If they are to be stored in refrigerators or larders, or transported to a venue, it is best to stretch a piece of clingfilm across the top of the mould to prevent the absorption of odours, dust, etc., or drying out.

Using these instructions it is easy to produce reliable, clear jellies. However, it is always best to try a small batch of any manufactured brand of gelatin before making larger quantities. Some have a yellowish tint, for example, and others, especially the leaf gelatines, are usually crystal clear. Some are made from bovine, and some from porcine bones or hides. In 1996 both the Spongiform Encephalopathy Advisory Committee and The World Health Organization issued reports which confirmed that manufactured gelatins were all considered safe for human consumption. They are filtered, concentrated and sterilized at approximately 140°C before drying to maintain this standard.

In addition to the major forms of gelatin considered in this chapter, there were others of lesser importance, such as hart's-horn and ivory gelatins, along with other starches and gums which were used to create moulded desserts. Their brief histories and methods of preparation will now follow.

CHAPTER TWO

OF JELLIES, GUMS & STARCHES

Jellies and blancmanges were not only reliant on calf, pig or fish gelatins, for similar rather than identical results could be obtained from a wide variety of other ingredients. Some, such as ivory and deer antlers, were animal products, but the majority were vegetable starches and gums. The flummeries thickened with fine starches extracted from oatmeal or bran which were made in Wales, the West Country and Welsh border counties for centuries were more of subsistence food than a delicacy. As one Merioneth couplet stated:[1]

Llymru llwyd da i ddim
Ond i lenwi bol rhag isho bwyd

[Pale flummery, good for nothing
But to fill the belly and suppress hunger]

From the early eighteenth century the expansion of seaborne trade with every part of the known world introduced new starches which had formed the staple diets of their distant communities. Instead of adopting their original methods of preparation, English cooks developed fresh recipes in order to produce a whole series of sweet, luscious desserts. In this way the sweet white-meat and almond blancmanges of earlier times were transformed into the moulded mixtures of starch, milk, sugar and flavourings which we recognize as blancmange today. However, not all of such dishes were to be eaten for pleasure. Some were intended for the sickroom, being considered both nutritive and easy of digestion to those with impaired appetites. The shape and enduring hardness of the elephant tusks used to

(1) Tibbott, 53–4.

make ivory jelly, as well as the deer antlers used for hartshorn jelly, were further believed to transfer their properties to gentlemen who lacked such characteristics.

The following paragraphs describe all the major gelling agents of the last 400 years, providing each with a typical recipe for its conversion into a jelly or blancmange. Quite a few are unsuitable for modern use, either because their principal ingredients are no longer available, or that, like biscuit or bread jellies, they are not required to sustain the sick. The remainder are all worth reviving, offering a range of economical, easily made and frequently vegetarian or vegan desserts. The oatmeal flummery should certainly be tried, its yoghurt-like acidity and smooth texture being an excellent foil for honey, fortified wines or thick creams.

AGAR-AGAR

In Japan the red *Gelidium* algae was gathered on marine shores and dried before being processed. Following a method reputedly developed in 1658, it was then beaten, washed, boiled, frozen and thawed, the impurities running off with the melt-water to leave the purified gum called kanten. When dried it would keep indefinitely, its use spreading from south-east Asia into Europe by the mid-nineteenth century. In England, where it was known by its Malay name of agar-agar, it was used as a domestic gelling agent up to the 1940s, when the War cut off supplies. This led to the development of alginates from other sources. The following is a typical version of the 1920s:[2]

¼ oz / 6 g agar-agar   *1 pt / 600 ml liquid*

Soak the agar-agar in ¼ pt / 150 ml cold water for 2 hours, then cut up, return to the water, and place over a low heat, stirring frequently, until it has dissolved. Stir in the remaining liquid, pour into a mould, and leave for about 1 ½ hours in a cold place to set. Turn out of mould just before serving.

(2) Beeton, (c. 1920), no. 1189.

ALGINATES

These gums are extracted from seaweeds, such as *Macrocystis pyrifera*, the Californian kelp, the genus *Laminaria* from the British coast, and various *Ascophylum* wracks. When processed, their gums are used in a wide variety of industrially-processed foods, only being used domestically as an ingredient in the squares and crystals sold for making vegetarian jellies.

AMYDON

In 1600 Richard Surflet's *Maison Rustique, or the countrie farme* described amydon as 'the best wheat meal, put into water several times so that all the bran etc. may float to the top and be skimmed off, the heavy meal being dried in the sun, broken into gobbets, and so made into fine meal.'[3] Similar instructions survive in early fifteenth-century recipe books.[4]

> For to make amydon
> Nym whete at midsomer & salt, & do it in a faire vessel, do water therto, that thy whete be yheled, let it stonde ix days & ix nyght, & everyday whess wel thy whete & at ye ix daye ende bray hit well in a morter & drie hit togenst ye sonne, do it in a faire vessel & kevere hit fort, than will it note.

> Amydon
> To mak amydon take whet and step it in water x dais and change the water evry daye then bet yt smalle in a mortair and sethe it with water and mylk and sye it throughe a cloth and let yt stond and setelle and pour out the water and lay it on a clothe and turn it till it be drye.

The result was a very fine starch, for which cornflour may be substituted for modern versions of early recipes.

(3) Surflet (1616 ed.), 572.
(4) Austin, 112; Napier, 101.

ARROWROOT

This West Indian plant, *Maranta arundinacea* produces tubers which would absorb poison from wounds, especially those of poisoned arrows, as Sir Hans Sloane noted in 1696. When a year old, they were also dug up, washed and peeled, rasped or beaten to a pulp, strained with rainwater to extract the fibrous elements, and then left for their starch to settle. Having poured off the clear water, the starch was washed and drained two or three times, spread on white cloths and set in the sun to dry.[5] The best came from the islands of Jamaica, Bermuda, St Vincent and St Kitts, retailing at up to 2*s*. 6*d*. a pound in the 1860s.[6] It had excellent gelling properties, its high reputation and price causing a number of lesser starches to be sold as 'arrowroot' during the nineteenth century. These included:

East Indian arrowroot	*curcuna starch*
Brazilian arrowroot	*cassava starch or tapioca*
Tahiti arrowroot	*tacca starch or salop*
Portland arrowroot	*from the wild herb* Arum maculatum, *'Wake Robin' or 'Lords and Ladies' found in many English hedgerows*
English arrowroot	*potato starch, for which Eliza Acton gave instructions in her* Modern Cookery *of 1855*.[7]

All those cooking with 'arrowroot' in the nineteenth century must have experienced jellies and blancmanges which were either rubbery or irretrievably liquid according to which 'arrowroot' they had purchased. Only with the passing of Acts of Parliament governing adulteration was it possible to achieve good, predictable results. This arrowroot 'shape' recipe is typical of those made in the nineteenth century:[8]

(5) O.E.D. sv
    Arrowroot',
    Garrett, I 45.
(6) Walsh, 123.
(7) Acton, 154.
(8) Garrett, I 47.

1 oz / 25 g arrowroot	*1 tbs sugar*
2 tsp orange-flower water	*pinch of ground cinnamon*
1 pt / 600 ml milk	

Beat the arrowroot to a smooth paste with the orange-flower water and a little of the milk in a saucepan. Bring the remaining milk, sugar and cinnamon to the boil and strain through a piece of freshly-rinsed muslin onto the arrowroot, while stirring. Continue stirring while simmering for 5 minutes, then pour into a buttered mould. Leave in a cold place for a few hours to set, then turn out as a jelly and serve with a cold custard sauce flavoured with vanilla or orange-flower water.

BISCUITS

Cream crackers or water biscuits were used to make a jelly which the Victorians considered to be ideal for invalids and those with a weak digestion.[9]

4 oz / 100 g cream crackers	*1 lb / 450 g sugar*
¼ tsp ground cinnamon	*4 tbs port*

Crush the cream crackers and simmer with the cinnamon and 4 pt / 2.4 l water for 60 minutes, stirring to prevent burning. Pass the liquid through a sieve into a clean pan using the edge of a metal spoon, until only the pulp remains. Rapidly boil the liquid, stirring continuously, until reduced to 1 pt / 600 ml, stir in the sugar and port, pour into a bowl, and leave to set.

BRAN

In the mid-seventeenth century Sir Kenelm Digby described how the fine particles of flour remaining in wheat bran were sufficient to convert water into a smooth, 'clear gelly'.[10] In 1726 John Nott called this dish a 'West Country Flummery', while Florence Jack published it as 'Bran Jelly' in 1914:[11]

(9) ibid., I 141.
(10) Digby, 170.
(11) Nott *sv*
Flummery; Jack,
541.

½ pt/300 ml bran, freshly sifted from wholewheat flour
juice of ½ lemon or 2 tbs each rosewater and orange-flower
water and 2 tbs sugar

Soak the bran in 1 pt/600 ml water for 3 days, then strain and squeeze off the liquid through a fine sieve or piece of muslin into a clean pan. Simmer until it forms a thick paste, then stir in the remaining ingredients.

Pour into a bowl, and serve with cream, milk, wine or ale.

BREAD

Bread jelly was a speciality of the Victorian sickroom, being 'of so strengthening a nature that 1 teaspoon does as much good as 1 tablespoon of any other.'[12]

1 large thick slice of bread	*1 tbs cream*
1 tsp sugar	*a little lemon juice or*
	grated nutmeg

Toast the bread on both sides until dry and brown, break into small pieces and simmer gently in ½ pt/300 ml water for 15 minutes, adding a little more water if required. Beat in the remaining ingredients, pour into a bowl, and serve either hot or cold.

CARRAGEEN

The purplish or reddish-green fronded seaweed *Chondrus crispus* has a long history as a coastal food in Ireland, but was only introduced into English kitchens around 1830, when, in addition to its name taken from Carragheen near Waterford, where it was particularly abundant, it became known as Irish Moss.[13] It grows around other parts of the British coast, however, as well as on the other side of the Atlantic. Domestically it was almost solely used to make a mould or blancmange:[14]

(12) Jack, 541.
(13) *O.E.D. sv*
    Carragheen.
(14) Fairclough, 625.

½ oz / 12 g dried carrageen   *1 lemon*
1 pt / 600 ml milk   *2 tbs sugar*

Cover the carrageen with plenty of water and leave to soak for
10 min. Drain the carrageen, place in a saucepan with the milk,
sugar, and finely-pared zest of the lemon, bring almost to the
boil, and simmer very gently for 15 min. while stirring. Pour the
liquid through a sieve into a jug, pressing out as much liquid as
possible with the back of a spoon, then stir in the juice of the
lemon, pour into a freshly-rinsed mould, and leave in a cool
place for a few hours to set.

CORNFLOUR

In Britain, the use of finely-ground maize or 'Indian corn' for
desserts, etc., was first promoted by Messrs Brown and Polson of
Paisley in the 1850s. From this period its use was recommended
by the very best authorities. *The Lancet*, the leading medical
journal, described it as being 'superior to anything of the kind
known' in 1858, while Dr Lankester lectured on its benefits at
the South Kensington Museum. Even Charles Francatelli, chief
cook to Queen Victoria, published recipes for its use, while
the *Illustrated London News* gave a 'Summer Recipe for Patent
Corn-flour with Preserved or Green Fruit' in 1860.[15] From this
time both Brown and Polson and other manufacturers used
cornflour to develop a wide variety of flavoured blancmange
and custard powders which were ideal for the busy cooks and
housewives of this increasingly industrialized country. However,
large quantities of the 'cornflour' sold in Britain were not made
from maize, but from very finely ground rice. There was no
attempt at deception, for leading companies such as Colman's
of Norwich clearly advertised their own brand as 'British
Cornflour (prepared from rice).'

[15] Francatelli,
(1888), 89,
421; *Illustrated
London News*
(1860), XX.

2 oz / 50 g cornflour   2 to 4 tbs sugar
1 pt / 600 ml liquid, such as strained orange, cranberry or
other fruit juice, coffee, chocolate or tea, or else milk simmered
for 5 minutes, with a vanilla pod or two bay leaves or a
stick of cinnamon, or with ½ tsp ground nutmeg or mace.
Alternatively use other essences, flavourings or food-colouring
to taste.

Put the cornflour into a basin and beat in sufficient cold liquid to produce a thin solution. Bring the remaining liquid to the boil, pour into the basin, stir, return to the pan, and stir in sugar (with 1 oz / 25 g butter if using milk). Simmer for 5 minutes, stirring continuously to prevent any sticking to the bottom and burning, then turn into freshly-rinsed moulds, basins or cups and leave in a cool place for a few hours, or overnight, until set.

Tilt the mould and ensure that none of the skin of the jelly / blancmange has stuck to the sides. Brush or sprinkle the skin all over with a little cold water, place a freshly-rinsed plate on top, and invert, allowing the jelly / blancmange to drop onto the plate. If it should stick, give the plate and mould a sharp, horizontal rotary twist, for shaking it up and down usually tears the jelly / blancmange in two, leaving half in the mould.

Remove the mould immediately and slide the jelly/blancmange into the required position, where it will rapidly absorb the water, and set itself in place.

FAROLA

James Marshall of 23 East Cumberland Street, Glasgow developed this 'highly refined preparation of Wheat, which conserves all the nutritive elements and fine flavour naturally belonging to the purest parts of the grain.' It won gold medals at the International Exhibitions in Edinburgh and Liverpool in 1886, was promoted in Mrs Marshall's recipe books, and used in the household of the Prince of Wales in the 1890s.[16] In use, it was a wheat version of cornflour.

(16) Marshall (1896), advertisements.

HARTSHORN

The use of shavings or raspings of deer-antler for making jellies was probably introduced from France in the mid-seventeenth century. Recipes are given in La Varenne's *The French Cook* of 1653 and Rabisha's *The Whole Body of Cookery Dissected* of 1661.[17] By this time hartshorn rasping mills had been invented so that the ready-rasped horn could be offered for sale.[18]

> Gelee of Harts horn[19]
> Take Harts horn rasped; for to make three dishes of Gelee, you must take two pounds of Harts horn, seeth it with white wine two houres, so that after it is boiled there may remain [enough] to make up your three dishes with. Strain it well through a napkin and then put it in a pan with one pound of sugar, and the juice of six lemons. When it is ready to boile, put in it the whites of a d ozen of new layd eggs, and as soon as you have put them in, poure all into the strainer and set it up in a cool place. Serve it natural, and garnish it with pomegranates and lemon slices.

Hartshorn jelly continued to be made into the 1890s, perhaps due to 'an exploded belief that the condition of the body was influenced by the hard and enduring quality of the Harts' horn', as the bowdlerizing Theodore Garrett commented.[20]

> 8 oz / 225 g hartshorn   6 egg-whites, beaten
> juice and pared zest of 3 oranges & 2 lemons
> 8 oz / 225 g sugar

Simmer the hartshorn in 4 pt / 2.4 l water until reduced to 2 pt / 1.2 l, strain through a fine sieve, and simmer for 10 minutes with the orange and lemon zests. Strain through a fine sieve, allow to cool, beat in the eggs, orange and lemon juice, allow to boil up three times without stirring, strain through a fine cloth, pour into moulds, leave to set in a cool place, overnight until set, then turn out as a jelly.

(17) La Varenne, 87; Rabisha (1682), 33.
(18) *O.E.D. sv* Hartshorn.
(19) La Varenne, 87.
(20) Garrett, I 756.

HOMINY

In 1629 Captain John Smith described how the native Americans fed 'upon Milke Homini, which is bruised Indian corne pounded, and boiled thicke, and milke for the sauce.'[21] By the nineteenth century the hulling and coarse-grinding of maize was being carried on an industrial scale in large mills. Quantities of the prepared meal were imported into England to make porridge, soup, cakes and blancmanges.[22]

½ pt / 300 ml hominy	*2 oz / 50 g sugar*
1 pt / 600 ml milk	*flavouring*
pinch of salt	

Simmer the hominy, milk and salt, stirring continuously, for about 10 minutes, adding more milk should it become too thick. When tender, stir in the sugar and a few drops of any flavouring essence [vanilla, ratafia, etc.], pour into a buttered mould, leave in a cool place for a few hours to set, turn out like a jelly and serve with stewed fruit.

IVORY

As the British Empire expanded in the eighteenth and nineteenth centuries, so London craftsmen used increasing quantities of ivory to make all manner of practical and decorative artefacts. Their waste turnings, chips and file-dust were collected, ground and sold as ivory powder for making jellies, as described in *The Lady's Companion* of 1740.[23] According to Theodore Garrett, writing around 1890, 'Extraordinary, and most probably fictitious, nutritive virtues are attributed to it', probably similar to those of rhinoceros horn.[24] In Victorian Sheffield, the huge cutlery factory of Joseph Rogers & Sons of 6, Norfolk Street, used tons of ivory every year to provide handles for their knives and forks. The ivory dust from the works was carefully collected and sold for jelly-making, its accompanying flysheet bearing the company's name and address, along with:

(21) *O.E.D. sv* Hominy.
(22) Garrett, I 767.
(23) *The Ladies Companion*, 575.
(24) Garrett, I 780.

IVORY POWDER

Parcels of 6, 12, 18 and 24 lbs. at 4*d*. a lb. To each lb. of Ivory Powder, put 3 quarts of water and stew in an earthenware vessel down to 3 pints (which will take 12 to 24 hours). When cooked, take the fat off and heat as you would jelly from calves feet, adding oranges, lemons or any flavouring to taste.

LOCUST BEAN GUM

Locust beans are the seeds of the carob tree *Ceratonia siliqua* cultivated in Africa and parts of Asia. The gum produced by grinding their endosperm is used as a gelling agent in the manufacture of vegetarian jelly powders, but is not available as a separate culinary ingredient.[25]

MAIZINE

This was a late nineteenth-century form of very finely ground maize flour used in the identical manner as cornflour for making blancmanges, bavaroises, etc.[26]

MANNA

In the mid-nineteenth century a kind of semolina made from the hard wheats of Odessa and the Taganrog was imported under the names of manna, manna croup, or manna groats.[27] Around 1890, Lady Constance Howard recorded that 'Mr Sanine imports Russian ... Manna for blancmanges or puddings', but it never achieved the popularity of cornflour or other mainstream thickeners.[28]

OATMEAL

In 1603 Gervase Markham described how 'small Oatmeal, by oft steeping it in water and cleansing it, and then boyling it to a thicke and stiffe Jelly, is made [into] that excellent dish of meat which is so esteemed in the West parts of this Kingdome, which they call Wash-brew, and in Chesheire and Lancasheire they call

(25) Davidson *sv* Carob.
(26) Garrett, I 780.
(27) *O.E.D. sv* Manna Croup; Howard (*c.* 1890), 133.
(28) Howard, 133.

it Flumerie or Flummerie.'[29] It continued to be made in this way by West Yorkshire, Lancashire, Cheshire and Shropshire working-class families well into the nineteenth century.[30]

5 oz / 150 g coarse oatmeal   2 pt / 1.2 l water

Soak the oatmeal in the water for 3 to 4 days until it has turned sour, then strain through a very fine sieve or a piece of muslin, squeezing out as much liquid as possible. Boil the liquid rapidly, stirring continuously until it forms a stream the size of a rat's tail when the stirring stick is raised a few inches above the surface. Pour into rinsed bowls and leave in a cool place overnight to set.

Just before serving, turn out on to plates or dishes and serve, as Markham recommended, 'with honey, which is reputed the best sauce; [with] sack, claret or white [wine] ... strong beer [or] milk.'

The surface skin of the flummery should remain perfectly smooth for, according to old beliefs, the women whose flummery cracked would all marry boys with ugly faces.[31]

RICE

Rice, the seed of the grass *Oryza sativa* which flourishes in soft, marshy lands, was being imported from the Middle East and southern Mediterranean from the thirteenth century. By the early-Victorian period, when it first began to be used for moulded desserts, England was drawing its supplies from many parts of south and eastern Asia, Australia and America, its preference being for the short-grained or 'pudding' varieties. In this form it was made into either a smooth rice jelly, or a soft-grained rice mould, the latter making an ideal border for stewed fruits etc. For rice jelly take:[32]

(29) Markham, VI
  220.
(30) *E.D.D. sv*
  Flummery;
  Jackson *sv*
  Flummery.
(31) Tibbott, 54.
(32) Garrett, II 332.

3 oz / 75 g short-grain rice   *2 oz / 50 g sugar*
2 tsp lemon juice and a little grated zest
1 tbs kirsch or other liqueur

Simmer the rice in a covered pan with 1 ½ pts / 900 ml of water for 60 minutes, pour through a strainer into a clean pan, add the sugar and lemon and simmer until the sugar has dissolved. Remove from the heat, stir in the liqueur, pour into lightly oiled moulds, leave in a cool place to set, then turn out like a jelly.

Should you wish to make a rice mould, proceed as follows:

3 oz / 75 g short-grain rice   *1 oz / 25 g butter*
1 pt / 600 ml milk   *2 oz / 50 g sugar*

Simmer the rice in ¼ pt / 150 ml water until all the liquid has been absorbed, add the milk and butter, and simmer gently, stirring regularly, until thick and soft. Pour into freshly-rinsed cups or moulds, leave in a cool place until set, turn out, and serve with custard, jam, stewed fruit etc.

In 1845 Eliza Acton published instructions for producing ground rice or rice flour in the domestic kitchen, carefully washing the grain before drying, grinding in a mortar, and passing it through a fine sieve.[33] This ensured that there was no adulteration, but was extremely time-consuming and laborious. It was far easier to purchase rice which had already been ground by commercial food manufacturers. The best-known brands of the 1890s included 'Rizene' and 'Marshall's Crème de Riz', but ground rice was also being marketed as arrowroot or cornflour, and used to make blancmanges or 'rice mange':[34]

(33) Acton, 155.
(34) Garrett, II 332.

1 oz/25 g ground rice	*1 slice lemon zest*
1 ½ tsp ground almonds	*2 oz/50 g sugar*
1 bayleaf	*1 pt/600 ml milk*

Mix the ground rice to a smooth paste with a little of the milk. Simmer the remaining ingredients together for 5 minutes, strain into a clean pan, stir in the rice, and simmer for 10 minutes, stirring continuously. Pour into a rinsed mould, leave in a cold place until set, turn out, and pour a cold custard sauce over it just before serving.

SAGO

Explorers such as Sir Francis Drake had tasted a 'meale which they call Sago, made of the tops of certaine trees' in Java in the sixteenth century.[35] However, the prepared starch of this South Asian palm did not arrive in English kitchens until the mid-eighteenth century, when it was used for gruels or baked puddings, or for thickening soups.[36] By the mid-nineteenth century the popularity of sago was guaranteed more by its low price, about half that of semolina, than by its rather slimy, lumpy texture and its relative tastelessness. It could produce flavoursome desserts, however, such as this rhubarb and sago mould:[37]

1 lb/450 g rhubarb	*3 oz/75 g sugar*
½ pt/300 ml water	*grated lemon zest*
2 oz/50 g sago	*few drops red food colour*

Chop the rhubarb (preferably the forced stalks) into short lengths and simmer with the water, sago and sugar for about 15 minutes until the whole is soft, tender and thickened. Stir in the zest and food colour, pour into a freshly rinsed mould, and leave overnight in a cool place to set. Turn out on to a dish and serve with either custard or cream.

(35) *O.E.D. sv* Sago.
(36) Glasse, 120;
    Raffald, 84–5.
(37) Jack, 437.

SEMOLINA

The hard durum wheat of Italy leaves brittle, sharp chips when coarsely ground, these forming the semolina imported into England from the eighteenth century. Its area of production was later extended to the United States and Canada, ensuring plentiful supplies for culinary use. By the mid-nineteenth century, semolina was also available in finer particles as semoletta, or in a processed high-gluten form called 'Semola', manufactured by Perrins & Barnitt of Conduit Street, London.[38] When used for moulded desserts, gelatin or eggs were usually included to add smoothness, while still retaining the characteristic slightly sandy texture of the semolina.[39]

1 oz / 25 g semolina　　　　　*2 tbs sugar*
1 ¼ pt / 750 ml milk　　　　　*few drops vanilla essence*
5 tsp gelatin

Soak the semolina in ¼ pt / 150 ml of the milk for 1 hour. Sprinkle and stir the gelatin into ⅛ pt / 75 ml cold water, and leave to soak.

Simmer the semolina with ½ pt / 300 ml of the milk for 10 minutes until tender, stirring regularly, then stir in the sugar and vanilla essence. Meanwhile bring the remaining milk to the boil, leave to cool to around 60°C, 140°F and beat in the soaked gelatin until completely dissolved. Mix the semolina and gelatin milks together, pour into a mould, leave in a cool place overnight, then turn out on to a plate, like a jelly.

TAPIOCA

In 1612 Captain John Smith noted that the native Americans used a root called *tockawoughe*: 'Raw it is no better than poison, and being roasted ... will prickle and torment the throat extremely.'[40] Spanish and Portuguese explorers had already discovered this starch extracted from the cassava or manihot root in South America, where it was known as *tipioca*. It was by this name, therefore, that it became known when imported

(38) Walsh (1860), 124.
(39) Garrett, I 416.
(40) *O.E.D. sv* Tapioca.

into England from Brazil in the late nineteenth century. When stewed with milk, it produced the 'frogspawn' remembered by generations of schoolchildren, but when cooked in water it was transformed into a jelly:[41]

2 oz / 50 g tapioca	*2 oz / 50 g sugar*
grated zest of a lemon	

Put the tapioca and lemon zest into an open jar with ½ pt / 300 ml cold water, stand in a pan of simmering water, and continue to cook, stirring from time to time for about 30 minutes, until it has thickened. Transfer to a saucepan, add a further ½ pt / 300 ml water, and simmer for 30 minutes more, stirring as before. Stir in the sugar until dissolved, pour into a rinsed mould, leave in a cool place overnight, then unmould as a jelly.

VEGETARIAN JELLIES

Packet jellies made with entirely vegetable ingredients, including carrageen, locust bean gum and quar gum, and in some brands natural sweetening, flavourings and colourings too, are now readily available. Instructions for making them up are included in each pack, but generally involve sprinkling their powder into a little cold water and then making up to 1 pt / 600 ml with either boiling water, or cold water which is then heated to boiling point. It should be recognized that vegetarian alternatives cannot be used as a direct substitute for gelatin. Some will set quite firmly, but they rarely attain crystal clarity. The best policy is to make a trial jelly of any particular brand and see how it behaves when unmoulded. Should it ever prove unsatisfactory, it may be slowly remelted in a pan or in a microwave and transferred to a shallow mould or a bowl.

Over previous centuries the status, place in the menu, shape and contents of jellies and blancmanges had progressed through many transformations. These will now be followed in chronological order from the medieval period through to the present time.

(41) Garrett, I 568.

CHAPTER THREE

MEDIEVAL JELLIES

Figure 2. Medieval jellies. (1) a 'partie jelly of two colours'; (2) a jelly garnished with laurel sprigs; (3) Bishop Clifford's 'brod custard with a castell, ther in with a stuff in the castelle of gille', bearing a demon debating with a priest defended with the text 'In Deo salutare meo' (In God I have the advantage/benefit).

Since the conversion of raw materials into clear, flavoursome and attractive jellies demanded great investment in time, labour and skill, it is not surprising that they were considered a royal and noble delicacy. In the fourteenth century the finest foods cooked 'for the kynge at home for his owne table' featured a 'potage callyd gele' served at the start of the second of his three courses.[1] Other recommended menus of the period included 'gele' as a second-course dish on Eastertime flesh-days, and as a first-course dish on fish days.[2] The 'Sotelteys' which terminated each course at the King's table were elaborate presentations of the finest foods, each being designed both to impress and to deliver a particular message through its symbolism or inscription. *The Forme of Cury*, the cookery manuscript compiled by Richard II's cooks about 1390, gave instructions for making them, in various forms. The installation feast of Bishop Clifford of London in 1407 featured one with a demon and a doctor of divinity on a jelly-filled castle amid a custard moat, for example.[3]

Jellies continued to appear as second-course pottages in the fifteenth century, John Russell's *Boke of Nurture* considering that 'Jely red and white ... is good dewynge' for fish days.[4] They were also to be found during the remainder of the meal, his menus including an amber jelly at the end of the second course and perch in jelly in the third.[5] Unfortunately there are no descriptions of the second-course jelly which Henry IV provided for his French guests and the heralds after jousting at Smithfield, or for those served in 1403 at his marriage to Joan of Navarre.[6] However, much more is known of those made for his successors. For the coronation of Henry V in 1413, for example,

(1) Hieatt & Butler, 39.
(2) ibid., 40 (4), 41 (8).
(3) Warner, 4; Napier, 6.
(4) Furnival, 49, 51.
(5) ibid., 49–50.
(6) Napier, 4; Warner, XXXIV.

the second-course pottage was a 'gilly with swannys of braun [meat] ther in for the king and ffor other Estates'.[7] The swans on this jelly lake were one of his father's badges, a tribute which all the diners would have clearly recognized.[8] When a feast was held to celebrate the coronation of his new wife Catherine of Valois in 1421 the second-course pottage was a 'Gely coloured with columbyne floures'.[9] The inverted flowers of the *Aqualegia vulgaris* resembled five doves clustered together, hence its 'columbine' name, meaning dove-like. Their appearance here therefore celebrated Catherine's dove-like qualities of maidenly innocence and gentleness. Henry VI also had a second-course jelly at his coronation feast in 1429, his being a 'Gely party wrytlen and noted with "Te Deum Laudamus" [Thee, God, we praise]'.[10]

Evidence of the importance of jellies at medieval feasts is provided by the accounts of the food served at the 1466 enthronement celebrations for George Neville, Archbishop of York and Chancellor of England, in his palace just to the north of York Minster. The menus for the various tables list tench in jelly, ling in jelly, 'Jelly, and parted raysing to pottage' and great jellies. Probably in addition to these there were a thousand dishes of plain jelly and a further three thousand 'parted' or multi-colour jellies, perhaps over five thousand jellies in all for a single feast.[11]

The earlier recipes for jelly are for an uncleared, meaty dish we would now recognize as a brawn. The following example dating from around 1381, could also be made with pig's ears, partridges or chickens.

(7) ibid., 7.
(8) Hasler 8.
(9) Warner, XXXVI.
(10) Strutt II 103.
(11) Warner, 97–9.

TO MAKE A JELLY[12]
[see fig. 2.2]

4 pig's feet	*½ pt / 300 ml white wine vinegar*
½ tsp ground cinnamon	*½ tsp ground galingal [or ginger]*
½ tsp ground cloves	*large sprigs of laurel or bay*

Soak the feet in cold water for a few hours, scrub clean, rinse, and chop coarsely. Cover with water, cinnamon, clove and vinegar, cover, and simmer slowly for 4–5 hours until the flesh falls off the bone. Pour the stock off into a clean pan, remove all the flesh from the bones, carve it in small pieces, return to the stock, briefly re-heat it and pour into a deep serving dish. Sprinkle the galingal over the surface, leave in a cool place to set, and finally stick with 'branches' of the laurel or bay (do not forget that other laurels than bay laurel are poisonous if eaten).

By the fifteenth century rather more elegant and delicate jellies of meat were being made by cooking calf's feet separately in the stock in order to extract their gelatin. This may still be done today, but in the recipe below modern gelatin has been used to obtain exactly the same result.

JELLY OF FLESH[13]

1 rabbit, prepared for cooking	*1 bottle [sweet] red wine*
1 small 'oven-ready' chicken	*gelatin*
1 lb / 600 g lean pork	*salt*
1 lb / 600 g kid [or lamb]	*[red] wine vinegar*

Joint the rabbit and chicken, and cut the other meats as for a stew, put into a pan with the wine, adding sufficient water to cover the meat, cover, and simmer gently for about 1 hour until tender. Pour the stock off [through a strainer] into a clean pan, and set aside. Dry the meat on a cloth [or paper kitchen towel]

(12) Hieatt & Butler, I 56.
(13) Hieatt 74 no. 100.

and arrange in a dish [for today's use, the bones may now be removed]. Take the fat off the stock. Measure the stock and stir in 5 tsp/7 leaves of gelatin to each 1 pt/600 ml, pre-soaking this for 5 minutes in a little cold water before adding. Stir over a gentle heat until the gelatin has completely melted, add salt and vinegar to taste, pour over the meats in the dish, and leave to cool and set. Just before serving it may be garnished with pared ginger.

The same methods were followed when making fish jellies for fish days, the place of the calf's-foot gelatin being taken by that obtained from 'barbell or congure, playc or thornebake or other good fisch that wil agely & ... the skynys of elys'. Here these are replaced by gelatin.

JELLY ON FISH DAYS[14]

2 lb/1 kg pike, tench, perch, eel	[white] wine vinegar
1 bottle [sweet] red wine	gelatin
½ tsp crushed black peppercorns	a few blanched almonds
large pinch saffron	whole cloves & mace
salt	a piece of root ginger

Cut the fish into small pieces, having first removed the skin of the eel and set it aside. Simmer the fish and the eel skin in the wine for about 10 minutes until tender. Strain the stock through a cloth into a clean pan, remove and discard the skin and bones from the pieces of fish. These you arrange in a large dish and leave to cool. Simmer the stock for 5 minutes with the saffron and the peppercorns tied up in a small piece of muslin, then add the salt and vinegar to taste. Remove the pepper, and measure the stock, stirring in 5 tsp/7 sheets of gelatin to each 1 pt/600 ml, pre-soaking this for 5 minutes in a little cold water before adding. Stir over a gentle heat until the gelatin has completely melted, pour over the fish, leave to cool, and just before setting

(14) ibid., 76 no. 102.

insert the almonds, cloves and mace. Finally garnish with the little pared root ginger just before serving.

As a further development, the pig's feet, calves' feet and gelatinous fish were first used to make a rich stock which was used as the cooking liquor for the main meats or fish. This is an example of around 1420.

JELLIES OF [PORK & CHICKEN] MEAT[15]

6 pork chops	[white] wine vinegar
1 small trussed chicken (if possible with the feet on)	
1 ½ bottles [sweet] white wine	salt
10 tsp / 12 leaves gelatin	a few blanched almonds &
pinch of saffron	whole cloves
½ tsp ground black pepper	a piece of root ginger

Trim most of the fat from the chops. Place in a pan with the chicken, wine and gelatin (pre-soaked in ½ pt cold water). Cover, gently simmer for about 1 hour until tender, remove the chops and arrange in one dish, the chicken in another. Skim the fat off the stock, add the pepper and saffron, simmer for a further 5 minutes, add vinegar and salt to taste, then strain through a cloth into a clean jug. When nearly cold, pour over the chops and the chicken, leave to set, then garnish with the almonds, cloves and pared ginger.

None of the jellies just described conform to our modern perception of what they should be like, since they contain meat or fish and have a predominantly sweet-and-sour taste. There were others, however, which were sweet, coloured and separated from any form of flesh, these being the ancestors of all later jellies. Some were flavoured and turned opaque white with almond milk, their appearance as a 'white food' giving them the title of 'blanc-mange' in the Stuart and Georgian periods.

(15) Austin, 25.

ALMOND MILK[16]

3 oz/75 g blanched almonds   *¼ tsp salt*
1 tbs sugar or honey

Scald the ingredients with 1 pt/600 ml boiling water, cover, and leave to cool for 1 hour. Strain off the almonds (saving the liquid), and either pound in a mortar or grind in a food processor with a little of the liquid to produce a smooth paste. Add the remaining liquid, pound or grind once more, then strain off the milk through a piece of freshly-rinsed muslin, squeezing it to produce about 1 pt/600 ml of almond milk. When stained with a variety of colourings, almond-milk jellies were used to make 'parted' jellies, as served at the Neville feast. Here again gelatin has been used to replace those originally based on pig, veal or chicken stocks.

PARTED JELLY[17]
[see fig. 2.1]

1 pt/600 ml almond milk   *5 tsp/7 leaves gelatin*
2 tbs sugar or honey   *4 oz/100 g pastry*
purple (turnsole), blue (indigo),
  red (alkanet), or yellow (saffron) food colouring

Sprinkle and stir the gelatin into the almond milk for 5 minutes in a pan, add the sugar or honey and heat while stirring until it is dissolved. Roll the pastry into a narrow strip and use to form a circular wall, fixed securely in the centre of a dish. Pour half the white jelly around the wall, leave it to set, remove the pastry, then melt and colour the remainder of the jelly and, when almost cold, pour it into the centre. Alternatively, both the middle and the outer jellies may be coloured.

(16) Napier, 76;
    Hodgett 24;
    Austin, 96.
(17) Warner, 61.

VYAUNDE LECHE[18]

1 pt / 600 ml jelly made as in the recipe above
¼ pt / 150 ml sweet [red?] wine   1–2 tbs sugar
¼ tsp ground ginger   red food colouring

Pour half the jelly into a dish and leave it to set, then melt the remainder, colour it red, allow to cool, and pour on top. Simmer the wine, ginger and sugar together for 5 minutes, allow to cool, and pour over the jellies when they are fully set.

If the almond-milk jelly was made from fish stock, it could be served on fish-day meals. One recipe for 'Brawn ryall in lentyn' describes how the jelly was to be made by soaking the swim-bladders of dried stockfish and changing the water twice. After being laid on a board and scraped with the edge of a knife, they were washed, boiled, re-boiled in conger or eel stock, and ground smooth with almonds and cooked eel to make a delicate white brawn. This was used to half-fill eggshells, saffron-coloured 'yolks' of the same mixture then being added, and finally more of the white to make a realistic looking egg. The conceit might then be completed by serving them in salt, or on 'cryspes', crunchy strands of deep-fried batter closely resembling straw. Alternatively, the eggs could be made entirely from jelly, as in this version of 'Eyren Gelide'.[19]

JELLY EGGS

1 pt / 600 ml jelly made as in the parted jelly recipe above but
with an extra 1 ½ tsp / 2 leaves of gelatin.

Take the tops off eggshells, pour out the contents and use for any other purpose. Wash out the shells, fill them with the jelly, and prop them upright until set. Remove the shells and stand the 'eggs' on a plate. [The recipe is unclear, but the tops of the eggs appear to have been stuck with gilt-headed cloves]

(18) Austin, 27.
(19) *Household Ordinances*, 471.

The fifteenth century also saw fruit juices being turned into jelly-like leaches by the use of amydon, the very fine wheat starch, or rice flour.

STRAWBERRY

8 oz / 225 g strawberries
¼ pt / 150 ml almond milk
3 tbs red wine
3 tbs cornflour (for amydon)
4 tbs sugar
1 tsp lard
large pinch saffron

½ tsp mixed ground pepper,
    ginger,
cinnamon and galingal
1 oz / 25 g currants
2 tsp [red] wine vinegar
red food colour (for
    alkanet)
1 pomegranate

Pulp the strawberries with the wine and rub through [a sieve or] a piece of muslin. Stir in all but the vinegar, food colour and pomegranate seeds, and simmer while stirring for 5 minutes until thick. Remove from the heat, stir in the vinegar and sufficient food colour to produce a fine red. When cold drop it in spoonfuls on a dish and sprinkle with the pomegranate seeds.

As these and other medieval recipes show, jelly was usually poured or spooned directly into any of the silver-gilt, silver and pewter dishes then in use in wealthy households. There might also have been dishes specially made for this purpose, one guild account of 1480 recording '9 dosen gely dishes' for the use of its members.[20]

(20) O.E.D. sv Jelly.

CHAPTER FOUR

TUDOR JELLIES

In July, 1517, Henry VIII entertained the newly arrived embassy from Spain with a joust followed by a great feast which lasted seven hours. It impressed Francesco Chiericati, the Apostolic Nuncio, with its lavish magnificence, 'but the jellies,of some twenty sorts perhaps, surpassed everything; they were made in the shape of castles and animals of various descriptions, as beautiful as can be imagined.'[1]

The cooks of the royal household were expert in the art of jellymaking, for, as stated in the Eltham Ordinances of 1526, King Henry and Queen Catherine's second course at dinner always commenced with a jelly hippocras costing 8*d.* as its pottage.[2]

JELLY HIPPOCRAS[3]

½ pt / 300 ml claret	*6 cloves*
4 oz / 100 g sugar	*¼ tsp coriander seeds*
2–3 pieces root ginger	*pinch of salt*
2 in. / 5 cm stick of cinnamon	*4 tsp / 5 leaves gelatin*
¼ nutmeg, crushed	*(for calf's feet &*
	isinglass)

Lightly bruise the spices and gently simmer with the salt and ½ pt water for 10 minutes. Pour the claret into a pan, stir in the gelatin, and leave to soak for 10 min. Strain the spiced water through a fine cloth [or coffee filter paper] into the pan, stir in the sugar and the gelatin mixture, and gently heat while stirring until fully dissolved, then pour into a dish and leave to set.

(1) *Calendar of State Papers Venetian,* II 918.
(2) *Household Ordinances,* 174.
(3) A.W., 31.

In addition to continuing its role as a second-course dish, jelly now became a feature of a new high-status, exclusive entertainment called a banquet. This was not merely a large communal dinner, as we use that word today, but a select gathering of the wealthy and great designed to impress through its display of costly dress, entertainment, tableware, food and drink. Frequently held in a separate room, in specially-constructed tents or leafy bowers, or in the open air, its tables were heaped with sweetmeats and sweet, spiced wines, the most expensive, aspirational and fashionable of fare. Such banquets and their 'banqueting stuff' had developed out of the 'void' of digestive sweet spices served at the end of medieval dinners, but had now become a major, competitive social display among the aristocracy and gentry. Their banquets could cost vast amounts in time, energy and materials, especially when entertaining Elizabeth I on her progresses around the country.

In 1591, when the Earl of Hertford entertained the Queen at Elvetham, for example, 'there was a banket served, all in glass and silver, into the low gallery in the garden ... by two hundred of my Lord of Hertford's gentlemen, every one carrying so many dishes, that the whole number amounted to a thousand [led by] a hundred torch bearers.'[4] Their sweetmeats included the most elaborate of sugarwork, as well as jellies and leaches, probably made by the army of professional cooks hired for the event. In many major houses the making of banqueting stuff became an interesting and rewarding hobby for their ladies, giving them a welcome opportunity to display their confectionery skills to their peers. In the latter part of Elizabeth's reign the London book-trade began to publish books such as *The Good Huswife's Jewell* of 1596 or *Delightes for Ladies* of 1600, which included recipes for all kinds of 'banqueting stuff', including the following for jellies and leaches. The original gelling agents of calf's feet, knuckles of veal and isinglass have here been replaced with gelatin, and the scented musk omitted.

(4) Nichols, II 20.

[AMBER] CRYSTAL JELLY[5]

4 tsp / 5 leaves gelatin
½ oz / 12 g root ginger
½ tsp white peppercorns
⅛ nutmeg

6 cloves
2 oz / 50 g sugar
1 tbs rosewater

Bruise the spices in a mortar and simmer them in 1 pt / 600 ml water in a covered pan for 15 minutes. Meanwhile soak the gelatin in ¼ pt / 150 ml cold water in a jug. Strain the spiced water through a fine cloth [or coffee filter paper] onto the gelatin, stir in the sugar and rosewater until all is dissolved, then pour into a dish and leave to set.

STRAWBERRY, MULBERRY OR RASPBERRY JELLY[6]

1 lb / 450 g soft fruit
¼ pt / 150 ml rosewater

4 oz / 100 g sugar
5 tsp / 7 leaves gelatin

Grind or liquidize the fruit with the rosewater and sugar, bring to the boil, and strain through a piece of fine cloth or muslin into a clean pan. Add the gelatin which has been pre-soaked in ¼ pt / 150 ml water for 10 minutes, gently heat and stir until it has dissolved, then pour into a dish.

(5) Platt.
(6) ibid.

CLARET JELLY[7]

½ pt/300 ml claret
4 oz/100 g sugar
2–3 pieces root ginger
2 in./5 cm stick cinnamon
¼ nutmeg

6 cloves
¼ tsp coriander seeds
pinch of salt
5 tsp/7 leaves gelatin

Bruise the spices and salt in a mortar and simmer in ½ pt/300 ml water in a covered pan for 15 minutes. Meanwhile soak the gelatin in ¼ pt/150 ml cold water in a pan for 10 minutes. Strain the spiced water through a fine cloth [or coffee filter paper] onto the gelatin, add the sugar and claret, and stir over a gentle heat until fully dissolved before pouring into a dish.

Being more solid than jellies, leaches were ideal for banquets, since they could be lifted to the mouth by the use of the fingers, rather than a spoon. The first recipe here might only be flavoured with milk and isinglass, but the real ostentation came in its covering of gold leaf. Pure gold leaf is edible, but not the base-metal 'gold leaf' usually sold in craft shops today, which should never be consumed.

A WHITE LEACH[8]

1 pt/600 ml whole milk
6–7 tsp/8–10 leaves gelatin
1 ½ tsp rosewater

4 oz/100 g sugar
gold leaf

Soak the gelatin in a quarter of the milk for 10 minutes in a pan, add the rest of the milk, rosewater and sugar, and heat gently while stirring until all is dissolved. Use a sugar-boiling thermometer to ensure the temperature does not exceed 60°C, beyond which it is likely to curdle. Leave to cool, then pour about 1 in./2.5 cm thick into a very lightly greased metal tray or

(7) A.W., 31.
(8) Dawson, II 19.

plastic box, and leave to set firmly, preferably overnight. Turn out onto a freshly-rinsed and smoothed cloth, cut into 1 in./2.5 cm cubes using a knife dipped in warm water, and arrange in a chequerboard pattern on a dish, at which point the gold leaf may be applied, a task best left to those with practical skills in gilding.

LEACHES OF ALMONDS[9]

Follow the previous recipe, but use the milk (instead of water) to make 1 pt of rich almond milk following the instructions given on page 60.

As in the medieval period, leaches made with pike, tench or isinglass were still being used to make artificial eggs. This recipe comes from *The Good Huswifes Handmaide for the Kitchen* of 1588.

TO MAKE EGGS IN LENT[10]

1 batch of leach, as in the recipe for a white leach, above
large pinch of saffron   *eggshells*

Save eggshells after they have been served as boiled eggs, prop them vertically in a bed of uncooked rice or flour, fill with the leach and leave to set. Using a teaspoon dipped in warm water, scoop out the holes for the yolks, melting the removed leach with the saffron to turn it a deep yellow. Allow this to cool, then pour into the whites to produce very realistic eggs.

(9) Platt.
(10) Peachey, 55.

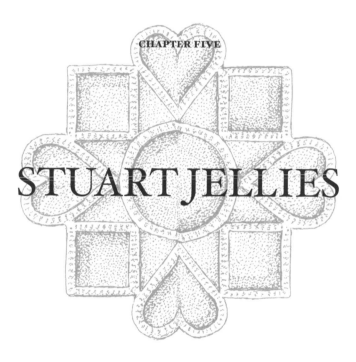

STUART JELLIES

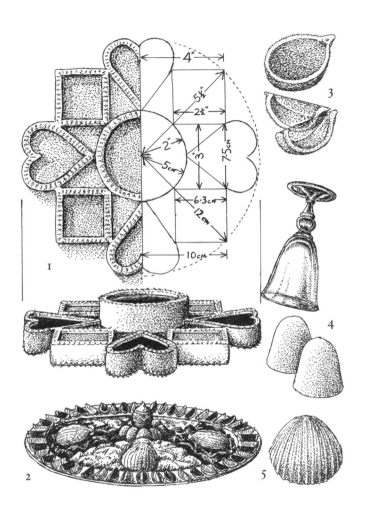

Figure 3. Stuart jellies. (1) William Rabisha's laid tart of jelly, 1661; (2) Robert May's great dish of jelly, 1660; (3) his orange and lemon jelly quarters; (4) Queen Henrietta Maria's piramidis creams of 1655; (5) jelly moulded in a scallop shell.

The court of Elizabeth, the Virgin Queen, had been one of regal, stately and dignified magnificence. For over forty years she had maintained her power throughout numerous political and military crises by means of commanding enormous respect. The arrival of James VI of Scotland as James I of England in 1603 therefore was something of a shock to the upper levels of English society. Though shrewd and learned, his laddish appetites and lack of personal dignity came as a complete revelation. He loved fruit and sweet wines, however, with the result that his reign saw sweetmeat banquets flourish as never before.[1] Frequently they accompanied one of Ben Jonson's masques, when this poet's incomparable verse, combined with lavish costume and awesome scenery, acted as a prelude to even more action around the banquet table. Just a few months after his accession, James visited Apethorpe in Northamptonshire, where the tables were:[2]

> covered with costly banquets, wherein every thing that was most delicious for taste, proved more delicate by the arte that made it seeme beauteous to the eye; the Lady of the house being one of the most excellent Confectioners in England, though I confess many honourable women very expert.

Three years later, when holding a banquet for King Christian of Denmark at the great mansion of Theobalds, James and all his guests fully indulged themselves, even to excess. As the 'Queen of Sheba' approached the kings, she tripped over the steps of the dais, tipping her caskets of wine, cream, jelly and

(1) Nichols, IV 554.
(2) ibid., I 97.

other good things into his Danish majesty's lap, then fell on top of him, both ending up on the floor. As Sir John Harington reported to Mr Secretary Barlow, all ended in a drunken sprawl: 'never did I see such lack of good order, discretion, and sobriety, as I have now done.'[3] Given this great boost to banqueting, it is hardly surprising to find that jellies became even more popular in the years leading up to the Civil War.

Even though more jelly recipes were both published and noted down in manuscript cookery books, most of them followed exactly the same methods as described by their Tudor predecessors. The only major introductions were cream, white wine, orange or lemon juice, along with hartshorn and ivory for gelatin. Robert May, one of the leading country-house cooks of the period, made his jellies with calf's feet, knuckle of veal and capon (here replaced by gelatin) and a large quantity of sugar:

ROBERT MAY'S COLOURED JELLIES[4]

4 tbs / 6 leaves gelatin	*juice of 1 lemon*
1 pt / 1.2 l white wine	*12 oz / 325 g sugar*
4 sprigs rosemary	

Stir the gelatin into ½ pt / 300 ml water in a pan and leave to soak for 10 minutes, then add the wine, lemon juice, sugar, and 1 pt / 600 ml warm water, and heat gently while stirring until all is dissolved. Divide into four pans for:[5]

CLEAR: 1 piece root ginger, sliced, 2 blades mace;

RED: red food colour (for alkanet), 1 nutmeg and 1 in. / 2.5 cm cinnamon stick, 1 piece root ginger, all bruised;

PURPLE: purple food colour (for Turnsole), as for red, plus 4 cloves;

YELLOW: yellow food colour or saffron, spiced as for purple.

Cover each pan, simmer with sprigs of rosemary for 5 minutes, strain through a fine cloth and leave to cool for use.

(3) ibid., II 72–3.
(4) May, 202–3.
(5) ibid., 203.

JELLIES & THEIR MOULDS

At this stage May would have clarified the jellies with egg-whites, but this should not be necessary with modern gelatins and sugar.

WINE, ORANGE OR LEMON JELLIES[6]

1 pt/600 ml white wine or ½ pt/300 ml grape juice mixed
with ½ pt/300 ml strained orange or lemon juice
1 ½ lb/625 g sugar   10 tsp/12 leaves gelatin
1 nutmeg, 1 piece root ginger, 1 in./2.5 cm stick cinnamon

Simmer the wine or fruit juices with ¾ pt/450 ml water and the spices for 5 minutes in a covered pan. Soak the gelatin in ¼ pt/150 ml cold water for 10 minutes in a pan, strain in the spiced juices through a fine cloth, and stir in the sugar over a gentle heat until all is dissolved.

This jelly was similarly cleared with egg-whites, and filtered through 'new bags, wash them first in warm water, and then in cold, wring them dry, and being ready strung with packethread on sticks, hang them on a spit by the fire [away] from any dust, and set new earthen pans under them being well seasoned with boiling liquor.'[7]

ORANGE & LEMON JELLY QUARTERS[8]
[see fig. 3.3]

batches of the coloured, orange   orange or lemon peels
or lemon jellies just described

Before taking the juices from the fruit, cut them in two from stalk to bud, and use a steel spoon to carefully remove all the pulp. Prop the shells horizontally on a bed of raw rice or flour, fill with the appropriate jellies, leave to set, then cut longways into quarters using a knife dipped in warm water.

(6) ibid., 204.
(7) ibid., 203.
(8) ibid.

The quarters I have just described were used either to form a border around a dish or, filled with red, blue and yellow jellies, were served on silver dishes.[9] Other jellies were served in elaborate pastry cases called laid tarts.

A LAID TART OF JELLY[10]
[see fig. 3.1 and plate i]

1 ½ lb / 675 g plain flour   *14 fl oz / 420 ml boiling*
4 egg yolks & 2 whites   *water*
a selection of coloured jellies

Make a well in the flour in a large bowl, drop in the eggs, stir, then rub in until completely absorbed. Make a well a second time, pour in the boiling water, mix, then knead until perfectly smooth.

Roll out a third of the pastry into a large round ¼ in. / 7 mm thick on a sheet of oven paper on a baking tray, prepare a paper pattern to the drawing on page 72, lay it on top, and lightly score the lines on to the pastry. Remove the paper.

Roll the rest of the pastry to the same thickness, cut out a rectangle 12 ½ in. x 4 in. / 32 cm x 10 cm, using a knife for three sides, and a jagged pastry wheel for one long side. Form this into a cylindrical tower, jagged edge on top, moisten and seal the joint, and seal into the centre of the base.

Cut the remaining pastry into strips 1 ½ in. / 4cm high, with one top edge jagged, fold into shape on the paper pattern, and stick in place onto the base around the tower. When all is complete, run the jagging-iron around the perimeter to remove all the surplus from the base.

Use a sharp metal skewer to prick the insides and bases of all the pastry walls to stop them blistering, then bake at 150°C / 300°F / Gas mark 2 for about 30 minutes, until just starting to brown, then remove and leave to cool.

Fill each compartment with as contrasting a series of coloured jellies as possible.

(9) Price, 171.
(10) Rabisha, 110.

Jelly might also be served in little round glasses, four or five in a dish, or silver trencher plates or glass trencher plates.[11]

As cooks became more confident in making jellies which would stand up, they began to experiment with the use of moulds. Some were natural, such as scallop and mussel shells (see fig. 3.5), or eggshells, while others were manufactured, including wineglasses or moulds made of wood or tin.[12] Unfortunately none of these purpose-made wooden or tin moulds appear to have survived to the present day. Moulding was particularly useful for shaping the thicker, creamier leaches, which were hence called piramidis creams.

QUEEN HENRIETTA MARIA'S PIRAMIDIS CREAM[13]
[see fig. 3.4]

2 oz / 50 g ground almonds	*2 tbs rosewater*
5 tsp / 7 leaves gelatin	*½ pt / 300 ml cream*
a few pine kernels and	*2 oz / 50 g sugar*
a little cream for garnishing	

Grind or liquidize the almonds with ½ pt / 300 ml water and strain the milk through a piece of muslin into a saucepan. Stir the gelatin into the cream and leave to soak for 10 minutes, add to the pan along with the sugar and rosewater, and heat gently while stirring until all is dissolved, keeping the temperature around 60°C (with a sugar-boiling thermometer) to prevent curdling.

Allow to cool, then:

> put it into an old fashioned drinking-Glass, and let it stand till it is cold, and when you will use it, hold your Glasse in a warm hand, and loosen it with a knife, and whelm it into a dish, and have in readiness Pine-Apple blown, and stick it all over, and serve it with cream or without as you please.

(11) May, 204; Price, 171.
(12) May, 204.
(13) W.M., I 32.

As in earlier periods, leaches and creams were still being moulded in eggshells, but now without necessarily having to fulfil any Lenten restrictions, even though jelly stocks were still being made from fish.

WHITE JELLY EGGS[14]

Follow the recipe for parted jelly (p. 60) but with an extra 1 ½ tsp/2 leaves gelatin, adding the juice of half a lemon when cold, along with food colouring to produce batches of white, yellow, blue and green leach. Pour these into rinsed eggshells, leave to set, and turn out onto a dish.

Using these jelly eggs, along with the jellies described above, cooks such as Robert May were able to produce great multi-coloured silver chargers of jelly ideal for making impressive additions to the banquet table.

A GREAT DISH OF JELLY[15]
[see fig. 3.2]

1 pt/600 ml each of red and amber wine jellies (pp. 67, 68)
2 pt/1.2l clear wine jelly
1 batch coloured jelly eggs, to the recipe above
4 scallop shells filled with different colours of
*   the jelly eggs leach*
1 batch of orange & lemon quarters (p. 75)
1 lemon, its peel carved in ornamental designs

Arrange a small circle of the eggs at the centre of the dish, fill opposing quarters with large spoonfuls of the red and the amber jellies separately, and the spaces between them with the spooned clear jelly. Turn out a scallop on to each quarter of the jellies, and set the carved lemon in the centre.

(14) May, 206.
(15) ibid., 327.

The same recipe used to make the jelly eggs was also used to make the first of the 'ribbon' jellies so popular in later years. Successive 'layers of divers colours in the French fashion' were built up in a dish, then being sliced and re-arranged to show their cross-section. This recipe, published by John Murrell in 1617, used saffron yellow, turnsole red and bluebottle blue, 'bluebottles' at this period being cornflowers, not enormous flies.

A LEACH IN THE FRENCH FASHION[16]

1 batch of leach as for white jelly eggs, above
yellow, red & blue food colouring

Divide the leach into four parts, leaving one white and staining the others yellow, red and blue. Pour the white when cold but not set into a lightly greased plastic or metal box measuring 5 x 3 in. / 13 x 8 cm and leave to set. Add the successive layers of yellow, red and blue, then turn out on to a freshly rinsed and smoothed cloth, cut into slices, and arrange on a serving dish.

As might have been expected, the Civil War and Commonwealth saw a lull in the most lavish and boisterous of the entertainments in the banqueting houses. Even so, the tradition did continue in a more restrained form, Elizabeth Cromwell, the Lord Protector's wife, making special wine jellies from calf's feet and knuckles of veal.

MRS ELIZABETH CROMWELL'S
EXCELLENT JELLY[17]

4 tsp / 5 leaves gelatin	*¼ pt / 150 ml dry sherry*
2 in. / 5cm stick cinnamon	*3 tbs sugar*

Stir the gelatin into ¼ pt cold water and leave to soak for 10 minutes. Meanwhile simmer the cinnamon in ¾ pt / 450 ml water for 10 minutes, strain onto the gelatin, stir until dissolved, then stir in the sherry and sugar. Turn into a dish or glasses, and leave to set.

(16) Murrell, in Lorwin, 148.
(17) Clinton, 77.

After the Restoration, both jellies and 'blancmanges' remained popular, blancmanges now being almond-milk jellies identical to the former 'leaches', and nothing at all like their white-meat and rice medieval namesakes. They even appeared at the great Coronation feasts held in Westminster Hall. On 23 April, 1685, 'Their MAJESTIES Table was furnished by Patrick Lamb Esq. the KINGS Master Cook [with] Plates of all sorts of Jellyes, Blancmange, &c.' They were all served in separate glasses, two dozen to the plate on most tables, three dozen at the royal table, over 166 in total. The table plans show their position as usually being along the centre-line of the nobles' tables, a convenient location from which they could be taken as required by the guests.[18] The royal household regularly purchased 5 lb of hartshorn every month, since Patrick Lamb preferred it to calves' feet for his jellies, warning the unwary not to buy the shaved bones often fraudulently sold in its place.[19] After boiling 1 lb/450 g of hartshorn in 12 pt/7.2 l of water until it formed a jelly, he left it overnight, removed the sediment, and then prepared it as follows (but here using gelatin).

PATRICK LAMB'S JELLY[20]

4 tsp/5 leaves gelatin	*1 oz/25 g sugar*
2 cloves	*6 tbs Rhenish wine (Hock)*
1 blade of mace	*juice of 1 lemon, strained*
½ in./12 mm stick cinnamon	

Soak the gelatin in ¼ pt/150 ml water for 10 minutes. Simmer the spices, sugar and wine in ¾ pt/450 ml water for 3 minutes, add the lemon juice, boil for 2 minutes more, skim, pour onto the gelatin, stir until dissolved, strain through a fine cloth, allow to cool, then pour into glasses or a china dish.

(18) Sandford, 108–115.
(19) *Household Ordinances*, 381, 384.
(20) Lamb, 110–111.

PATRICK LAMB'S BLANCMANGE[21]

1 batch of Patrick Lamb's jelly, to the previous recipe
6 oz / 150 g whole almonds

Pour boiling water over the almonds, leave to soak for 30 minutes, then drain and either finely chop or grind with 3–4 tbs of the jelly, grinding them to a smooth paste. Heat the remaining jelly, mix in the almond paste, and strain though a fine cloth or muslin, pressing out as much liquid as possible. Grind the almonds again with a little of the strained jelly, and repeat the process twice more to extract as much of the almond's milk as possible, finally straining the blancmange into a glass or dishes. [For an easier modern substitute, flavour a milk jelly with sugar and almond flavouring.]

Lamb also provides very useful information as to the use of jellies and blancmanges at table in the late seventeenth and early eighteenth centuries. When presented in its old-established role as a second-course dish, it was served in a china bowl or plates or, if in glasses, arranged on the table alternately, jelly-blancmange-jelly-blancmange and so on. He even provides a plan of the plate of jellies he made for Queen Mary's dinner in February, 1704. A blancmange stood in the centre of a group of four jellies, while two clear, two yellow and two green jellies, with two more blancmanges, all in jelly glasses, were spaced in opposing pairs all around the rim.

Some blancmanges made in the early seventeenth century had their veal jellies stiffened and textured with rice flour.[22] Later these developed into sweet, rosewater-flavoured rice-flour moulds, each shaped as a creamy white tall dome by being cast in a wine-glass. For obvious reasons, they became known as Spanish Paps.

(21) ibid., 30–31.
(22) Fettiplace, 82.

SPANISH PAPS[23]

2 ½ oz / 65 g ground rice or rice flour	3 egg-whites lightly beaten
	1 tsp rosewater
2 ½ oz / 65 g sugar	1 pt / 600 ml cream

Beat all the ingredients together, stir while heating gently until boiling and thickened, then pour into wine glasses with rounded conical bowls which have been freshly rinsed with a little more rosewater. Leave to set, then turn out on to a dish.

Before we move on to the contemplation of jellies in the eighteenth century, it is worthwhile to revisit the years before the Civil War for this unusual recipe originally intended to assist those suffering from tuberculosis. It remains one of the best of all dried-fruit jellies.

EXCELLENT RECIPE FOR THE CONSUMPTION[24]

8 dates	a small piece of liquorice
4 figs (dried)	5 tsp / 7 leaves gelatin
8 prunes	few drops red food
½ tsp mixed ground cinnamon, ginger, mace, clove & nutmeg	colouring
	2 tbs sugar

Slice the dried fruits and gently stew with the spices and food colouring in ¾ pt / 450 ml water for up to 4 hours until tender. Soak the gelatin in ¼ pt / 150 ml water for 2 hours, stir into the fruit with the sugar, until completely dissolved. Leave to set.

(23) Brears (1989), 90.
(24) May, 207.

CHAPTER SIX

GEORGIAN JELLIES

Figure 4. Georgian jellies. (1) jellies served in glasses on an epergne of c. 1765; *(2) a salver bearing jellies in glasses around a sweetmeat dish,* c. 1745; *(3) an epergne of jelly glasses for a City banquet, after an engraving by J. Williams, 1772; (4) James Gillray's depiction of Captain Birch enjoying a jelly at Kelsey's shop in St James's in 1797.*

In the reign of George I (1714–27) most jellies were being served in purpose-made jelly glasses arranged on a dish to form part of the second course at dinner, but their use here was far from universal. As late as the 1730s, professionals such as Charles Carter, cook to the Duke of Argyll, Earl of Pontefract and Lord Cornwallis, rarely included jellies in their dinner menus, preferring fruit, tarts and custards instead. They were still a part of the third 'Dessert' courses, however.[1] By the 1740s jellies had become much more popular, even provincial cook-housekeepers preparing them on a regular basis. Mrs Elizabeth Moxon of Pontefract set them in the middle of her symmetrically arranged second courses and suppers, where, catching the light, they would look most attractive.[2] The pyramids of jellies which had first graced the royal tables were now to be found on those of the gentry and merchant classes. English glassmakers were supplying all that was required. The tiered structures were formed by a number of tall-stemmed glass salvers of diminishing sizes, each set one on top of the other and terminating in a goblet-like sweetmeat glass. Cookson, Jeffreys and Dixon of Newcastle upon Tyne were offering pyramids comprising four salvers, one top glass, five top sweetmeat glasses and up to thirty-two jelly and custard glasses for £2 2s. 6d. in 1746, for example.[3]

Jelly glasses were also used to serve the products of Georgian jelly-shops, the predecessors of the early twentieth-century ice-cream parlours. Tomlin's Jelly House, late Oswald's, stood at the corner of Ryder Street and Bury Street in the fashionable heart of St James's in London. It must have been founded around 1700, since *The Epicure's Almanack or Calendar of Good*

(1) Carter, plates 41, 45.
(2) Moxon, monthly menus.
(3) For an excellent introduction to jelly glasses, see Hughes (1982).

Living of 1815 stated that it had already been trading for over a century.[4] Nearby, at the corner of St James's Street and Blue Bird Yard, James Kelsay opened his fruit and confectioner's shop in 1760. In 1793 his son Francis moved to No. 7 St James's Street, almost opposite the gates of the Palace, an ideal location from which to serve its Guards and Dragoons. The interior of the shop formed the setting for James Gillray's 'Heros recruiting at Kelsays, or Guard-day at St. James's'. This fine satirical print published in 1793 shows Thomas Birch of the 16th Light Dragoons enthusiastically spooning his jelly from a jelly glass (see fig. 4.4).[5] We know the recipe for the jelly served at the St James's Coffee House, which operated at 87 St James's Street from 1705 to the 1840s. It was noted down in the manuscript recipe book of Sir Walter Ffarington (1730–1781) of Shaw Hall, Worden, Lancashire, as:

THE ST JAMES'S COFFEE HOUSE JELLY[6]

juice and pared zest of 1 ½ lemons, strained
1 oz / 25 g soft brown sugar   4 tsp / 5 leaves gelatin

Sprinkle and stir the gelatin into ¼ pt / 450 ml water and leave to soak for 10 minutes. Simmer the lemon juice and zest in ¾ pt / 450 ml water for 10 minutes, skim, strain, pour onto the gelatin, stir until dissolved, leave to cool, then pour into jelly glasses.

Returning to the domestic table, jellies were also served in glass or china bowls. Mrs Elizabeth Raffald's *Experienced English Housekeeper* of 1769 showed a 'Transparent pudding cover'd with a Silver Web' at the centre of her Grand Table's second course.[7]

(4) Hughes, p.204.
(5) Burford, 157.
(6) Private collection, 60.
(7) Raffald, plate p.195.

TRANSPARENT PUDDING[8]

1 pt / 600 ml lemon-flavoured white wine jelly

1 oz / 25 g flaked blanched almonds	*2 oz / 50 g lexia raisins, sliced*
2 oz / 50 g candied lemon & citron peels	*1 oz / 25 g currants*

Pour a thin layer of this jelly into a bowl, leave it to set, stick in part of the almonds, peel, raisins and currants, and cover with another layer of jelly, continuing in alternate layers until the bowl is full. Lexia raisins are the large seeded raisins from Muscatel grapes.

SILVER OR GOLDEN WEB

6 oz / 150 g sugar   *[pinch cream of tartar]*

Gently heat the sugar and 2 tbs water to boiling, stir in the cream of tartar dissolved in a little water, then boil rapidly until it rises to 150°C on a sugar-boiling thermometer, then dip the base of the pan in cold water for a second or two to stop the sugar boiling any further. Have a dish or bowl large enough to cover the transparent pudding set upside down on a large jar over a sheet of paper, the domed surface of the dish being very lightly oiled. As soon as the sugar is ready, dip the blade of a knife into it, and trail thin thread across the dish in both directions and also around it to form a 'trellis'. Trim the surplus from below the rim, lift off, and place over the pudding just before serving. If allowed to stand where there is virtually any humidity, it will rapidly soften and collapse.

While jellies occupied the centre-spot on the table, flummeries or blancmanges, both of almond-milk jelly, were usually relegated to the role of side-dishes. This made good

(8) ibid., 97, 92.

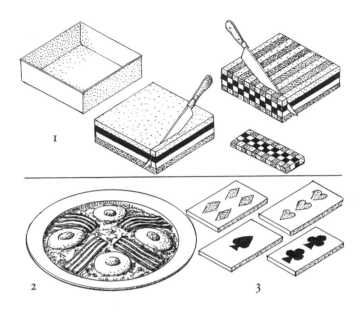

Figure 5. Georgian leaches. (1) Charles Carter's checker'd leach of 1730; (2) Katherine Foulis' spinach, eggs and bacon; (3) Ann Peckham's cards of 1767.

sense, for most of them were served in dishes, rather than individual glasses. Firmer and more opaque than jellies, flummeries and blancmanges were ideal for taking on more interesting shapes. They might simply be left in china dishes until set and then either 'cut ... out in the Shape of Dice' or 'cut ... with a Jagging-Iron in long Slips [and tied] in Knots on the Dish or Plate you serve it up in.'⁹ If built up in layers of different colours, it became a 'ribbon', Charles Carter suggesting a repeated sequence of red, yellow and clear, or green and white. With rather more time and trouble, it could even be made into:

(9) Schoonover, 98; Eales, 84.

CHECKER'D JELLY, OR LEACH [OR FLUMMERY / BLANCMANGE][10]
[see fig. 5]

*equal quantities of red, clear [or white], purple and yellow
jelly or flummery, etc., 7 tsp or 10 leaves to the pint*

Lightly grease a deep square metal or plastic tray, and pour in successive layers (each ⅜ in. / 1 cm deep) of the red, white, purple and yellow jellies. Do not add a layer before the jelly or flummery you are adding has completely cooled. Then, allow it to set before adding subsequent layers. When all are very firmly set, turn them out on to a freshly-rinsed and smoothed cloth. Prop the tray at a slight angle, and, having used a knife blade dipped in warm water to cut a ⅜ in / 1 cm slice from the flummery, set it red side up against one side of the mould. Cut another slice, turn it yellow side up, brush its face with a little warm, clear jelly, and set it against the first slice, continuing with alternate-coloured jellies until the tray is full. Turn out onto the rinsed cloth once more, and slice across the stripes to produce chequered slices to be arranged as a dish.

Ribbon jellies could also be made to represent the red and white stripes of bacon, and then be dished up with appropriate jelly accompaniments. This version is from the manuscript recipe book of Katherine Foulis of York:[11]

SPINACH, EGGS & BACON
[see fig. 5]

*1 pt / 600 ml [spinach] green jelly
¾ pt / 450 ml white [milk or cream] jelly (p. 68)
½ pt / 300 ml [redcurrant] red jelly
¼ pt / 150 ml orange jelly*

(10) Carter, 178–180.
(11) Private collection, 46.

Make the green jelly, leave to set in a dish, then chop to represent spinach. Pour a 3 in./7.5 cm circle of white jelly into 4 lightly greased saucers, and the orange jelly into 1 ½ in./4 cm circles in the bottom of 4 lightly greased cups. Fill a rectangular 1 pt/600 ml mould with alternate layers of white, then red jellies, to represent the fat and lean of bacon (follow the same rules as set out in the checker'd jelly, above), leave to set, turn out, and slice with a knife blade dipped in warm water. Arrange these slices of 'bacon' on the spinach, with the egg 'whites' turned out beside them, each topped with its orange 'yolk'.

Other cooks made their bacon with a layered chocolate rind, 1 in./2.5 cm of white 'fat' and 3 in./7.5 cm red 'lean', and cast their yolks in half eggshells, pouring a little white flummery over them to give a more realistic effect.[12]

Flummery was also used to make imitation playing cards:

TO MAKE CARDS[13]
[see fig. 5]

1 pt/600 ml flummery/leach made with cream (p. 68)
dark chocolate   *red food colouring*

Pour ¾ pt/450 ml of the flummery into a lightly greased baking tray when almost cold, and leave it to set. Colour half the remainder by mixing red food colouring into it, and melting sufficient grated chocolate into the other half to give a dark brown, then leave to set the same thickness as the white flummery. Turn the white flummery onto a freshly rinsed and smoothed cloth, cut into the shape of playing cards, and arrange them on a flat dish. Using small tinplate cutters, cut out hearts, diamonds, clubs and spades where appropriate for the chosen numbers, then cut out the matching shapes from the chocolate or red flummery, and slip them into the vacancies to produce 'cards'.

(12) Peckham, 165.
(13) ibid., 166.

Ann Peckham's table-plans include one for a supper which had a 'Jelly turned out' at its centre.[14] This would probably have been one of the newly-invented jellies in which fruit, flowers or shapes moulded in flummery had been layered and embedded in jelly set within an ordinary hemispherical pottery bowl. Sir Walter Ffarington's manuscript has a typical early example:

TO MAKE A NEST OF EGGS[15]
[see plate ii]

2–3 pts / 1.2–1.8 l stiff lemon-flavoured white wine jelly
¾ pt / 450 ml stiff white flummery / leach (p. 68)
yellow & green orange peels & 'Indian Sweetmeats'

Pour a quarter of the jelly into a basin and leave it to set. Blow eggshells, block one end with a piece of pastry, fill with flummery, allow to set firmly, then remove the shells and arrange in the centre of the jelly, half-submerging them in more cold but unset jelly. [Cut the peels into fine straws, poach in water with a little sugar until just tender] then arrange around the eggs and fill the bowl before leaving to set.

To turn the jelly out, the cook was to put 'the Bowl in hot Water to soften it, & when it is ready to Turn out put the Dish upon the Bowl & turn it out upon it.' Hopefully the bowl had walls of the same thickness, but since most had narrow rims and thick bases, the bottom might still be stuck firm when the sides had already melted. This was the standard method of unmoulding at this time but, as Elizabeth Raffald explained, 'putting it into water ... takes off the figures of the mould and makes the flummery look dull.'[16] She advised making the flummery stiff and wetting the moulds, so that it would turn out without the need of warming. Martha Bradley preferred to use orange-flower water since 'it gives the Flummery a very high Flavour, and makes it come out of the Cups easily'.[17] The best solution to the problem, one rarely repeated elsewhere, came

(14) ibid., October menu.
(15) Private collection, 22.
(16) Smith, 187; Kidder, 91; Raffald, 92.
(17) Bradley, II 197.

from Charles Carter. He advised washing the interiors of the moulds with almond oil, then pouring in the flummery when cold but still liquid.[18]

There are numerous references to jelly and flummery being moulded in cups, glasses and scallop shells, but the first purpose-made moulds began to appear around the middle of the eighteenth century.

WOODEN MOULDS

These were made of sycamore, a close-grained white timber already in regular use for dairy utensils. Turned from solid blocks, their interiors measured some $3\frac{1}{2}$–5 in. / 9–13 cm in diameter by up to $1\frac{3}{4}$ in. / 4.3 cm in depth. They had smooth side walls, only their bases being carved with floral plants or rosettes as decoration.[19] It is probable that they were treated like butter-prints, first scalded and then plunged into cold water to stop their contents sticking within.

STONEWARE MOULDS

The white salt-glazed stonewares made from the middle to the late eighteenth century in Staffordshire were of exceptionally high quality and practicality. They were hard, robust and impervious, their semi-matt off-white surfaces retaining the sharpest moulded details. Some of the blocks, the original shapes used to shape them in the pottery, still survive in the City Museum at Stoke-on-Trent. They include one with a high-relief arrangement of peaches and blossoms on a squat, fluted plinth which is inscribed 'Ralph Wood 1770'. Ralph Wood (1715–1772) was employed as a block cutter by Thomas and John Wedgwood at the Big House Pottery in Burslem. Other Ralph Wood blocks for jelly-moulds include one with a spiral-fluted dome known as a 'Turk's cap', incised 'R.W. 1768', and another shaped as a flat-topped hexagonal pyramid with a step part-way up each fluted side and known as a 'double star petty', marked with 'Ralph Wood, 1768'. From the 1740s to around the 1780s,

(18) Carter, 177.
(19) Pinto, 187 & plate 186.

white saltglazed stoneware moulds were made in the shapes of scallop-shells, melons, eggs, hedgehogs, fishes, swans, hens, chickens, suns, moons and stars. Ann Cook of Newcastle upon Tyne referred to them in her book of *Professed Cookery* of 1753 as 'Shapes of various Forms, such as Scallops, Shells, Harts &c.'[20] The latter were actually made as 'heart pickle plates', but they doubled up as useful jelly-moulds.

Some of the moulds, particularly hearts and suns, were unusual in having their decoration moulded on their converse outer surfaces. The reason for this is that they were designed to float in a bowl of clear jelly and then be removed so that the negative shapes they left behind could be filled with opaque jelly:

A MOON AND STARS IN JELLY[21]
[see fig. 6]

clear jelly   *jelly coloured with*
                                 chocolate and cochineal

Fill a dish with the coloured jelly, float a moon and seven star-moulds in it, weighting them to sink to their brims, and leave to set. Remove the moulds and fill the hollows with clear jelly. Allow to set, then turn out.

Alternatively, fill a bowl with clear jelly, float the moulds as just described, remove them when set and fill with opaque white jelly, finally adding a thin layer of chocolate / red jelly. This produces a jelly 'planetarium' just as attractive and interesting now as in the eighteenth century.

Sun, moon and star moulds with their details inside could be made in a similar way, as in the Fish Pond below.

Most of the other moulds were made in the usual way with their modelling on their inside surfaces. Some were for particular jellies, including Mrs. Raffald's 1769 versions of:

(20) Cook, 150.
(21) Raffald, 99.

Figure 6. *Elizabeth Raffald's jellies, 1769. (1) moon and stars, using saltglazed moulds made from the 1740s; (2) a fish pond, with its salt-glazed mould; (3) green melon in jelly with its saltglazed or creamware mould; (4) a hen's nest, using egg-shells as moulds; (5) fresh peaches and grapes in jelly.*

JELLIES & THEIR MOULDS

HEN AND CHICKENS IN JELLY[22]

almond-milk jelly, some left   clear white wine &
white, some turned brown   lemon jelly
with chocolate, some yellow
with beaten hard-boiled egg yolk
Lemon peel poached to tenderness

Fill the hen mould and one chicken mould with brown jelly, three other chicken moulds with white jelly and three with yellow. Turn out and arrange in a deep dish, surround with narrow 'straws' cut from the lemon peel. Pour in sufficient clear jelly to hold all in place.

GILDED FISH IN JELLY[23]

almond, rosewater and cream jelly   clear white wine &
gold leaf   lemon jelly

Fill two large fish moulds with the almond jelly. When set, turn them out into a large dish, cover them with real gold leaf, and cover them with the clear jelly.

A FISH POND[24]

jellies as above

Fill four large and six small fish-moulds with the almond jelly. Set ½ pt / 300 ml of the clear jelly in a bowl, turn two of the small fish out onto a piece of smooth wet cloth and carefully invert onto the jelly, moulded side down, then cover with more clear jelly. Repeat this process for the four remaining fishes, crossing each other in a circle, then add a thick layer of clear jelly before repeating again with the four large fishes. Leave overnight before turning out.

(22) ibid., 97.
(23) ibid., 97.
(24) ibid., 94.

GREEN MELON IN FLUMMERY[25]
[see fig. 6 and plate ii]

jellies as above   *a little green colouring*
fresh flowers

Colour the almond jelly green with food colouring [originally spinach juice] and use to fill a melon mould. Set 1 pt/600 ml of the clear jelly in a bowl, half-fill the rest of the bowl with more clear jelly, then turn the melon out, moulded side downwards, in the centre. Arrange the fresh flowers around the melon, and top up the mould with clear jelly before leaving overnight to set before turning out.

EARTHENWARE MOULDS

The mid-eighteenth century saw the development of Wedgwood's creamware, a fine off-white earthenware of smooth hard-firing off-white clay, covered in a glossy pale yellow glaze. It was ideal for both throwing and moulding and was so instantly popular that it largely replaced pewter dining- and kitchen-ware. By the last quarter of the eighteenth century its production had spread to other factories in Staffordshire and particularly in Yorkshire, Lancashire and Derbyshire. Wedgwood's 1774 *Creamware Catalogue* listed 'Shapes for Blancmange, great variety'. The majority of the Turks' head, melon, fish and other salt-glazed forms were now adopted into the creamware repertoire, but these were soon joined by many other new designs.

The late eighteenth-century moulds are usually relatively shallow, having low fluted sides supporting a flat top bearing a high-relief depiction of its chosen subject. Some were naturalistic, as in the beautifully modelled bunch of grapes and vine leaf patterns (plate ii). In these, it is obvious that the modeller had no experience of culinary matters, for each grape acts as a virtual suction-cup intent on holding its jelly inseparably in place. There were pineapples too, then the recognized symbol

(25) ibid., 96.

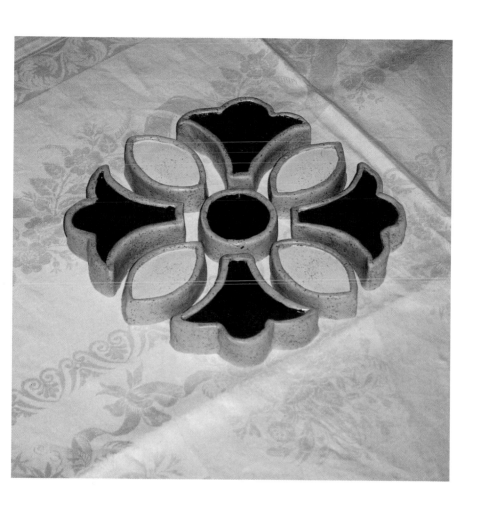

Plate i. A seventeenth-century laid tart or tart royal, filled with jellies.

Plate ii. Mrs Raffald's jellies of the 1760s. From top to bottom: two fruits in jelly (and a bunch of grapes in flummery at the top left); a green melon in flummery encased in jelly; and, foreground, Sir Walter Ffarington's nest of eggs.

Plate iii. Oranges en Rubans *or* à la Bellevue *were introduced in the Regency, but remained a Victorian favourite.*

Plate iv. Louis Ude published a recipe for this marbled cream in 1813.

Plate v. The Belgrave mould of 1850 introduced spiral columns of coloured creams into jelly.

Plate vi. The Brunswick Star mould of 1864 (left) and the Alexandra Cross mould of 1863 both used inner liners to form internal star- and cross-shaped columns of white jelly.

Plate vii. Mrs A.B. Marshall's mosaic jelly of 1891 is lined with rings of set custard.

Plate viii. Some High Victorian jellies. Clockwise from the top: little eggs; strawberry chartreuse; a lemon and wine jelly pyramid; strawberry ballettes; Dantzig jelly; coloured ballettes. In the centre is a ribbon jelly.

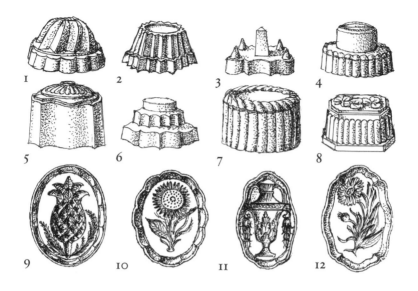

Figure 7. Wedgwood moulds. (1 & 2) a Turk's cap and 'double star petty' by Ralph Wood, 1768; (3) Solomon's Temple, c. 1780–1800; (4–7) designs from Charles Gill's drawing book c. 1807; (8) with the shamrock of Ireland, c. 1805–10; (9–12) typical moulds of c. 1800–1820.

of welcome, along with ears of Indian corn or maize, perhaps already seen as an ingredient for making cornflour blancmange. Closer to home, there were wheatsheaves symbolic of harvest, as well as sunflowers, anemones, shells, crayfish, etc., which had no particular significance. Perhaps the most popular subjects of all were classical, reflecting the interest in new discoveries in Italy, Greece and Egypt. An antique gem by Protarchos showing a lion pacified by the music of a lyre to symbolize the power of love provided the inspiration for one rectangular mould, for example. Similarly an engraving of a canopic jar in Bernard de Montfaucon's *L'Antiquité expliquée* was transformed into a finely-detailed oval mould, its scarab beetle and every other feature reproduced with archaeological accuracy.[26]

Made by pressing a sheet of clay over a positive mould, these early pieces were thin-walled, their backs being smoothly rounded and closely following the shape of the underlying design. They were therefore very unstable when rested on a flat surface, readily rolling this way and that and totally impossible to fill with liquid jelly. Initially cooks had to set them in dishes or bowls of sand to keep them level, but around the 1780s and '90s the potters provided an initial solution by modelling three narrow conical feet onto the underside of each mould. In practical kitchen use these were certainly a great improvement, but, being brittle, they often broke off, as may be seen on many surviving examples.

By the 1760s some jelly moulds were being made to explore the possibilities of achieving more verticality, always a challenge with an uncertain combination of calf's-foot gelatin and isinglass. The earliest were the Solomon's Temple moulds, which had a tall central obelisk and four short pinnacles, all set on a low, wavy-edged square plinth. Mrs Raffald provided instructions for its use in 1769:

SOLOMON'S TEMPLE[27]
[see fig. 7, no. 3]

1 ½ pt / 900 ml strong almond milk, rosewater and cream jelly
red food colour   a little black coffee
3–4 tbs grated dark chocolate   sprigs or flowers
*   with stiff stems*

Mix sufficient red colour into enough jelly to fill the obelisk with bright pink, fill the pinnacles with the plain white, and the base with sufficient chocolate melted in black coffee mixed into the remaining jelly to produce a light stone colour. Turn out after leaving overnight to set, then stick a sprig (for instance of rosemary with the lower leaves stripped off) or a flower on its

(26) Montfaucon, II pl. CXXXII.
(27) Raffald, 100.

stem down the centres of the obelisk and pinnacles in order to keep them erect.

Unmoulding such a jelly, preventing the whole creation from collapsing either before the stems were inserted, or as it was perilously carried upstairs to the dining table, must have been a constant challenge to even the most resolute of cooks. If jellies were to stand higher, and take a meaningful place amid the tall candlesticks, centrepieces, dress-stands and high-modelled confectionery pieces which now were adorning fashionable tables, they had to acquire much more substantial and reliable internal supports. This led to the invention of the core mould and cover by the Wedgwoods around 1780 (see fig. 8). The cores were usually tall obelisks, either round or square in section, or flat-sided rectangular wedges tapering to a narrow top strip, similar in shape to the Egyptian pylon. Others were tall domes, their sides having concave flutes like a lemon-reamer, while others introduced in the early nineteenth century adopted the form of straw lipwork beehives. All the vertical surfaces, and the flat area around the base which extended to a U-shaped rim, were delicately painted with sprays and wreaths of flowers or fruit all in their natural colours.

A contemporary document in the Wedgwood Museum describes how such cores were used. 'A Mould for Jelly a Square Pyramid with cover to fit on it with 5 holes in it to pour the Jelly through, and the Middle (columnar) part is left in the Jelly and showing the painting through.'[28] In practice, this meant that the cover or outer mould had to have its interior at least a quarter-inch bigger all round than the obelisk core, and a foot which exactly fitted into its U-shaped rim. In use, the cook would prop the cover upside down in a pot or pan of sand, then carefully lower the inverted core inside until the two parts fitted snugly together. She would then pour her crystal-clear jelly through the holes to fill the space between them. Once it had set, she would turn the moulds right-way up, and remove the cover, revealing the obelisk now ensheathed in a thick layer of glass-like jelly.

(28) Hughes (1969), 628.

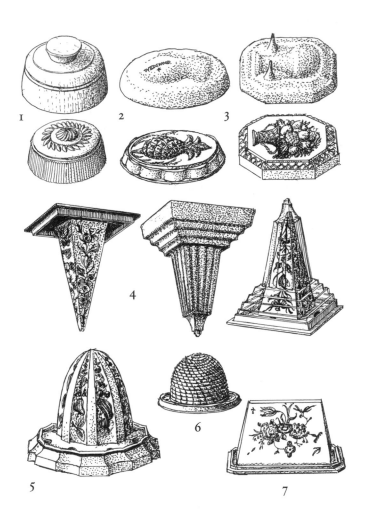

*Figure 8. Georgian moulds. (1) a turned sycamore mould of the later 18th century;
(2) a Wedgwood mould of c. 1800–1820 without feet; (3) a Spode mould of c.
1810 with typical pointed feet; (4) a Wedgwood core mould, its case and resulting
jelly, c. 1780; (5) a Wilson core mould; (6) a 19th-century Staffordshire beehive
core mould; (7) a late 18th-century wedge-shaped Wedgwood core mould.*

The overall effect was enhanced by two important design features. Firstly, the clear jelly acted like a lens on all curved surfaces, giving the fine painted decoration both magnification and movement, and secondly, these effects, coupled with additional sparkle, were complemented by the narrow fluted surfaces provided by relief modelling on the interior of the cover. By both sunlight, and especially by candlelight, these moulds gave delightful decoration on the dining table but no more than that. These were never intended to be eaten, that role being fulfilled by their dormant counterparts.

The appearance of core moulds on the fashionable table is best described in the diary entry made by Parson Woodforde on 28 March 1782, when he had just dined at Weston House. Here the table had 'a very pretty Pyramid of Jelly in the centre, a Landscape appearing thro' the Jelly, a new Device and brought from London.'[29] Hostesses wishing to obtain similar effects, but without a core-mould, could adopt the advice of John Bell, the Scarborough and Newcastle confectioner. He considered that painting a piece of wafer paper with sprigs of strawberries, cherries or peaches, or with a landscape, laying this in the base of a dish and turning a clear jelly out on top of it, gave 'a very good effect.'[30] Ann Cook was using an even simpler method in 1770, merely arranging three laurel leaves on the surface of her jellies just before they were unmoulded.[31]

Probably by experimenting with the use of a core-mould cover, it was realized that a stiffly-made jelly could support itself without a core. As a result, conical jelly moulds began to be made in the opening decade of the nineteenth century by companies such as Spode. Entitled steeples in the catalogues, they don't appear to be of any great interest, just a round fluted base supporting a stepped or spiral cone. In use, however, they are among the favourite moulds of any experienced jelly-maker. No other mould has ever exploited jelly's wobble factor so efficiently and delightfully. The slightest vibration of a table will set it off, sinuously gyrating in sensuous succulence. Just

(29) Woodforde 28/3/1782.
(30) Bell 63.
(31) Cook 149.

unmoulding one at a demonstration produces instant grins, these increasing as it performs its two-hundred-year-old routines. It is not surprising that it remained in continuous production through to the early twentieth century.

Core moulds were still popular through into the early nineteenth century, other producers including Wilsons and James Neale of Church Works, Hanley, Staffordshire, as may be seen by their impressed marks.

The standard forms of ordinary creamware moulds began to change around 1800, both by the replacement of the applied feet with a narrow strip of clay to form a strong and secure foot-ring, and by having rather deeper bodies. This change can be seen in some of the designs shown in Wedgwood's shape book of around 1805, and the set of moulds that company produced to celebrate the popular union of the Parliaments of Great Britain and Ireland in 1801. These had their respective rose, thistle, shamrock and harp raised in relief on their flat tops, but were now raised on taller fluted or scalloped sides. Charles Gill's drawing-book of Wedgwood shapes, dating from around 1807, shows blancmange moulds with almost vertical sides, showing that much firmer jelly solutions were now being used.

From this period up to the 1830s fine earthenware moulds were made by most major potteries, their walls gradually becoming thicker, and their narrow foot-rings being broadened and smoothed on to the bases in a much coarser manner. Most moulds are unmarked, but others are identifiable. Moulds of about 1810–15 made and stamped at Liverpool's Herculaneum pottery, for example, have a cockerel on top and leaves descending the sides.[32] The sherds excavated from the Humber Bank Pottery in Hull are thin-walled and stand on three feet, showing them to have been produced by the partnership of J. & J. Smith, J. Ridgway and J. Hipswell shortly after it was founded in 1802. They are oval, with fluted sides and an anchor on top, a device which must have sold well to the local seafaring and merchant community.[33]

(32) Hyland 73.
(33) Kingston, 2, 15.

COPPER MOULDS

Tin-lined copper is the best combination of materials for making jelly-moulds. The copper itself is extremely ductile, so that it can be pressed and formed into deep shapes without the need for seams. This property also enables it to hold sharp details, although not as fine as those of the best Wedgwood moulds. It is its excellent conductivity, however, which makes it so good for unmoulding jellies.

It is difficult to establish when copper moulds were first commercially manufactured. The inventories of great aristocratic kitchens such as those at Petworth House and Aston Hall make no mention of them in the 1760s and '70s, but they are certainly in evidence by the 1790s. The Harewood House kitchens had '1 Basket mould, 6 large moulds 65 small moulds' listed in its copperware in 1795,[34] for example. In 1808 there were eight 'large jelley molds' of copper in the kitchen at Temple Newsam House, near Leeds, while in 1822 William Vickers of Manchester billed John Poole, house-steward to the Earl of Stamford at Dunham Massey, £1 1s. 0d. for re-tinning the jelly moulds there, showing that they must have been in use for some time.[35] From this, it would appear that copper jelly moulds probably began to come into use around the 1780s.

Unfortunately the recipe books of the period rarely, if ever, specify the material from which any mould was made, and so can give no closer clues as to when copper was introduced for this purpose. Neither have any well-provenanced Georgian pieces yet been found, nor any bearing an early maker's mark. It is known, however, that some of the best-known mould manufacturers of the Victorian period were founded during the Regency. These included A.F. Crook in 1810 and Benham & Sons who started in Wigmore Street in 1817.[36]

(34) Harewood House Archives, 1795, Inventory no. 306.
(35) Temple Newsam Archives, 1808; Sambrook, 84.
(36) Kevill-Davis, 44.

TINPLATE MOULDS

Tinplate was used for mould-making in Georgian England, the inventory of Harewood House listing '6 large Tin moulds' in the kitchen in 1795.[37] Cooks such as 'Meg Dods', writing in 1829, certainly had experience of them, having found that they 'give red jellies a bad colour.'[38] Regrettably none are known to have survived to the present day.

Since copper and tin moulds were both made from thin sheet metal, confectioners soon realized that two could be used together to create macédoine jellies. G.A. Jarrin, the Italian confectioner of Bond Street, provided the following instructions in 1827:

MACÉDOINE JELLY[39]

clear fruit jelly with a variety of fresh fruit, the larger ones cut into pieces	or	*clear wine or liqueur jelly with a variety of preserved [or tinned] fruits*

'These jellies are best made by using two moulds of different sizes; the smaller one is put inside the larger one, and surrounded by jelly; when it is fixed the inner is taken out by using a little warm water, and the hollow it leaves behind is to be filled up with layers of fruit and layers of jelly, which must be put in gradually, and each allowed to set before the next is added; when the whole is set, it is to be turned out on a dish and served up.'

Considering the great advance of the jelly mould in Georgian England, it is surprising that some of the best jellies remained unmoulded, their appeal being in either their decoration or their taste. Few jellies were more attractive than Mrs Raffald's 'Islands' such as:

(37) Harewood House Archives, 1795, Inventory no. 306.
(38) Dods, 418.
(39) Jarrin, 142.

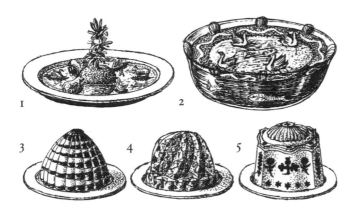

Figure 9. Regency jellies. (1) Mrs Raffald's rocky island of 1769 had gilded fish swimming in a lake of jelly, the island, shimmering in silver bran and glitter and topped with a 'tree' of myrtle, being surrounded by lambs or ducks on green leaves. Such jellies inspired (2), John Bell's fish pond, with its gold and silver fish, white swans, and orange sugar path encircling its green sugar banks; (3–5) Louis Ude's marbled, macédoine and mosaic jellies of 1813.

A FLOATING ISLAND[40]
[see fig. 9.1]

2 pt / 1.2l any clear set jelly   1 sprig of myrtle
1 medium turnip [or swede]   ½ tsp gum tragacanth
green 'hundreds & thousands' [for green comfits]
small model sheep, swans, snakes or wild animals
any flat green leaves, washed and dried

Slice the bottom off the turnip, trim the top, and drill a small hole in it. Brush the upper half with a paste made by stirring the gum into 2–3 tbs cold water and use this to cover it with the 'hundreds-and-thousands'. Set this in the centre of a large dish of jelly (having stirred the jelly a little to break it up), and place the myrtle sprig in the top. Finally arrange the lambs or swans on leaves on the jelly, looking towards the island.

(40) Raffald, 98.

The major development of jelly recipes in England took place just after the end of the Napoleonic Wars in 1815, when the already large number of French cooks working in this country was boosted by the arrival of even more. Of these, the most highly-skilled, prestigious and influential was Antonin Carême (1783–1833). In 1815 he left the service of Talleyrand to work for the Prince Regent, preparing the most superb dinners for that most portly of monarchs. However, disappointed with the standards of English cookery, he returned to live in France in 1818. In 1834 his translated recipes were published in London as *The Royal Parisian Pastrycook and Confectioner*. It includes recipes for thirty-six fruit and wine jellies, six macédoines, numerous whipped jellies, ten blancmanges, thirty-two bavarois, and nineteen French creams, as well as creams plombières thickened with rice flour. They are all of the very highest quality, inventiveness and subtlety. The following may serve as an example:

JELLY OF ROSES[41]

Put the leaves [petals] of about thirty fine roses and a pinch of cochineal into twelve ounces of clarified sugar: cover the whole close, and as soon as it is lukewarm strain it through a sieve; then add half a glass of distilled rosewater, half a glass of kirschwasser, and one ounce of clarified isinglass to it nearly cold ... stir the whole with a silver spoon, and then pour it into a mould, into which you have previously put ten pounds of pounded ice, taking care that the ice reaches nearly to the rim, and is everywhere of the same thickness. Cover the mould with a stewpan-lid, on which put a little ice, then let it stand three hours. When you are ready to serve, dip the moulds quickly in a large stewpan filled with hot water, then turn the jelly immediately out into the dish.

(41) Carême, 267.

Carême's influence on English jellies was not so much directly from his own work here, but from the generations of his Continental students and successors who subsequently served in English households. Their recipes can frequently be seen to have originated in his kitchens, as in:

APPLE JELLY THE REGENT'S WAY[42]

6 small crisp eating apples
4 oz / 100 g sugar
juice & pared zest of 1 lemon
2 in. / 5 cm stick cinnamon
2 oz / 50 g redcurrant jelly
3 tbs whipped cream

¼ pt / 150 ml stiff wine jelly
pinch grated nutmeg
3 tbs brandy
1 oz / 25 g gelatin
½ pt / 300 ml thick custard

Line a plain cylindrical 1 ½ pt / 900 ml mould with a central tube with the wine jelly, and set aside. If the redcurrant jelly is too soft to be sliced, add 1 tsp gelatin soaked for 10 minutes in a little water, warm and stir until dissolved, then set firm ¼ in. thick on a lightly greased plate. Peel the apples, rub them with the lemon juice, and simmer with the sugar, cinnamon, lemon zest and ¾ pt / 450 ml water until nearly done, then strain off the syrup into a pan, and plunge the apples into cold water. Drain the apples and cut across in ¼ in. / 7 mm slices, and cut into squares or diamonds as large as the flat part of the mould will take, using a tin cutter to remove the cores from their centres. Use the same cutter to cut out small pieces of the redcurrant jelly, and insert these in the middle of each slice of apple. Arrange these in the mould.

Rub the trimmings from the apples through a sieve, and add with the grated nutmeg and brandy to the cold syrup, in which the gelatin has soaked for about 10 minutes. Warm and stir until dissolved, fill the mould when cold, and leave to set firm. When turned out, fill the central tube with the custard beaten with the cream.

(42) Simpson, 269.

Among other French cooks finding ready employment in noble households and in gentlemen's clubs, Louis Eustache Ude was perhaps the most notable. He had been ci-devant cook to Louis XVI and the Earl of Sefton, steward to the Duke of York, and latterly maître d'hôtel at the exclusive Crockford's Club in St James's. In 1813 he had published his *The French Cook* as a 'system of Fashionable and Economical Cookery adapted to the use of English Families'. Many of its recipes were already familiar, the calf's foot jelly, strawberry jelly, etc., but no-one had ever prepared them with such refinement of method and taste. His practice of chilling jellies in ice both during their preparation and until they were unmoulded just before serving, was certainly not an English practice. It soon became a standard procedure, however, reducing the required strength of the jelly, and making it much fresher on the palate. Here is an example of one of his fruit jellies, which can also be used for raspberries, red or white currants:

STRAWBERRY JELLY[43]

Put some strawberries into an earthen pan, squeeze them well with a new wooden spoon; mix some pounded sugar with the fruit, and let them infuse for an hour, that the sugar might draw out all the juices; next pour in a little water. If the strawberries are very ripe, squeeze the juice of two lemons to restore the acid taste to the strawberries, for such preparations which are too sweet are insipid. Put all this into a bag that is nearly new, that the juice may be strained clear and limpid; mix some melted isinglass with the juice, but mind that the whole must be very cold. Now put half a spoonful of the jelly into a mould over ice to ascertain of what substance it is. If thick enough, put the whole into the large mould in ice, and cover it also with ice, but no salt, for it would spoil the bright colour of the jelly.

(43) Ude, 358.

Such frozen jellies could only be made in metal moulds, those made of pottery for the use of English cooks being very poor conductors of heat. Even if the contents of a pottery mould eventually froze when set in ice, they would have melted to a shapeless mass by the time they could be released by dipping in warm water. The introduction of the frozen jelly around the Regency period explains why there was such an increase in the manufacture of tinned copper moulds. Their use is fully described by Guglielmo Jarrin, a native of Colorno, close to Padua in northern Italy, who had become a leading New Bond Street confectioner by 1820:[44]

> take a copper mould of any form you please, according to the dish you mean to make; place the mould in a box full of pounded ice, quite to the edge of the mould, and surround it on all sides; pour your jelly into it, cover it with a tin cover, or any other equally thin, and put some ice on it; three hours is sufficient to ice this sort of jelly; when you wish to serve it up, take a basin of warm water, plunge your mould quickly into it, and instantly turn it out on the plate.

Although he doesn't mention it, it is always essential to ensure that the plate has been set on ice beforehand, otherwise it melts the bottom of the jelly, leaving it so unstable that the slightest movement is likely to send it over the rim and onto the floor.

Jarrin is also useful for providing many more recipes for jellies to be made using the freezing method. Here, his isinglass is replaced by gelatin.

(44) Jarrin, 138.

JARRIN'S CLEAR JELLY STOCK[45]

1 oz / 25 g gelatin   *3 oz / 75 g sugar*

Sprinkle then stir the gelatin into ½ pt / 300 ml of water, leave to soak for 10 minutes, then add the sugar, pour on the fruit juices, etc., listed below, made up to 1 pt / 600 ml with water, all almost at boiling point, and stir until completely dissolved. Allow to cool before moulding as described above.

VENUS'S CLEAR JELLY

6 tbs rosewater, 3 tbs brandy, a little red food colouring

ORANGE-FLOWER JELLY

6 tbs orange-flower water, strained juice of 3 oranges or lemons, 1 glass champagne, a little red food colouring

STRAWBERRY JELLY

strained juice of 1 lb / 450 g ripe strawberries, juice of 2 lemons, a little red food colouring

RED & WHITE CURRANT JELLY

strained juice of 1 lb / 450 g currants and 4 oz / 100 g raspberries, a little red food colouring

CHERRY JELLY

strained juice of 2 lb / 900 g very ripe cherries, and of 4 oz / 100 g redcurrants

GRAPE JELLY

strained juice of 2 lb / 900 g grapes, and of 2 lemons

LEMON JELLY

strained juice of 2 or 3 lemons

(45) ibid., 136–141.

VANILLA JELLY

simmer 2 finely-chopped vanilla pods with ½ pt / 300 ml of the hot water used to make the jelly, strain, 1 glass maraschino

COFFEE JELLY

4 oz / 100 g freshly-ground coffee, scalded with 1 pt / 600 ml of the water used to make the jelly and then strained clear

TEA JELLY

¼ oz / 6 g green or black tea, scalded with 1 pt / 600 ml of the water used to make the jelly, strained clear, 1 glass brandy, a little red food colouring

RUM JELLY

1 glass rum, zest of 2 lemons rubbed off on sugar-lumps, strained juice of 5 lemons

Along with other confectioners and cooks, he was still making almond-milk blancmanges (now sometimes described as 'orgeat jellies'), and macédoine jellies which had layers of fruit and jelly built up in a mould lined with clear jelly. He was one of the first to publish details of a new technique which was to become a regular household favourite well into the mid-twentieth century. In his words:

WHISKED JELLIES[46]

Are nothing more than the preceding jellies whisked, when cold, with a rod of birch twigs; they must be put in their moulds as soon as they are set [i.e. fully frothed], like a soft cream; they must not have time to fix [i.e. set firm] before they are whisked, as they would not take the smooth form of the moulds; the jelly thus whisked is not so long taking ice.

(46) ibid., 142.

Later known as Venetian or Russian jelly, this method is applicable to all clear jellies, giving them an almost marble-like translucent appearance and a satisfyingly fresh, light spongy texture.

Most of the flavoured creams which had been served in individual glasses amid the pyramids of jellies were liquids. By the 1820s many were being set with additional egg yolks and gelatin, to produce moulded creams of unrivalled smoothness and richness. Some of the best were published by Ude. His recipes are not the easiest to follow, since, like many highly skilled professionals, he is so busy giving the finer details that the basic techniques tend to get rather lost.

UDE'S MOULDED CREAMS[47]

½ pt / 300 ml single cream	8 egg yolks
½ pt / 300 ml milk	4 tsp / 6 leaves gelatin
4 tbs sugar	flavourings – see below
pinch of salt	

Beat the yolks and strain them into a large bowl. Stir the gelatin into ¼ pt / 150 ml cold water and leave to soak for 10 minutes. Bring the cream, milk, sugar, salt and one of the flavourings given below to the boil, pour onto the yolks from a height while beating with a whisk, so that the mixture thickens evenly. Beat in the gelatin, leave to cool, then pour into a mould previously brushed with clarified butter, and leave in a cool place to set.

One of his variations mixed the ingredients cold, poured them into a buttered mould, covering the top, and set it by poaching in water below boiling point. If the water boils, the cream separates into a curd, like over-cooked scrambled eggs. In another, half the yolks were omitted from the hot mixture and the mould set in ice and salt to freeze like an ice-cream. In yet another the hot mixture was whipped when cold and about to set, then put into the mould for freezing.

(47) Ude, 342–44.

COFFEE CREAM

Ude's method was to heat ground coffee scalding hot in an omelet pan and add it to the above mixture while it was still hot. Today it is best to boil the milk, pour it onto 2–3 tbs ground coffee, leave to infuse, then strain through a muslin into a clean pan, before adding the cream and proceeding as above.

TEA CREAM

As for coffee cream, pouring the boiling milk onto 2–3 tsp leaf tea.

CHOCOLATE CREAM

Add 2 oz / 50 g grated dark chocolate to the cream, etc., before boiling.

VANILLA CREAM

Boil a chopped stick of vanilla in the cream before straining it onto the yolks.

ORANGE OR LEMON CREAM

Add the finely-pared zest of an orange or lemon to the cream before boiling, then strain onto the yolks.

ORANGE-FLOWER CREAM

When soaking the gelatin, replace half the water with orange-flower water.

CRÈME À LA GENET, BARLEY-SUGAR CREAM, OR CARAMEL CREAM

Dissolve 2 tbs sugar in 1 tbs water in a small pan, boil, then stir continuously over a reduced heat until it is golden brown, then dip the base of the pan immediately into cold water to stop it cooking. Add ¼ pt / 150 ml cold water, and re-heat with 1 tbs additional sugar to form a caramel-flavoured syrup. When cold, use this to dissolve the gelatin as in the main recipe above.

Rather confusingly, some of the moulded creams introduced at this time were called cheeses, fromages, or iced Bavarian Creams. They were made by mixing raw fruit purées, purposely uncooked to retain their fresh flavours and colours, with whipped cream and gelatin before moulding and freezing.

FRUIT CHEESES, FROMAGES OR ICED BAVARIAN CREAMS[48]

¼ pt / 150 ml whipping cream   2 tsp / 3 leaves gelatin
3–4 tbs sugar
1 pt / 600 ml fresh strawberries or raspberries or 3 ripe apricots or 1 stewed peach with its kernel reduced to a paste, or ½ a pineapple, stewed tender in syrup.

Grind or liquidize the fruit to a purée and rub through a fine cloth or muslin. Stir the gelatin into 3 tbs cold water, leave to soak for 10 minutes, then warm until completely dissolved. Mix the cream, fruit purée and the cool gelatin, whip over ice until thick, turn into a mould, and freeze until solid. To release the cream, either dip the mould into warm water or wrap in a towel freshly dipped in hot water. Turn out onto a dish already chilled to freezing-point.

INFUSED CHEESES

½ pt / 300 ml single cream   4 tbs sugar
1 pt / 600 ml double cream   2 tsp / 3 leaves gelatin
small pinch of salt
2 vanilla pods or 2 tbs coffee or 4 oz / 100 g grated dark chocolate

Simmer the vanilla, coffee or chocolate, the salt and the sugar in the single cream until it has acquired a strong flavour, strain through a fine muslin, and leave to cool. Soften the gelatin in

(48) ibid., 366–69.

3 tbs cold water for 10 minutes, then warm untill completely dissolved. Reserve. Partly whip the double cream, add the flavoured cream, whip over ice until thick, add the cool gelatin and proceed as above.

New and attractive ways of moulding the unfrozen jellies and creams were now developed, these including

MARBLED CREAMS[49]
[see fig. 9.3 and plate iv]

any two of the creams (p. 113) of contrasting colours, such as
vanilla and chocolate or coffee, cold but not set

Oil the interior of a mould and embed in ice or iced water. Mark one point on the rim with a little adhesive tape, raise this a little by tilting the mould, and pour in a little of the darker cream. When set, level the mould, pour in sufficient of the lighter cream to just cover the darker one, and leave to set. Continue in this way until the mould is nearly full, then pour in the last layer with the mould level. Leave to set and turn out in the usual way. The finished cream is both attractive and eats well.

MARBLED JELLIES[50]
[see fig. 9.3]

any opaque whipped jellies or creams of different colours,
already firmly set
clear orange jelly, cold but unset

Using a knife blade freshly rinsed in warm water, on a freshly rinsed, wrung out and smoothed cloth, cut the opaque jellies into pieces of different sizes. Set a lightly oiled mould in ice or iced water, pour in a little of the orange jelly, and drop in pieces of the opaque jellies, allow to set and continue in this way until the mould is full. Leave to set, then turn out as usual. As Ude explained 'this jelly will be as good to the taste as it will be pleasing to the eye.'

(49) ibid., 348.
(50) ibid., 365.

MOSAIC JELLIES AND CREAMS[51]
[see fig. 9.5]

¼ pt/150 ml orange cream (p. 113), 1 pt/600 ml orange jelly OR
*¼ pt/150 ml chocolate cream (p. 113), 1 pt/600 ml vanilla
cream (p. 113)*

Set the orange or chocolate creams in a small rectangular mould
until very firm, then turn out onto a freshly rinsed, wrung out
and smoothed cloth, and cut into thin slices with a knife freshly
rinsed in warm water. Use tin cutters to stamp out floret or
other small shapes. Take a metal mould, lightly oil the interior,
and arrange some of the shapes around the lower part of its
interior. Dip this part into iced water, and pour in enough of
the orange jelly or vanilla cream respectively to just cover them.
Continue in this way until the mould is full. 'This jelly looks
beautiful when well made.'

With their tables groaning under the weight of magnificent
ormolu, gold and silverware made by craftsmen such as Thomire
of Paris and Storr of London, porcelain and fine earthenware
by the best Continental and English factories, heavy lead-
glass cut-crystal from Sunderland and the West Midlands,
and magnificent heraldic damask from Northern Ireland and
Yorkshire, the nobles of Regency England dined in a splendour
to vie with Imperial Rome. The old two-course dinners were
too clumsy and primitive to continue at this level of society,
their place being taken by *service à la Russe*: a regular sequence
of many separate services within the two main courses. In the
first came the soups, fish, *entrées*, *relevés*, in the second the roast
and *entremets*, then the dessert of fruits and confectionery, after
the servants had departed. Since they had to be served, jellies
and creams always formed part of the *entremets*, never, as it is
often imagined, the dessert. Given this degree of spectacle and
formality, it is not surprising that the jellies and creams of the
Regency were so subtly flavoured and elegantly presented.

(51) ibid., 360.

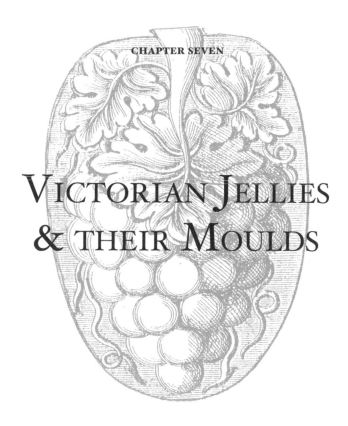

CHAPTER SEVEN

VICTORIAN JELLIES & THEIR MOULDS

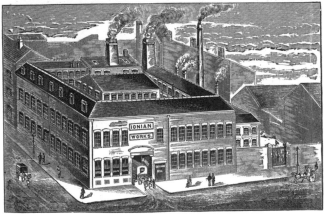

Figure 10. Metal moulds were manufactured in factories centred around London and the West Midlands. Typical of these were the works of Sellman & Hill, founded in Wolverhampton in 1880 as tinsmiths and japanners. Their London showroom was at 71 Queen Street, in the heart of the City.

The late eighteenth and early nineteenth centuries had seen great changes in English society. This country's natural resources of water, coal, clay, metallic ores, wool and sheer muscle, supplemented by cotton and other imports from across the entire world, were now being exploited as never before. The combination of capital and inventiveness, boosted by the demands and successes of international military campaigns, fostered a spirit of entrepreneurial expansion which was already reaching across the globe. To service its needs, the first great steam and water-powered factories had been built, together with new roads, canals and railways linking them to the mines, to other fast-growing urban centres of trade and industry, and, most importantly, to the ports. The world had never seen anything to compare with this economic, industrial and social phenomenon, but it was soon to realize that it was only the start of things to come. In the long reign of Queen Victoria, from 1837 to 1901, Britain and its Empire was the greatest ever naval, military and trading power.

All those who experienced British influence through its colonies and protectorates, its diplomatic, military and trading activities, were left in no doubt as to the country's great wealth and might. They believed that all their labour, raw materials and taxes, and the wealth they produced, was going back to Britain to fund the most lavish and luxurious of lifestyles for all its inhabitants. Although most of their descendants still assume this to be true, the majority of the population of England was subject to severe poverty and oppression. They had no vote, worked in industries which frequently killed or maimed them for starvation wages and without any compensation, and usually lived in squalid, overcrowded and disease-ridden houses, whether in town or countryside. These circumstances explain why the development of Victorian jellies followed two quite different routes, one meeting the needs of the poor, and the other those of the fashionable and wealthy.

In the 1830s jelly was seen as either a sick-room food, or as a delightful and delicate addition to the *entremet* course for middle- and upper-class dinners. To make it still took hours of boiling up raw ingredients, painstakingly filtering them through thick flannel jelly-bags, and flavouring them with expensive almonds, fruits, wines and spirits. Most women had neither the financial resources nor the inherited knowledge to waste their time in this way. They usually had large families to bring up and busy homes to run without any labour-saving devices. Many also had long hours to work as domestic servants, agricultural labourers, factory hands or, like some of my ancestors, as underground mineworkers. The combination of low life-expectancy, poverty, child labour and removal to mushrooming urban centres, meant that most never grew up in homes where they could learn even the most basic of the domestic skills needed to operate an efficient household. These circumstances even affected those who climbed up into pretentious lower-middle classes. They would now be expected to give dinner parties such as they could never previously afford, offering dishes they didn't know how to make.

It was to serve this group in particular that the first mass-produced and mass-marketed processed gelatins were manufactured. Swinborne's patent refined isinglass and gelatins were among the most successful, being widely advertised from the 1840s. Alexis Soyer's *Modern Housewife* of 1848 gave instructions for how such prepared products were to be used.[1]

GELATINE AND ISINGLASS JELLY is made using one ounce and a half of either, and boil in one quart of water, reduce to half; if not required very clear, as for

(1) Soyer (1848), 350.

JELLIES & THEIR MOULDS

lemon jelly, it need not be run through a bag, but merely through a fine sieve.

Much still depended on the quality and purity of the different brands, however, for some retained traces of their boneyard, tanyard, and slaughterhouse origins. To quote 'Wanderer', writing in 1885, 'As to the jelly, with its ancient and fish-like flavour, the less said about it the better. This, with blanc-manges and bread puddings, may be classified under the head of "minor atrocities", because they can be left alone.'[2]

By the time Mrs Beeton had compiled her great *Book of Household Management* in 1861, prepared isinglass and gelatin were in regular use. She gives some 26 recipes for using them to make jellies and creams, explaining that:[3]

> Substitutes for calf's feet are now frequently used in making jellies, which lessen the expense and trouble in preparing this favourite dish; isinglass and gelatine being two of the principal materials employed; but, although they may look as nicely as jellies made from good stock, they are never so delicate, having very often an unpleasant flavour, somewhat resembling glue, particularly when made with gelatine.

For this reason, she and many other cookery writers continued to give recipes for the seven-hour process for transforming calf's feet into jelly stock.

It is interesting to compare her costings for making jellies from different materials. One pint of calf's foot jelly required one calf's foot costing at least 6*d.*, or cow-heel at about 4*d.*[4] Most isinglass jellies cost between 2*s.* 6*d.* and up to 5*s.* each in raw materials alone – about £10–15 in modern values – which explains why they were still a luxury even in middle-class homes. Her recipes include the usual fruit jellies, almond-milk and lemon gelatin blancmanges, jaunemanges, rich set creams, macédoines and ribbons (see plate viii), as well as other varieties such as;[5]

(2) D'Avigdor, 76.
(3) Beeton, no. 1411.
(4) ibid., no. 1411.
(5) ibid., no. 1426.

DUTCH FLUMMERY

1 oz / 25 g gelatin
zest & juice of ½ lemon
sugar to taste

2 eggs, beaten
½ pt / 300 ml sherry or
Madeira
½ tbs brandy

Soak the gelatin in ¼ pt / 150 ml water in a jug for 10 minutes, meanwhile simmering the pared zest in a further ¼ pt / 150 ml of water. Strain the hot lemon-flavoured water on to the gelatin, stir until dissolved, then add the wine and eggs, and sugar to taste. Stand the jug in a pan of simmering water and stir until it has thickened, but not boiled, then stir in the brandy, strain into an oiled mould and leave to set.

LEMON SPONGE[6]

1 oz / 25 g gelatin
6 oz / 150 g sugar

juice and pared zest of 2
lemons
2 large egg-whites

Stir the gelatin into 1 pt / 600 ml water, leave to soak for 10 minutes, then add the sugar and zest, and stir over a gentle heat until the sugar and gelatin have completely dissolved. Strain into a bowl and leave until just about to set. Beat the eggs to stiffness, then beat them in the jelly until all is a stiff, white froth. Pour into a lightly oiled mould, and leave to set.

[N.B. this recipe should be avoided by anyone liable to experience problems through eating raw eggs.]

Those for whom these recipes were too troublesome, or who had little faith in their culinary skills, could always find acceptable substitutes. One was to buy ready-made bottled jellies from companies such as Crosse and Blackwell who made:

(6) ibid., no. 1448.

JELLIES of unequalled brilliance, consisting of Calf's Feet, Orange, Lemon, Noyeau, Punch, Madeira etc. In pint and quart bottles for the Convenience.

as advertised in Francatelli's *Plain Cookery for the Working Classes* of 1861. Alternatively they could have their jellies delivered directly from a nearby confectioner. These professionals found that ice was more economical than gelatin for keeping their product upright. Ude had known balls where, in spite of the pillage of a pack of footmen, which was enormous, the jellies had melted on all the tables or been heaped up in the kitchen, completely disfigured by the manner in which they had been removed from the serving dishes.[7] John Jorrocks, Surtees' famous fox-hunting London grocer, experienced similar problems when holding a large dinner party in his own home. He had his jellies delivered fresh from Mr Farrell, the confectioner in Lamb's Conduit Street near Great Ormond Street Children's Hospital, only to find that they 'had all melted long before it came their turn to be eaten.' Elsewhere Surtees described how an 'ornamental cake basket of the prize candelabrum makes a grand plateau for the usual group of calves feet jelly-glasses.'[8] He also perceived how the below-stairs servants, succumbing to temptation and devouring the jellies and creams intended for their master's table, fell back on the barely believable excuses that 'the cat upset the cream – the cat eat the jelly'![9]

Later in the century, tinned jellies were invented as a convenience food. In 1880 T.F. Blackwell patented a tin mould with a hole in the base for inserting molten jelly, this then being soldered to create an airtight seal. A small flap projected from a [deeply scored?] strip around the base, a split ended rod or key slipping over this so that it could be wound up, opening the mould just like a traditional tin of sardines or cooked meat. T.B. Browne came up with a similar tin with an easily removable lid, its interior being formed into 'grooves, corrugations or other means for imparting an ornamental configuration to the jelly'.[10]

(7) Ude, 435.
(8) Surtees (1838) (1949 ed.), 200, 205.
(9) Surtees (1859), 430.
(10) Pat. No. 1880–3018 July 26; & 1891 – 8375 May 15.

Being relatively expensive to produce, and only used to contain foods which could be easily made at home, they can never have been produced in significant numbers.

One of Mrs Beeton's most useful contributions to household knowledge was to publicize the fact that jellies were not nutritive, and should no longer be relied upon to sustain invalids and the sick. It is worthwhile to read her well-founded opinions:[11]

> JELLIES are not the nourishing food they were at one time considered to be, and many eminent physicians are of the opinion that they are less digestible than the flesh, or muscular parts of animals ... Animal jelly, or gelatine, is glue, whereas vegetable jelly is rather analogous to gum. Leibig places gelatine very low indeed in the scale of usefulness. He says 'Gelatin, which by itself is tasteless, and when eaten, excites nausea, possesses no nutritive value; that, even when accompanied by the savoury constituents of flesh, it is not capable of supporting the vital process' ... It is this substance which is most frequently employed in the manufacture of the jellies supplied by the confectioner; but those prepared at home from calves' feet do possess some nutrition, and are the only sort which should be given to invalids.

As far as most of the poor were concerned, sweet jellies were a luxury beyond their means, and calf's feet jellies only an expensive sick-room necessity. If they wanted any for that purpose, they could buy it ready-made in stoneware jars printed with texts such as;

(11) Beeton, 696.

INVALID JELLY
SPECIALLY PREPARED FROM CALVES FEET
BY
PARKER & SONS
CONFECTIONERS BY APPOINTMENT
18 ST. MARYS GATE AND 12 ST. ANNS SQUARE
MANCHESTER

Jellies formed no part of the culinary curriculum at the National and Industrial Schools for servants, wives and mothers in Finchley in the 1850s.[12] By the 1870s, however, practical, pioneering educationalists were insisting that children should have a real knowledge of nutrition, not only learned from books, but demonstrated before their eyes using real ingredients. In the syllabus developed by Mrs Catherine M. Buckton, for teaching girls in the Leeds Board Schools, the teacher explained that:[13]

If I were to boil beef or any butcher's meat for a very long time I would boil away all ... except 'gelatine', – here it is in the bottle. The gelatine we buy in packets to make jelly or stiffen any dish like blanc-mange is the same substance ... The gelatine in this packet is made from bone. Gelatine is nourishing when mixed up with different substances, as we find it in meat; but it is not nourishing when eaten by itself, and only takes away the appetite; for this reason we do not give delicate patients jelly which is almost entirely made of gelatine.

An ignorant cook would tell you that this stiff stock [of pure gelatine] is very strong and nourishing, but a doctor would tell you that if a man, woman, child, or dog, were to be fed on nothing else for some time, they would first suffer from diarrhoea and then die of starvation. I should recommend all cooks ... to buy some gelatine sold in packets and add it to the stock, or any food they wish to make stiff, instead of ruining meat and wasting their

(12) Finchley.
(13) Buckton, 69–71.

time in trying to send away all the other good substances it contains up the chimney.

Needless to say, there were no recipes for sweet jellies in her book, but she did include one for semolina and ground-rice moulds. Mrs Beeton had priced her rice blancmange at about 6*d.* the pint, one-sixth that of most of her jellies, showing how economical it was, especially for poorer families.[14] In addition, as Mrs Buckton explained to the girls:[15]

> Semolina is roughly ground wheat of a hard kind that contains a great deal of gluten and is very nutritious, because besides gluten it has all the other good things which wheat possesses. I shall put one tablespoonful into half a pint of milk, sweeten it with two teaspoonfuls of sugar, and let it simmer very gently on top of the oven for half an hour [she used a Yorkshire range with a hotplate over the oven]. It must be well stirred for the first ten minutes. As soon as it is ready I shall pour it into this basin that has been well rinsed out in cold water. When the semolina is cold it will turn out, and be very nice eaten with treacle, sugar, or preserve.

Semolina, ground rice, whole rice and cornflour were the moulded sweets of working-class households, not jellies. They could be flavoured by mixing in custard powder as a substitute for costly eggs, or flavoured with any of the essences produced by Langdale's and similar manufacturers.[16] Alternatively, they could be made with packeted blancmange powders made by Greens of Brighton, Goodall and Backhouse of Leeds, Alfred Bird of Birmingham and Chivers of Cambridge, among many others. 'By the simple addition of Milk, without the use of [additional] sugar, the housewife can prepare a delicious dish,' stated one of Chivers' advertisements. This was perfectly true. Starch-based blancmanges could be made in minutes, cost

(14) Beeton, no. 1476.
(15) Buckton, 83.
(16) Howard, 124.

very little, were good to eat, satisfied the appetite, provided nourishment and, when moulded, looked attractive, even luxurious on any ordinary kitchen / living-room table. This is why the well-designed and robust, cheap mass-produced pottery moulds of the Victorian period were always sold as blancmange moulds. Blancmange was the working family's dish, one which always turned out of its water-rinsed mould without any trouble, and only had one real disadvantage – its often too-frequent appearance at the end of main meals, high teas, and social events such as picnics and chapel teas.

At the other end of the social scale, in houses where professional housekeepers and cooks were employed to prepare all the food required by the family and its servants, the jelly and cream *entremets* of the Regency remained as popular as ever. Manufactured isinglass and gelatins were certainly used since they were convenient and saved time and trouble, but Jules Gouffé still maintained that the:[17]

> pastrycooks having continuous work [should] make their own stiffening, say either pork rind or calf's foot ... a clean and wholesome stiffening, far preferable to the gelatine to be had from the trade, which frequently lacks both these qualities.

His recipe for using pork skin was simple and effective.

PORK RIND JELLY STOCK[18]

4 lb / 1.8 kg fresh pork skin   *juice of 2 lemons*
8 egg-whites

Scald the skin, leave to soak for 10 minutes, scrape it clean, and leave overnight in cold water. Next day cut it into fine strips, put in a pan with 10 pt / 6 l cold water, bring to the boil, then simmer very gently, without a lid, until it can be rubbed to a paste between the fingers and the volume is reduced to

(17) Gouffé, 353.
(18) ibid., 355.

4 pt/2.4 l. As it simmers, add a little cold water from time to time and skim off all the rising scum. Strain the liquid through a freshly rinsed cloth into a clean pan, and leave to chill.

When cold, remove the fat from the top, and wipe the surface clean with a little hot water and a clean cloth. Beat the egg-whites, lemon juice and ½ pt/300 ml water to a froth, beat this into the jelly with a wire whisk, continuing until it comes to the boil, then simmer for 4 minutes before straining through a jelly-bag. This produces sufficient jelly to set 12 pt/7.2 l of liquid in moulds.

If for future use, Gouffé poured the strained stock onto the cold marble slab of his pastry kitchen, allowed it to become firm, then dried it off to brittleness in his hot closet, storing the finished gelatin in a dry place.

The conical jelly bags were now usually made with four loops of tape sewn at intervals around their open end. This enabled them to be tied open, either into a supporting iron ring, or to hooks screwed around the insides of the top rails of an enclosed wooden jelly-stand. These square stands usually stood about 3 ft/90 cm high, their planked walls sloping inwards, the top hinging up to allow the jelly stock to be poured in, and the front door opening to admit the basin which caught the dripping jelly. In this way the jelly was kept warm, fluid, and uncontaminated by the dust of the kitchen. Those without such equipment were advised to up-end a stool or chair onto a table and tie a piece of fine cloth or flannel between its legs to create an impromptu jelly-bag.

It is well known that as the era progressed, there was an ever-increasing demand for every artefact to become more elaborate and fussy. In the dining-room, for example, this was to be seen in the design of furniture, tableware, cutlery, light fittings, flower arrangements and interior decoration. Unsurprisingly, jellies followed suit. Soyer's recipes of the 1840s had already changed from those of Ude; there were similar fruit jellies, creams, and bavarois, but these were now supplemented by new ingredients and techniques. Richer creams were made using both eggs and whipped cream, for example:

PISTACHIO CREAM[19]

4 oz / 100 g pistachio kernels	*1 oz / 25 g gelatin*
6 oz / 150 g sugar	*5 egg yolks, beaten*
zest of 1 lemon	*¾ pt / 450 ml whipping*
few drops of almond essence	*cream*
¾ pt / 450 ml milk	*green food colouring [for*
	spinach juice]

Grind the pistachios, sugar, almond essence and a little of the milk to a smooth paste. Soak the gelatin in ¼ pt / 150 ml cold water. Bring the rest of the milk to the boil, remove from the heat, stir in the pistachio paste, then pour onto the yolks, while beating. Return to the pan, and stir while heating until it thickens as a custard, but does not boil. Allow to cool a little, then stir in the gelatin until dissolved, pass through a fine sieve into a bowl, and leave in a cool place until almost set. Finally beat in the whipped cream and sufficient colouring to give a good green, and pour into its mould to set.

Another major new arrival was variously called Dantzig Goldwasser, Eau de Vie de Danzic, or Eau d'Or, a clear liqueur made in Germany, Holland and France which was characterized by its glittering flakes of pure gold leaf. Added to a clear jelly, they gave it an opulent sparkle, especially by the candlelight of a formal dinner.[20] Soyer let the gold settle to the bottom of a glass, draining off most of the clear before mixing in a little jelly and using it to line the base of an inverted mould before filling it up with layers of clear liqueur jelly and fresh strawberries. This ensured that the top displayed most of its gold when turned out (see plate viii). He used similar methods for macédoines of fresh fruits, or apricots, peaches and black grapes.

(19) ibid., 325.
(20) Soyer (1847), 518, 519, 521.

As champagne was then as popular as today, this too was set as a jelly, the skilful cook enabling it to retain much of its fizz, so that it tingled on the tongue:

GELÉE DE FLEURS D'ORANGE AU VIN DE CHAMPAGNE[21]

6 oz / 150 g sugar	*1 oz / 25 g gelatin*
⅛ pt / 75 ml rosewater	*½ pt / 300 ml champagne*

Stir the gelatin and sugar into ½ pt / 300 ml cold water, soak for 10 minutes, then gently heat and stir until dissolved, and leave to cool. When cold but unset, fold in the rosewater and champagne as gently as possible, and chill until set. Do not make too far in advance, otherwise the gas separates into large bubbles.

By the 1850s cooks such as Charles Elmé Francatelli, one of Carême's pupils who rose to become Maître d' Hôtel and Chief Cook to Queen Victoria, were making jellies of even greater elaboration for the *entremets* of the royal tables. Some of the most effective were relatively simple:

CELESTINA STRAWBERRY CREAM[22]

small ripe strawberries	*1½ oz / 35 g sugar*
any clear strong jelly	*¼ pt / 150 ml whipping*
½ pt / 300 ml strawberries	*cream*
	1 oz / 25 g gelatin

Dip the small strawberries individually in the clear jelly, set as a solid wall around the base and sides of a mould, and chill. Bruise the ½ pt / 300 ml strawberries with the sugar, rub through a sieve, and stir in the gelatin which has been soaked in ¼ pt / 150 ml water for 10 minutes, warmed and stirred to dissolve, and

(21) Soyer, 524.
(22) Francatelli (1855), 467.

allowed to cool but not set. Whip the cream until stiff, mix into the strawberry jelly, and as it is about to set pour into the lined mould before leaving it to become completely firm before turning out.

ORANGES OR LEMONS À LA BELLEVUE[23]
[Carême's *Oranges en Rubans*]
[see frontispiece no. 2 and plate iii]

oranges or lemons	white gelatin blancmange
orange jelly coloured pink, or lemon jelly	

Use a tin cutter to remove a ½ in./12 mm hole from the stalk end of each orange or lemon, then a steel teaspoon to scoop out all the pulp. Soak the shells in cold water for 1 hour, then use the spoon once more to smooth the insides. Block any accidental holes from the outside with a little butter, and set the shells on ice. Carefully fill the interiors with alternating layers of the appropriate orange or lemon jelly and blancmange (ensuring that each layer is set enough to take the next), leave to set completely, then cut vertically into four segments. These may be dished as a cone or pyramid, with fresh bayleaves emerging from between them.

JELLY À LA VICTORIA
[WITH DANTZIG JELLY][24]
[see plate viii]

7 tsp/10 sheets gelatin	¼ pt/150 ml Danziger
3 tbs sugar	Goldwasser
1 tsp strained lemon juice	3 oz/75 g pistachio kernels, blanched and sliced into 6

Stir the gelatin and sugar into 1 pt/600 ml water and leave to soak for 10 minutes, then stir and warm until dissolved. When

(23) ibid., 464.
(24) ibid., 463.

cool, stir in the liqueur. When about to set, pour a little into a mould, scatter with some of the pistachios, then continue to layer the jelly and pistachios until the mould is full, and leave until completely firm.

Other jellies were becoming far more ornate as well as more interesting to the diner:

JELLIES EN SURPRISE[25]

¼ pt / 150 ml any clear jelly
½ pt / 300 ml any dark cream jelly
1 oz / 25 g flaked almonds
5 tsp / 8 sheets of gelatin to the pint

1 pt / 600 ml any pale cream jelly [e.g. a cream flavoured with toasted flaked almonds with pistachio cream, apricot with vanilla, or chocolate with white coffee]

When the clear jelly is close to setting, dip individual flakes of almond into it, and use them to decorate the inside of the mould. Pour in some clear jelly and rotate within the mould to build up a thin layer around the base and sides. Once this has set, put in the darker cream jelly and rotate to form a layer about ⅓ in. / 1 cm thick all round. Finally fill up with the pale cream jelly and leave to become firm.

The 'Panachée' jelly offered the cook a real opportunity for display. Its name was derived from the tricolour plume of feathers worn by Representatives during the French Revolution, when it was apparently invented. At its simplest, it was merely a ribbon jelly of ¼ in. / 6 mm alternating layers of pink and pale jellies. In practice these work well in jelly glasses but visually merge inseparably in a large mould. Its mature form was much more impressive.

(25) Francatelli (1855), 468.

PANACHEE JELLY[26]

*½ pt / 300 ml each of 2 jellies of contrasting colours made with
6 tsp / 9 leaves gelatin to the pint
1 pt / 600 ml any firm cream jelly, or macédoine jelly with
fresh or stewed fruits*

Pour the 2 jellies into separate moulds, leave overnight to set
firmly, then turn out onto a freshly rinsed and smoothed cloth,
and cut into ¼ in. / 6 mm slices using a knife blade dipped in
warm water. Cut these into diamond, triangle or other shapes
which will fit together like a tiled floor to completely cover the
base of a charlotte mould. To do this, it is best to draw a full-
size design on paper beforehand. Then dip each piece in clear
jelly and set in place in a lightly oiled mould. Cut the remaining
set jellies into strips, and apply these in the same way vertically
around the sides of the mould. Finally fill the centre with the
cream or macédoine jelly, and leave to set.

During the 1850s gastronomes were becoming critically
concerned with their jelly *entremets*. By this stage of the meal,
already having consumed the soup, fish, *entrée*, *relevé* and *rôti*,
their appetites and palates were already rather jaded:[27]

> As to our jellies, even the calf's foot, they are, generally
> speaking, not approachable by a prudent epicure, being
> on the one hand, of almost india-rubber toughness, and
> on the other hand, but slightly qualified by their proper
> natural corrections, the juice and the aroma.
>
> Yet such delicate dishes are easily designed but to
> appear at the close of a dinner. They should be well
> elaborated and nutritively prepared, or they become not
> only superfluous, but absolutely injurious to health.

The cooks responded to this challenge by creating jellies
which satisfied and sometimes almost overwhelmed all the
senses, except that of hearing. By the 1890s not only were all

(26) ibid., 463.
(27) Pierce, 81–2.

the earlier recipes and techniques still in use, but now they were joined by others offering a whole range of rich flavours and new visual effects. The delicacy of the Regency was replaced by the full-blown richness of the over-self-confident High Victorian. Even though they still came at the end of dinner, they now commanded the full interest of the diners, re-awakening them with stimulating scents, tastes and sparkling colours.

With regard to their flavours, some new recipes used fruits with sharper, more refreshing tastes, such as:

GÂTEAU DE RHUBARBE, GOOSEBERRIES OR RED OR WHITE CURRANTS[28]

1 lb / 450 g fruit	*1 oz / 25 g gelatin*
juice & pared zest of 1 lemon	*a few drops of red or green*
3 oz / 75 g sugar	*food colouring*

If using rhubarb, choose the pink forced stems, cut into lengths, with every trace of leaf removed. Stew the fruit, lemon and sugar in ½ pt / 300 ml water for about 15 minutes until very tender, then rub through a fine sieve. Meanwhile soak the gelatin in 2 fl oz / 4 tbs / 60 ml cold water for 10 minutes. Stir the gelatin into the fruit purée while warming gently until completely dissolved. Add the food colouring as appropriate, turn into a mould and leave to set.

CRANBERRY JELLY[29]

1 lb / 450 g cranberries	*1 glass maraschino syrup*
8 oz / 225 g sugar	*few drops red food*
½ oz / 12 g gelatin	*colouring*

Stew the cranberries and sugar in ½ pt / 300 ml water for 30 minutes, then follow the instructions above, adding the maraschino just before pouring into the mould.

(28) de Salis, 22.
(29) ibid., 18.

TANGERINE CREAM[30]

8 tangerines
8 oz / 225 g sugar
3 egg yolks, beaten

1 tbs brandy
1 pt / 600 ml cream
1 oz / 25 g gelatin

Boil the whole tangerines for one hour, cut them in half, and rub them through a fine sieve. Meanwhile soak the gelatin in 2 fl oz / 4 tbs / 60 ml cold water and leave for 10 minutes. Mix the fruit, yolks, brandy and gelatin, pour in the boiling cream, and stir until nearly cold before pouring into the mould.

PINEAPPLE BAVAROISE[31]

1 fresh pineapple
8 oz / 225 g sugar

½ oz / 12 g gelatin
1 pt / 600 ml whipping
    cream

Peel the pineapple, cut in ⅓ in. / 7 mm slices, stew until tender with the sugar and ¼ pt / 150 ml water, stirring continuously, then rub through a fine sieve. Soak the gelatin in 2 fl oz / 4 tbs / 60 ml cold water for 10 minutes, then stir into the purée, warming and stirring if necessary until completely dissolved. Leave to cool, then fold in the whipped cream and pour into the mould to set.

GINGER CREAM[32]

8 oz / 225 g contents of a jar of preserved ginger in syrup
½ pt / 300 ml double cream   1 oz / 25 g sugar
1 oz / 25 g gelatin

Drain the syrup into a pan, stir in the gelatin and the cream, leave to soak for 10 minutes, then stir over a gentle heat, not exceeding 70°C, until the gelatin has dissolved. Chop the preserved ginger into small pieces, stir into the cream when cold, and stir occasionally until just about to set, then turn into its mould.

(30) ibid., 45.
(31) Garrett, II 192.
(32) Garrett, I 680.

There was also a growing taste for alcoholic jellies using wines, fortified wines and liqueurs such as curaçao, kirsch, kümmel, maraschino and noyeau. They varied considerably in strength, one of the more potent being the Danish jelly:

DANISH JELLY[33]

¼ pt / 150 ml each of brandy, sherry and cherry brandy
7 fl oz / 225 ml claret   *3 oz / 75 g sugar*
juice & pared zest of 1 lemon   *¾ oz / 20 g gelatin*

Soak the gelatin in the claret for 10 minutes, add the remaining ingredients, warm and stir until all have dissolved, allow to cool, then pour into a mould and leave to set firm.

CHERRY BRANDY JELLY[34]

8 oz / 225 g black or dark red cherries
6 oz / 150 g sugar   *1 oz / 25 g gelatin*
juice of ½ lemon, strained   *¼ pt / 150 ml cherry brandy*

Stone the cherries. Crack the stones and blanch and peel the kernels. Simmer the cherries with the sugar, lemon juice and ¾ pt / 450 ml water for 10 minutes, then stir in the gelatin (pre-soaked in ¼ pt / 150 ml water for 10 minutes), until dissolved. Strain out the cherries, and mix the brandy into the jelly when cold. Pour a little of the jelly into a mould. When set, add a layer of cherries, cover with more jelly, and continue building up in layers, scattering the blanched and peeled kernels as you progress, until the mould is full. Leave to set firm before turning out.

Other wine jelly and fruit combinations made in this way included moselle and grapes, maraschino and quartered peaches, noyeau and apricots and champagne and macédoines of fresh or preserved fruits.[35]

(33) Garrett, I 784.
(34) de Salis, II.
(35) ibid., 20, 31, 34.

CLARET & BRANDY JELLY[36]

1 pt / 600 ml claret	*1 tsp redcurrant jelly*
6 oz / 150 g sugar	*4 tbs brandy*
pared zest & strained juice of	*½ oz / 12 g gelatin*
1 lemon	

Soak the gelatin in ¼ pt / 150 ml water for 10 minutes, add all but the brandy, and stir and warm until the gelatin has dissolved. Leave all to cool, mix in the brandy, pour into the mould and allow to set firm.

MARSALA JELLY[37]

4 oz / 100 g sugar	*1 bayleaf*
strained juice & grated zest of	*¼ pt / 150 ml marsala*
½ lemon	*1 tsp muscovado sugar*
large pinch nutmeg	*1 oz / 25 g gelatin*
3 cloves	

Soak the gelatin in ¼ pt / 150 ml water for 10 minutes. Simmer the sugar, lemon and spices in ¾ pt / 450 ml water for 6 minutes, strain onto the gelatin, stir until dissolved, then mix in the marsala and muscovado sugar. Pour into a mould and leave to set firm. It may be decorated with crystallized fruits and angelica points.

As well as new recipes, there were also new developments in decoration. One of the simplest methods depended on the principles outlined by Francatelli in his jellies 'en surprise' (above) by using different linings for the moulds. A ⅛ in. / 4 mm lining of clear but coloured jelly was filled with an opaque cream jelly to give the appearance of having a thick, ceramic glaze. It worked particularly well with moulds having a lot of surface detail, throwing this into a higher visual relief by being thinner over the raised parts, and thicker in the deeper grooves.

(36) ibid., 14.
(37) Garrett, I 913.

Lining a mould in this way also ensured that any successive linings, in different colours, would not melt together when being unmoulded as for:

MALTOISE À LA CHANTILLY[38]

1½ pt / 900 ml lemon jelly, made with 1½ oz / 40 g gelatin

A. Purée of Tangerines
8 tangerines
3 oz / 75 g sugar
½ oz / 12 g gelatin
yellow food colouring
1 tbs apricot jam
3 tbs maraschino
3 tbs white rum
¼ pt / 150 ml whipping cream

B. Lemon Cream
⅜ pt / 225 ml double cream
vanilla essence
red food colouring

C. Chocolate Cream
2 oz / 50 g grated dark
chocolate
2 oz / 50 g icing sugar
¼ oz / 6 g gelatin
1 tsp vanilla essence

A. Purée of Tangerines
Rub the sugar on the tangerine peels to extract their oils, then squeeze the juice and the pulp from the fruit. Beat the sugar and gelatin into ½ pt / 300 ml of the lemon jelly you have prepared earlier, stir and warm until all is dissolved, leave until cool, stir in the tangerine pulp and juice, the yellow colouring and apricot jam, and rub through a fine sieve. Whip the cream to stiffness and stir into the tangerine mixture with the maraschino and rum.

B. Lemon Cream
Warm ¾ pt / 450 ml of the lemon jelly until melted, leave until cool, stir in the cream and vanilla, and divide into two basins, colouring one pink, and keep tepid.

C. Chocolate Cream
Mix the chocolate and sugar with ½ pt / 300 ml water, simmer for 15 minutes, allow to cool, beat in the gelatin and vanilla, warming until dissolved, and keep tepid.

(38) Marshall (1888), 390.

Use the remaining lemon jelly to line an ornamental 2 pt/1.2 l mould, and when firmly set mask over its various divisions with the white, pink and chocolate creams to give good contrasts when turned out. When these have set, fill up with the tangerine mixture, and leave until very firm before turning out.

Garnish with whipped vanilla-flavoured cream and chocolate.

Other linings were made from set custards, fruits or fruit purées:

TIMBALE À LA VERSAILLES[39]
[see frontispiece no. 3]

½ pt/300 ml lemon jelly made with ¾ oz/20 g gelatin
3 tbs whipping cream

A. Chocolate Custard
¾ pt/450 ml milk
2 oz/50 g sugar
2½ oz/65 g dark chocolate
½ tsp vanilla essence
2 egg yolks, beaten
pinch instant coffee
¾ oz/20 g gelatin
1 tbs brandy
2 tbs maraschino

B. Vanilla Custard
½ pt/300 ml milk
½ a split vanilla pod
2 oz/50 g sugar
¼ oz/6 g gelatin
3 egg yolks, beaten
2 tbs cream

C. Strawberry Custard
½ pt/300 ml milk or cream
1½ oz/40 g sugar
½ oz/12 g gelatin
3 egg yolks, beaten
3 tbs white rum
¼ pt/150 ml strawberry
purée
red food colouring

Make each custard separately by mixing the gelatin with 4 tbs of the milk and leaving to soak for 10 minutes. Beat the remaining

(39) Marshall (1891), 514.

ingredients together, except the food colouring, strawberry purée and spirits, and heat gently while stirring until thickened as a custard, but not boiled. Leave to cool for about 10 minutes, then stir in the gelatin until dissolved. Stir in sufficient dissolved instant coffee to the chocolate, and the strawberries and red colouring into the strawberry to give a good colour, then rub each custard separately through a sieve. Pour some of each into three lightly greased trays in layers ¼ in./6 mm thick, and leave until set very firmly.

Use half the lemon jelly to line a plain cylindrical mould. Using metal cutters dipped in warm water, cut each set custard into 1 in./25 mm discs, each with a hole in the centre, reserving all the off-cuts separately. Dip each in turn in the cold but still melted lemon jelly that you have reserved, and arrange alternately, one just overlapping the other, across the base and round the sides. When these are set, melt the remains of each of the custards separately, leave to cool, beat 1 tbs whipped cream into each and when cold but unset pour each in turn (having allowed the previous one to set) until the mould is full. Leave to set firmly before turning out.

MOSAIC JELLY[40]
[see frontispiece no. 1 and plate vii]

2 pt/1.2 l lemon jelly made with 1½ oz/40 g gelatin
1 batch vanilla custard, as in the previous recipe, cut into
1 in./25 mm discs with holes in the centre

Line a plain mould with ¼ pt/150 ml of the jelly and leave to set. Dip each ring in turn in cold but unset jelly, set side by side across the base and one tier up the sides, cover with jelly to that level, allow to become semi-firm, then add another tier of rings, cover them with more jelly, and continue until the mould is full. Leave to set very firmly before turning out.

(40) ibid., 498.

APPLES À LA PRINCESSE MAUDE[41]

½ pt/300 ml lemon jelly made with ¾ oz/20 g gelatin

A. Apple Rings
1½ lb/675 g cooking apples
6 oz/150 g sugar
2 bayleaves
finely pared zest of 1 lemon

¾ oz/20 g gelatin
5 tbs white rum
red food colour
2 tbs cream

B. The Filling
½ pt/300 ml whipping cream

C. Decoration
angelica & whipped cream

Use ¼ pt/150 ml of the lemon jelly to line a plain cylindrical mould. Peel and core the apples, cook with the sugar, bayleaves and zest in ½ pt/300 ml water until tender, stir in the gelatin which has been soaked for 10 minutes in ¼ pt/150 ml water, add the rum and rub through a fine sieve. Divide the mixture into two, colouring one red with the food colour, the other white with the cream, pour ¼ in./6 mm deep into lightly greased trays, and leave until set firm. Cut out a number of long leaf shapes and, dipping them in the cold but unset lemon jelly, arrange them as a rosette on the base of the mould. Cut the rest into 1 in./25 mm discs, each with a hole in the middle, dip them in turn in the jelly, and arrange as a tier of alternating pinks and whites around the sides, a piece of angelica [or glacé cherry] in the central holes. Continue adding further tiers until the mould is fully lined. Melt the remaining pink and white jellies separately, each with 3 tbs lemon jelly and ¼ pt/150 ml whipped cream, and use when cold but unset to fill each tier of the interior with a separate colour, allowing each to become semi-set before adding the next.

A further lining technique was called the chartreuse. For this, a layer of clear jelly embedding fruits or creams was set in

(41) Marshall (1888), 412.

the base of a plain cylindrical charlotte mould, and a smaller mould set on top. The space between the two was then filled with further layers of clear jelly, fruits or creams, left to set, and a little warm water poured into the smaller mould so that it could be removed. The centre was then filled with an opaque gelatined cream or blancmange, and left to set. Examples of chartreuses for different fruits are given in the repertoire in the final chapter (and se plate viii).

Given such combinations of flavours and colours, *entremets* such as these were sure to stimulate the flagging palates of the diners. The group just described were all developed by one of the most remarkable of all culinary entrepreneurs, Mrs Agnes B. Marshall (1855–1905). In January 1883 she opened her cookery school at 31 Mortimer Street in London, off the north end of Regent Street and not far from the later BBC building. This was later expanded to include a cooks' employment registry and a shop / warehouse for all kinds of culinary equipment and materials, many being of her own invention or brand. In addition, she gave probably some of the best-ever cookery demonstrations, both in London and the provinces, and published a magazine called *The Table* to promote her recipes and products. It was through her books, however, that she exerted her greatest influence. As far as jellies were concerned, they are clearly described and often illustrated by excellent wood engravings in her *Mrs A.B. Marshall's Cookery Book* of 1888, and her *Mrs A.B. Marshall's Larger Book of Extra Recipes* of 1891. They are both collectors' items today, being particularly valued for the practicality of their recipes and the splendid results they produce for the table.

The period from the 1890s to the outbreak of the First World War marked the apogee of the English jelly. Never before, or since, had its place on the dinner table been so assured, or its contents blended, manipulated and moulded to such exceptionally high standards. Evidence of this is provided in the finest and most comprehensive cookery book ever published in

England, perhaps even in the world. This is Theodore Garrett's 1,852-page *Encyclopaedia of Practical Cookery* of c. 1893. Consulting the leading chefs of the period, he assembled here a hundred or more jelly recipes, along with many more for creams, bavarois and blancmanges. It is still the best source of inspiration for anyone wishing to explore the full range of recipes, although Mrs Marshall has the edge when it comes to elaborate decoration.

Partly because starch-based blancmanges were associated with poorer households, and partly because they lacked the glamorous colour and sparkle of jellies, they remained relatively undeveloped. Most could be improved by stirring in a few spoonfuls of the numerous food colourings and essences produced by companies such as Langdale's, the juice of lemon or a tablespoonful of cocoa, mixed with 1 tbs sugar. The most useful blancmanges were now usually made with cornflour, either plain, or as an enriched:

BLANCMANGE SPONGE[42]

2 oz/50 g cornflour	*2 eggs, separated*
1 pt/600 ml milk	*2 oz/50 g sugar*
1 tsp butter	

Beat the cornflour, butter, yolks and sugar into ¼ pt/150 ml of the milk in a basin. Bring the remainder of the milk to the boil, pour into the cornflour, etc., return to the pan and simmer while stirring for 10 minutes. Beat in the egg-whites which have been beaten to thickness, pour into a freshly rinsed mould and leave to set.

ORANGE CORNFLOUR JELLY[43]

1¼ oz / 30 g cornflour	*2 oz / 50 g sugar*
1 large orange	*juice of ½ lemon*
1 oz / 25 g lump sugar	

Rub the sugar lumps on the orange to absorb its oils. Mix the cornflour and sugar with ¼ pt / 150 ml of water, scald with ½ pt / 300 ml boiling water, return to the pan stirring vigorously, add the squeezed and strained orange and lemon juices, and continue simmering and stirring for a further 3 minutes. Pour into a freshly rinsed mould and leave to set.

Other flavours may be made by using the juices or purées of other soft fruits.

RICE À LA FRANÇAISE[44]

4 oz / 100 g Patna rice	*½ tsp orange-flower water*
1 oz / 25 g butter	*½ oz / 12 g candied orange*
3 tbs sugar	*peel*
1 pt / 600 ml milk	*12 glacé cherries, halved*
½ tsp almond essence	*12 lexia raisins, sliced*
	¼ oz / 6 g angelica, chopped

Boil the rice in water for 10 minutes, then drain. Put into a pan with the remaining ingredients, the orange peel narrowly sliced, and simmer and stir over a gentle heat until thick. Turn into a freshly rinsed mould, press down, and leave to set firmly before turning out.

Serve with a sauce of ¼ pt / 150 ml sherry, rum or kirsch thickened with a little cornflour cooked with water and 1 tbs sugar.

(43) ibid., 11.
(44) Garrett, II 327.

BAVAROIS DE RIZ AUX POMMES[45]

1 oz / 25 g short-grain rice	¾ oz / 20 g gelatin
2 oz / 50 g sugar	½ pt / 300 ml whipping
½ vanilla pod	cream
1 pt / 600 ml milk	½ lb / 225 g stiff apple,
2 large egg yolks, beaten	apricot, or peach purée,
	sweetened to taste

Simmer the rice, sugar and vanilla in ¾ pt / 450 ml of the milk for 30 minutes, stirring to prevent burning, until it has become soft and thick. Soak the gelatin in a few tbs of the remaining milk for 10 minutes. Beat the eggs into the remaining milk, stir and heat gently until thickened, but not boiled, leave to cool for 20 minutes, then mix in the gelatin until dissolved. When cold but still unset, mix in the cream which has been whisked to stiffness, mix with the rice, then pour into a mould and leave to set firmly. Spoon a deep hole in the centre, fill with the fruit purée, melt the scooped-out rice, pour on top to seal the fruit inside, then leave until set firm before unmoulding.

BORDER OF RICE À LA PARISIENNE[46]
[see frontispiece no. 8]

glacé cherries	1 in. / 25 mm stick cinnamon
angelica	1 pt / 600 ml milk
¼ pt / 150 ml lemon jelly	¼ oz / 6 g gelatin
3 oz / 75 g short-grain rice	6 drops vanilla essence
1 bayleaf	½ pt / 300 ml whipping
4 oz / 100 g sugar	cream

Decorate the top of a border mould with small rounds stamped out of angelica and strips of glacé cherry curved into half-moon shapes, all set in a little of the lemon jelly.

Cover the rice with cold water, bring slowly to the boil and drain. Add the bayleaf, cinnamon, sugar and most of the milk,

(45) Landon, 236.
(46) Marshall (1888), 441.

bring to the boil and simmer gently, stirring occasionally until most of the liquid has been absorbed. Meanwhile soak the gelatin in the remaining milk for 10 minutes. Remove the pan from the heat, remove the cinnamon and bayleaf, then stir in the gelatin and vanilla until completely dissolved. When cold, mix in the cream whisked until thick, and pour into the mould just before setting.

When set firm, turn out on to a dish, fill the centre with a stiff purée of stewed fruit, piled in a cone, cover this with more whipped cream, and edge the junction of the cream and the rice with either points of angelica or glacé cherries.

GROUND RICE FLUMMERY[47]

1 pt / 600 ml milk	*2 oz / 50 g sugar*
grated zest ¼ lemon	*2 oz / 50 g ground rice*
¼ oz / 6 g ground almonds	

Boil all together for 15 minutes, then pour into a freshly rinsed mould and leave to set firm.

In addition to these wider ranges of recipes and decorative techniques, the appearance of the jellies was improved by the use of new shapes of moulds. Some were designed with particular recipes in mind, but other moulding methods relied on very simple yet effective concepts. The following example dates from 1890, but if made with a range of coloured *'tesserae'* still proves highly popular with parties of archaeologists and (minus alcohol) children, or makes an interesting finger-food at receptions.

(47) Garrett II 325.

A ROMAN PAVEMENT[48]

3 pt / 1.8 l white blancmange made with 6 tbs gelatin and 6
   tbs sherry or cherry brandy
red, yellow and blue food colouring, chocolate, coffee
⅛ pt / 75 ml sweet sherry or cherry brandy

Pour a third of the blancmange 1 in. / 25 mm thick into a flat
mould, leave overnight and turn out into a glass dish or bowl.
Meanwhile divide the remainder into six trays, leaving one
white, and colouring the others red, orange, slate-blue, brown
and fawn and also leave to set 1 in. / 25 mm thick overnight.
Next morning cut the coloured blancmanges into 1 in. / 25 mm
'tesserae', and 'place each in an irregular manner in the shape of
the bowl, making it as high and romantic as you can, then pour
into the glass bowl a little sack or cherry brandy and serve.'

EDGINGS FOR BLANCMANGES[49]

Make white, pink, green and yellow blancmanges as in the
previous recipe, leave to set overnight in separate dishes, then
cut out into strips or stamp into star, heart or diamond shapes
and arrange these around the unmoulded blancmanges.

The Victorian period saw a great increase in the use
of moulds. Potteries and metal-works turned them out in
thousands for all those who wished to serve their cold *entremets*
or puddings in fashionably elaborate but easily made shapes.
Most were for general use, but others were made for particular
recipes. As in all culinary matters at the time, the aspiring
classes had distinct views on which were the most appropriate
designs. As one young lady informed her friend:[50]

I need not tell you, Lesbia, that you can make jellies of
every colour and shape. If you can afford them, there

(48) Wells, 46.
(49) ibid.
(50) Burrill, K. &
   Booth, A.M.,
   243.

are numbers of pretty little moulds. Simple dariole moulds can be filled with jelly and cream half-and-half, or three-quarters cream and a quarter jelly ... Moulds that represent fish and animals are not pretty. I have frequently met Canova's lions in white cream, and a sleeping cupid in chocolate shape, the result being grotesque. I have also seen small white cream swans with currant eyes floating gracefully on a lake of pale green jelly. Don't have over-elaboration; it tends towards vulgarity.

Such advice was lost on the majority of people. They liked their shaped jellies and blancmanges, and what could be wrong in having a patriotic lion lying in the middle of the table? To many, the shape of the jelly was one of its significant features, so much so that it began to be popularly referred to simply as 'shape', novelists such as Robert Surtees using expressions such as 'She had just stolen a shape of blanc-mange', in the early 1850s. This usage continued well into the second half of the last century: 'Anyone for shape?'[51]

EARTHENWARE MOULDS

In 1857, when planning her monumental *Book of Household Management*, Mrs Isabella Beeton was advised by her friend Henrietta English to consult the 34-year-old Joseph Orpwood, chef to the Duke of Rutland at Belvoir Castle who, in her opinion, operated the best-run kitchen in England.[52] Had she visited this vast noble establishment, where hundreds of meals were served each day, she would have found that he used dozens of white earthenware jelly moulds, their surfaces crazed as a result of their constant re-filling. The fact that so many pottery moulds were used in such a high-class household is significant since it shows that they were not a cheap product intended only for poorer homes.

Perhaps the finest Victorian pottery moulds were those made by Wedgwood. The design, observation of fine detail and quality

(51) *O.E.D. sv* Shape, 14.
(52) Hughes (2008), 189–192.

of the modelling is quite exceptional. Every minor vein on every leaf, every feather on every bird is rendered as close to nature as possible. It would be virtually impossible to describe all the moulds made by Wedgwood and all the other potteries working in England, even if all were identifiable by a mark, which by and large is not the case. The illustrated sales catalogues of the major companies offer the best clues to the range of available shapes and their names. Those issued by Minton in 1884 and Copeland [late Spode] in 1902 are particularly useful, since they include most of the standard lines produced over previous generations. It is interesting to follow the different approaches to pricing. In 1854 Copelands sold their 'B. Mange Moulds [at] 1*d*. Per in.' By 1872 they were being sold by the dozen, from 4-inch moulds at 5*s*. the dozen up to massive 12-inch moulds at 24*s*. the dozen. In the 1880s they were 1*d*. per inch up to 3 inches, with prices rising proportionately up to 10 inches, hollow centres and steeples being two sizes higher in price, pierced curd moulds at a price and a half, 6- and 7-inch hens at 10*d*. and 1*s*., and chickens large or small at 3*d*. each. The 1902 price list was based on the individual shapes, all being the same price per inch, except for the hollow centres, steeples, hens and chickens, which demanded extra work. From these it can be shown that an average 6-inch mould cost 6*d*. in 1854, 7*d*. in the 1880s, and 7½*d*. in 1902, remarkably stable prices over half a century.

It would be a mistake to think that the moulds listed in the price lists were the only ones made by any particular pottery, for there are many examples of unlisted shapes bearing identifiable pottery marks. Copeland's list does not include their tennis pattern, for example, but these are easily recognized by their design and impressed 'COPELAND' mark. They take the shape of a flat-topped rectangular pyramid, a post at each corner supporting nets which sag across each fluted side. On top, crossed racquets are arranged between four balls, the ideal motifs for a relaxed lawn tennis tea-party on a summer afternoon.

1 2 3 4
5 6 7 8
9 10 11 12
13 14 15 16
17 18 19 20
21 22 23 24

Figure 11. Minton jelly moulds (1), from their shape-book of 1883, with their pattern numbers.

Figure 12. Minton jelly moulds (2), from their shape-book of 1883, with their pattern numbers.

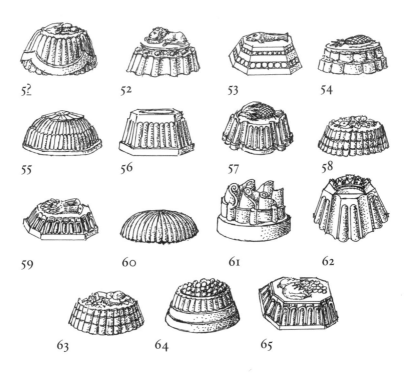

Figure 13. Minton jelly moulds (3), from their shape-book of 1883, with their pattern numbers.

A number of white earthenware moulds are extremely small, usually about 3 in. / 75 mm long. It might be imagined that they were used to make individual portions of jelly, but this is not the case. Throughout the Victorian period the children of prosperous parents learned their table-manners in the nursery. To assist in this process they were often provided with complete one-third scale ceramic dinner services and usable metal cutlery. With everything reduced down to suit child-sized fingers, complete dinner and tea tables were set with small quantities of real food, and the meal eaten with due ceremony. The whole

JELLIES & THEIR MOULDS

exercise was both practical and responded ideally to children's love of all things special and miniature. These moulds were made for the *entremet* course of such meals, fitting exactly on the round or oval serving dishes.

STONEWARE MOULDS

In contrast to the fine white salt-glazed stonewares of the eighteenth century, those of the Victorian period were decidedly coarse, lumpish and heavy. Made in unrefined fireclays and usually salt-glazed to a range of buff, brown and purplish semi-matt finishes, they were cheap to produce, strong, practical, and ideal for making cornflour blancmanges. However, to turn a jelly out of them successfully required a degree of knowledge and skill. Their shapes are usually those of the earthenware potters, either taken from blocks made for that industry, or just as likely pirated from the finished moulds. At this period stoneware moulds were hardly, if ever, stamped with a maker's mark, so that they may only be allocated to a particular pottery or region by their physical appearance. Most of the clear-glazed grey-buff moulds probably originated in the north Derbyshire potteries for example, while many of the dark purplish-brown moulds found in West Yorkshire museum collections probably came from the Eccleshill potteries near Bradford. Stonewares are such relatively similar products, however, that their attribution must always remain uncertain and problematic.

COPPER MOULDS

By the mid-nineteenth century most well-to-do households had a selection of copper jelly moulds for use in their kitchens. They were made by a number of companies, especially in London and the West Midlands. The leading manufacturers had been founded in the Regency. These included A.F. Crook, who took over Temple & Reynolds in the mid-Victorian period to trade as Temple & Crook, suppliers to Queen Victoria and the Prince of Wales. Benham & Sons of Wigmore Street, London, had begun

No.1 HOLLOW CENTRE. 4217   ACORN, 4215   FILBERT 4207

No. 2, HOLLOW CENTRE. 4221   No. 3. HOLLOW CENTRE. 4223   No.4 HOLLOW CENTRE. 4222

STAR. 4204   GAME. 4202

PYRAMID. 4211   TURK'S CAP. 4218   STEP. 4214   ROUND MELON. 4219

KHIVA. 4213.   NEW GOTHIC. 4209   PIPE AND PINE. 4216   STEEPLE. 4212   PIPE AND STAR. 4201

STRAWBERRY. 4189   FRUIT. 4202   DORIC. 4187   SHELL. 4195   VINE. 4197

OVAL MELON. 4188   PLUM. 4193   DOLPHIN. 4200   PINE CONE. 4194   OLD GOTHIC. 4192

PINE APPLE. 4184   CHARLOTTE. 4186   NEW PINE. 4190   DOME. 4191

GRAPE. 4185   CONCH. 4205   HEN 4196   CHICKENS 4206 & 8   BANDRINGHAM. 4201

Figure 14. W.T. Copeland & Sons' catalogue of shapes, with their pattern numbers and names, probably issued in the 1880s.

trading as ironmongers in 1817, while Benham & Froud were founded in 1855 and became one of the greatest of all designers and manufacturers of kitchen plant and equipment. They fitted out kitchens for the Reform Club, the royal yacht, Harrods and countless great country houses, as well as making a vast number of jelly moulds.[53] The illustrated catalogue published after they were reconstituted as Herbert Benham & Co. in 1906 shows 67 different designs, in addition to many small cup, dariole, egg and bomb moulds, but they also produced many others. Their mould no. 547, for example, had a triangular shaft topped by a square and compasses which could be filled with different colours of jelly for great Masonic dinners. Their moulds all bear both their pattern number and their trademark of a cross mounted on top of a ball. This represents the 23-foot ball and cross on the top of St Paul's Cathedral, made in 1821 by company they had taken over. The third major producer was Adams & Son of 57 Haymarket and 14 Norris Street, London, 'Manufacturing and Furnishing Ironmongers By Appointment to Queen Victoria and the Prince of Wales'. Their moulds were probably used by Charles Elmé Francatelli 'Pupil to the celebrated Carême, and late Maître d'Hôtel and Chief Cook to Her Majesty the Queen'. His *Cook's Guide* of 1853 includes a full-page illustrated advertisement for Adams, featuring ordinary moulds from 11s. 6d. to 14s. 6d., and Belgrave moulds at 30s., about six weeks' wages for a kitchen maid.

Other makers included Johnson & Davey of Conduit Street, London, Henry Fearncombe of Wolverhampton, and Villiers & Wilkes (previously Birch & Villiers, 1780–1818), Ash Brothers & Heaton (1828–), and E.T. Everton, all of Birmingham.

Figures 15, 16, 17 (overleaf). Copper jelly moulds, from the catalogue of Herbert Benham & Co., successors to Benham & Froud Ltd., of London. Although published in the opening years of the twentieth century, this catalogue includes many shapes introduced from the formation of the company. It is not comprehensive, however, since other shapes are known to bear the Benham trademark of the St Paul's cross.

(53) Kevill-Davis, 44.

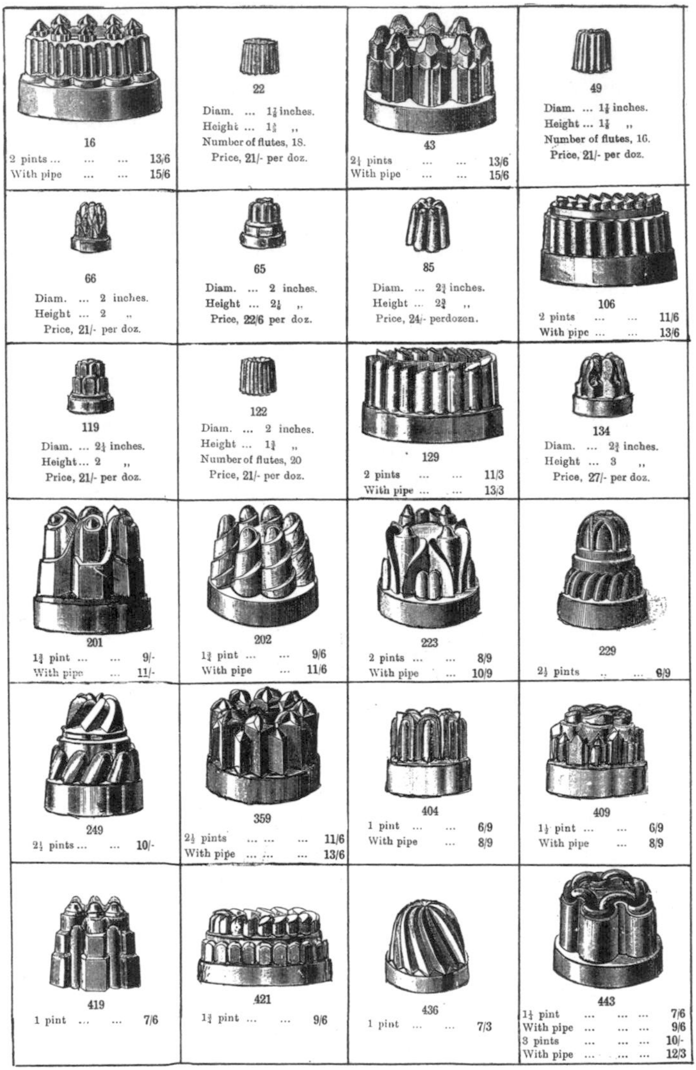
16
2 pints 13/6
With pipe 15/6
22
Diam. ... 1⅞ inches.
Height ... 1½ ,,
Number of flutes, 18.
Price, 21/- per doz.
43
2¼ pints 13/6
With pipe 15/6
49
Diam. ... 1⅛ inches.
Height ... 1⅛ ,,
Number of flutes, 16.
Price, 21/- per doz.
66
Diam. ... 2 inches.
Height ... 2 ,,
Price, 21/- per doz.
65
Diam. ... 2 inches.
Height ... 2⅛ ,,
Price, 22/6 per doz.
85
Diam. ... 2¼ inches.
Height ... 2¾ ,,
Price, 24/- perdozen.
106
2 pints 11/6
With pipe 13/6
119
Diam. ... 2¼ inches.
Height ... 2 ,,
Price, 21/- per doz.
122
Diam. ... 2 inches.
Height ... 1¾ ,,
Number of flutes, 20
Price, 21/- per doz.
129
2 pints 11/3
With pipe 13/3
134
Diam. ... 2¾ inches.
Height ... 3 ,,
Price, 27/- per doz.
201
1¾ pint 9/-
With pipe ... 11/-
202
1¾ pint 9/6
With pipe ... 11/6
223
2 pints 8/9
With pipe ... 10/9
229
2½ pints 6/9
249
2½ pints 10/-
359
2½ pints 11/6
With pipe 13/6
404
1 pint 6/9
With pipe ... 8/9
409
1½ pint 6/9
With pipe ... 8/9
419
1 pint 7/6
421
1¾ pint 9/6
436
1 pint 7/3
443
1¼ pint 7/6
With pipe 9/6
3 pints 10/-
With pipe 12/3

Figure 15. See caption on previous page.

Figure 16. See caption on page 155.

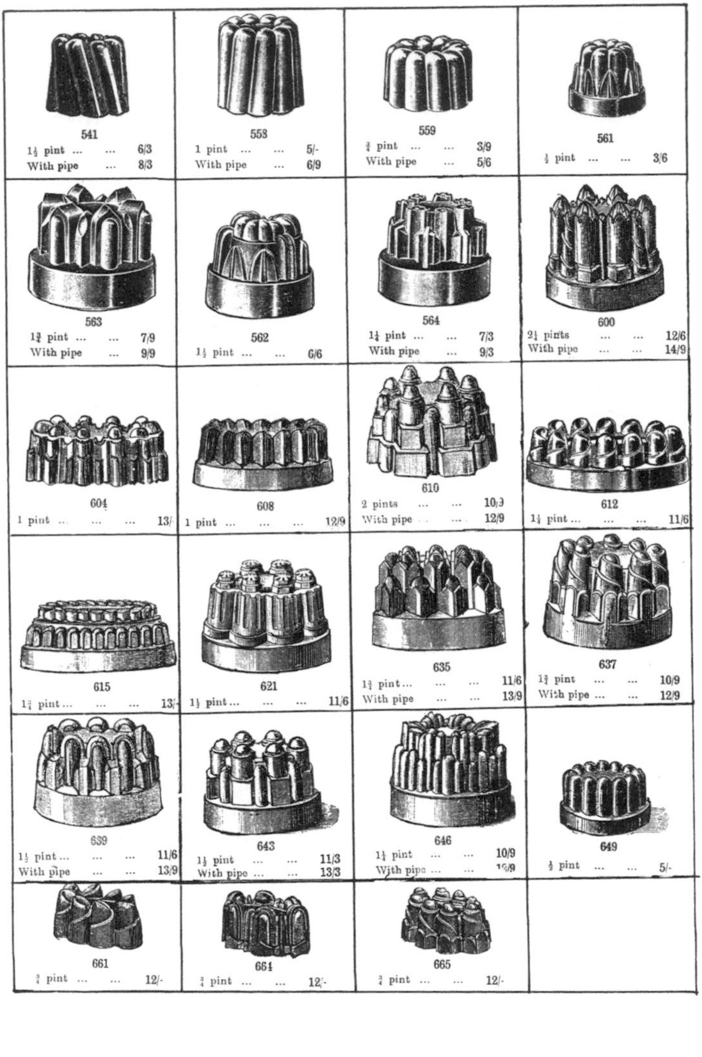
541
1½ pint 6/3
With pipe ... 8/3
558
1 pint 5/-
With pipe ... 6/9
559
¾ pint 3/9
With pipe ... 5/6
561
½ pint 3/6
563
1¾ pint 7/9
With pipe ... 9/9
562
1½ pint 6/6
564
1¼ pint 7/3
With pipe ... 9/3
600
2¼ pints 12/6
With pipe 14/9
604
1 pint 13/-
608
1 pint 12/9
610
2 pints 10/9
With pipe 12/9
612
1¼ pint 11/6
615
1¾ pint 13/-
621
1½ pint 11/6
635
1¾ pint 11/6
With pipe 13/9
637
1¾ pint 10/9
With pipe 12/9
639
1½ pint 11/6
With pipe 13/9
643
1½ pint 11/3
With pipe 13/3
646
1¼ pint 10/9
With pipe ... ...
649
½ pint 5/-
661
¾ pint 12/-
664
¾ pint 12/-
665
¾ pint 12/-

Figure 17. See caption on page 155.

Unless bearing a maker's mark, many of the designs cannot be attributed to any particular company as the moulds they produced were virtually identical. This can be seen by comparing those shown in Benhams' catalogue, for example, with those in the 1881 catalogue of A.F. Leale of the Vulcan Engineering Works, Castlenau, Barnes, London (figs. 18, 19).

In addition to the maker's name and pattern-number marks, many copper moulds were stamped with the names of their retailers. The stamps of Jones Brothers of Down Street, London, who operated from the mid-nineteenth century to the 1930s, are probably the most widespread. Others include Bennington of Jermyn Street, Kepp & Co. of Chandos Street, Harrod's of Knightsbridge, James Williams & Sons, The Army and Navy Stores, and Mrs Marshall's School of Cookery in Mortimer Street, all in London. The Harrods and Army and Navy Stores catalogues both illustrate a selection of moulds, with their prices, a practice which continued well into the following century. By far the most interesting and influential of the London retailers was Mrs Agnes B. Marshall. The cookery school she opened at 31 Mortimer Street in January 1883 taught 'High Class Cookery' to both ladies and their cooks, its courses and the recipes developed there being promoted through public demonstrations, a magazine called *The Table* and a number of well-written cookery books. In all of these she specified and advertised the moulds required, which could then be purchased from her extensively stocked showrooms at 32 Mortimer Street and her warehouse at Union Place, Wells Street. They also advertised her publication:

THE BOOK OF MOULDS
May be had gratis on application,
or is sent free to any address,
68 PAGES AND OVER 400 ENGRAVINGS, ILLUSTRATING, IN
DIFFERENT SIZES AND DESIGNS, ABOUT ONE THOUSAND KINDS
OF MOULDS

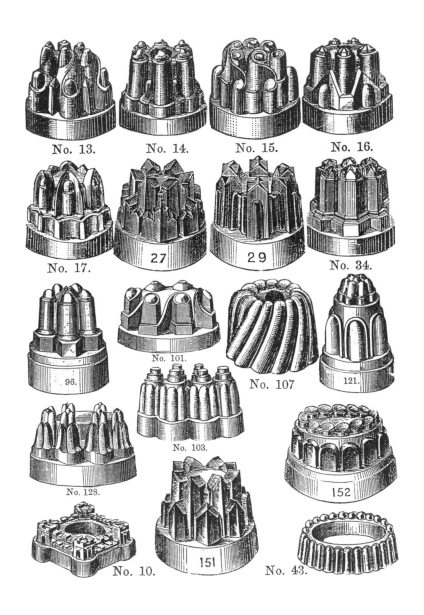

No. 13.　　No. 14.　　No. 15.　　No. 16.

No. 17.　　27　　29　　No. 34.

No. 101.

96.

No. 107

121.

No. 103.

No. 128.

152

No. 10.　　151　　No. 43.

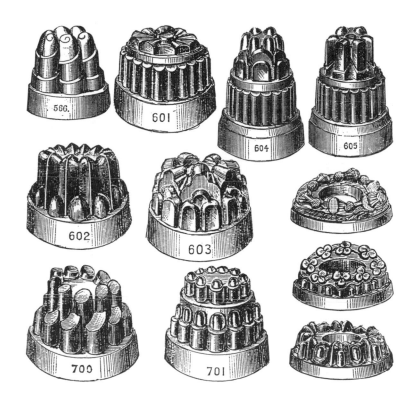

Figures 18, 19 (left and above). Copper jelly moulds, from the 1881 catalogue of A.F. Leale of the Vulcan Engineering Works, Barnes, S.W.7. The usual prices were as follows: 1-pint – 5s.; 2-pint – 8s. 3d.; 3-pint – 12s. 6d.; 1 ½-pint – 6s.; 2 ½-pint – 12s. 6d. Moulds with pipes 1s. 6d. each extra, re-tinning 1s. 3d. to 1s. 6d. each.

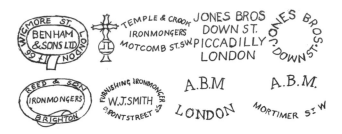

Figure 20. A selection of late nineteenth-century makers' and retailers' stamps found on copper jelly moulds. They include the St Paul's cross of Benhams, one of the most important manufacturers of kitchen equipment, and that of Benham & Sons, a separate company. The 'A.B.M.' stamps are those of Mrs Agnes Bertha Marshall, a leading retailer of the 1890s.

Unfortunately not a single copy of this catalogue has ever been found, its contents only being represented by a few sample pages printed at the ends of her various books.

As well as stamped marks, some moulds are also engraved with initials and numbers. These were to identify them as the property of their owner, partly to deter pilfering by in-house staff or visiting servants, and to ensure their safe return from the coppersmiths whenever they were sent off for re-tinning. Sometimes the owner's heraldic crest and initials are beautifully engraved into the external surface, but plain initials are more usual. Below these might be an L, for the family's London house or, in the largest of establishments, either the name of the particular house, or its department such as 'Stillroom' or 'Kitchen'. There may be a number too, either stamped or engraved, which related the mould to its particular place in the property's inventory of kitchen equipment. The engraving of 'L*L [Earl's Coronet] H' on a tube-mould at Harewood House indicates L for the family name of Lascelles, L for their London home, and H for their Harewood title. Sometimes it is possible to attribute moulds by archival means, as at the Duke of Rutland's seat at Belvoir Castle. Here, on 6 June 1900,

SPECIMENS FROM

THE BOOK OF MOULDS,

Containing 68 pages of Illustrations, published by

MARSHALL'S SCHOOL OF COOKERY

And sent POST-FREE on application.

COPPER JELLY AND CREAM MOULDS.

No. 369.
ALEXANDRA MOULD AND LINING.

No. 364.
BRUNSWICK STAR MOULD AND LINING

No. 1—Price 13s. 6d. complete.
Without lining, 9s. 9d.
No. 2—Price 18s. complete.
Without lining, 13s. 6d.

No. 1—Price 13s. 6d. complete.
Without lining, 9s. 9d.
No. 2—Price 18s. complete.
Without lining, 13s. 6d.

No. 307A.

No. 365.

No. 366.

No. 367.

2 pints.   Price 8s. 3d.

Price 10s. 9d. each.

Price 9s. each.

Price 6s. each.

No. 368.

No. 370.

No 380

No. 381.

Price 9s. 9d. each.

Price 7s. 6d. each.

Price 6s. each.

Price 9s. 9d. each.

COPPER BORDER MOULDS.

No. 348D.

No. 348E.

No. 343A.

Diameter 6 in., Capacity ¾ pt.
Price 10s. 9d. each.

Length 6½ in., Capacity 1¾ pts.,
Price 13s.

6 in. diameter 9s. 9d.

Figure 21. This specimen page from Mrs. Marshall's Book of Moulds *was published in her* Larger Book of Extra Recipes *of 1891.*

the chef, M. Louis Thevenot, took delivery of six new copper jelly moulds costing £2 5s. from 'Smith & Matthews (late Eitel), English and French Mould Manufacturers and Coppersmiths', these presumably being the moulds which still remain in the Castle's kitchens.[54]

Most moulds were filled with the usual range of clear or opaque jellies and creams, perhaps layered or used for embedding. Others were designed for use when making specific jellies, as in the following examples (see fig. 22).

THE ALEXANDRA CROSS MOULD[55]

The design of this mould was registered on 22 April 1863, its name and white cross set on a red jelly celebrating the marriage of Edward, Prince of Wales, to Princess Alexandra of Denmark. It is cross-shaped in plan, standing on a round base. In use the top part of the cross was filled with opaque white jelly and the next part with pink jelly, after which, when set, a cross-shaped liner was inserted and the space around it filled with very clear pink jelly to the level of the base ring. When this had set, the cross was filled with warm water, removed, and its place taken by more white jelly. After the base had been filled with golden yellow jelly, 'it will present a very beautiful representation of the Danish Cross in proper colours, upon a golden base'. When served in horizontal slices it produced a Danish flag on each plate. Around 1900 this sold wholesale for 12s. 9d. for a 1½-pint and 15s. for a 2½-pint mould. Miniature versions were also made.

THE ASPARAGUS MOULD[56]

Made by Temple & Crook of London, and illustrated in Garrett's *Encyclopaedia of Practical Cookery* of c. 1893, this mould represents a vertical bundle of asparagus tied with a band. In use, the tips were filled with a green jelly (probably opaque) and the section down to the band with a very pale green jelly. The band itself had a bright orange jelly coloured with apricot jam, followed by more very pale green jelly for the rest of the stalks.

(54) Belvoir Castle archives.
(55) Jewry, 25. And see plate vi.
(56) Garrett, I 738.

BALLETTE MOULDS

Made in seven sizes from 1½ in. at 11½*d.* each to 3 in. at 1*s.* 9½*d.*, these copper spheres had tinned interiors and a lapped joint about their equators. For a plain ball of jelly, the joint was sealed with cold butter and the cold jelly solution poured in through an integral funnel at the top, its capacity being calculated to compensate for any shrinkage as the jelly cooled and set. If clear and often coloured, each ballette jelly acted as a lens, reacting with its surrounding light. In 1905 Burrill and Booth considered that 'Round moulds ... half-coloured cream and half jelly, make a pretty dish. If you can afford them, there are numbers of pretty little moulds.'[57] They were perhaps best used for embedding fruits such as raspberries, strawberries or grapes in clear or golden jelly. The moistness of the jelly served as a varnish to enhance their natural colours, while the ball shape acted like a magnifying glass, making them look even larger and more succulent, ever-moving with every turn of the head. Jelly balls are among the most unpredictably mobile of all dishes, and have to be stood on either individual dimple-topped bouche-cup bases, in the channel of a hollow-topped border mould, or on a bed of chopped jelly. Since they are not supported on a flat base, the jelly for ballette moulds has to be made very stiff using twelve sheets of gelatin to the pint / 600ml (see plate viii).

THE BELGRAVE MOULD[58]

This mould took its name from the fashionable Belgrave Square in the heart of London's Belgravia. Messrs. Temple & Reynolds had a shop there at 80 Motcombe Street and another at Princes Street, Cavendish Square. As its kite mark shows, the design was registered on 16th April 1850, and by 1853 was being illustrated in William Adams & Son's advertisement in Francatelli's *Cook's Guide and Housekeeper's and Butler's Assistant.* The exterior has six round columns each topped by a hexagonal boss. When inverted, the top was seen to have a tinplate lid pierced by seven holes, one in the centre and one over the

(57) Burrill & Booth, 243.
(58) Acton, 470. And see plate v.

centre of each column. Into each of these was dropped a hollow spiral tube, hanging there while the mould was filled with a stiff, transparent jelly as Eliza Acton described in her *Modern Cookery* of 1855. When this had set, each tube was filled with warm water and carefully unscrewed from its surrounding jelly, a narrow internal tube through the base allowing air to enter the vacuum below. Cold jellies or creams of different colours were then poured into the outer ring of holes, and the centre one either left open or filled with a white or pale-tinted whipped cream [or creamy jelly]. When turned out, each coloured tube was seen to rise up magnified within each clear jelly column, the central white column providing them with an excellent contrasting background.

Most copper Belgrave moulds are marked with the St Paul's cross of Benham, the manufacturers, only the older examples having the names of the inventors and the royal arms within an oval stamp. In the 1890s, tinplate versions with straight-sides and slightly tapering tubes were being sold by Mrs A.B. Marshall. Her recipe filled the outer mould with wine-flavoured lemon jelly and the eight perimeter tubes with jellied whipped creams coloured and flavoured with coffee, vanilla, pineapple and banana to present multi-coloured columns.[59]

THE BRUNSWICK STAR MOULD[60]

Registered on September 15th, 1864, and usually made by Benham, this mould has a replica of the order of Brunswick, an eight-pointed star, on top of a tall faceted column. It was filled in the following order: the topmost central circle with red jelly, the top star with silver-leaf in the jelly, and the bottom star with more red jelly. After all these had set in turn, an eight-fluted column mould was placed within and the space around it filled with clear jelly up to the level of the foot-ring of the outer mould. When this had set, the column mould was filled with warm water and removed, its place being taken by an opaque white jelly. Finally the base-ring was filled with red jelly, to complete

(59) Marshall (1888), 431.
(60) Jewry, 26. And see plate vi.

JELLIES & THEIR MOULDS

the moulding process. When served in horizontal slices, most portions had a white star set within a clear red jelly border. Around 1906 Herbert Benham & Co. were wholesaling this mould at 14s. 6d. for a 1½-pint mould and 16s. 6d. for the 2½-pint.

THE IMPERIAL CROWN MOULD[61]

To celebrate the coronation of Edward VII in 1902, Mrs A.B. Marshall introduced a two-piece, two-inch diameter pewter mould in the shape of St Edward's crown. It was designed for individual ices, savouries, desserts, etc., but involved considerable expense, costing 18s. the dozen, and considerable skill to use, as evinced by this recipe:

STRAWBERRIES IN JELLY À LA ROYALE

½ pt / 300 ml lemon jelly with 3 tsp gelatin
½ pt / 300 ml plain jelly with 4 tsp gelatin
½ pt / 300 ml whipped cream
2 tubs maraschino syrup
red, green and purple food colour
6 strawberries

Pour 10 tbs of lemon jelly into a cup, and colour deep purple and 2 tbs lemon jelly into two more cups, colouring one red and the other green. Chill until set.

Set the open moulds face up in iced water, line with the rest of the lemon jelly, and leave to set. Cut slices of the purple jelly to represent the lining of the crown, set them in place within the moulds, then add small rubies and emeralds of red and green jelly around the base and crosses, etc.

Close the mould, half fill with a cream made by thoroughly mixing the plain jelly, whipped cream and maraschino, insert a strawberry in each mould, top up with more of the cream, and chill until set.

Serve on individual dish papers on a silver dish.

(61) *The Table* (1902).

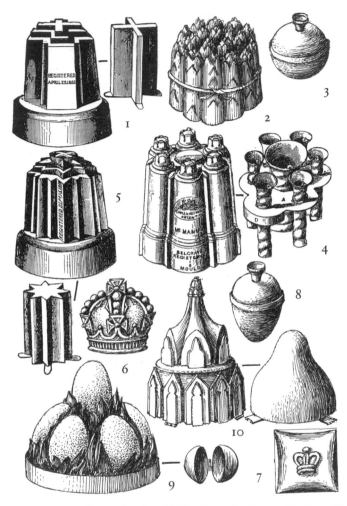

Figure 22. Moulds for specific jellies. (1) The Alexandra Cross and its liner, 1863; (2) asparagus mould by Temple & Crook; (3) ballette mould; (4) Belgrave mould and its liners, made by Temple & Reynolds of Belgravia in 1850; (5) Brunswick Star, which had a star-shaped liner, and was introduced in 1864; (6 & 7) Imperial Crown and Crown Cushion of 1902, made for Mrs Marshall; (8) egg mould; (9) Temple & Crook's hard-boiled egg mould; (10) macédoine mould and its liner.

Mrs Marshall's second mould for the 1902 coronation was a one-piece tinned copper square cushion with a low-relief crown embossed at its centre. They cost six shillings the dozen, and for dessert could be filled as in the recipe above.

EGG MOULDS

Two-part tinned copper egg moulds were of about one and two pints in capacity, Mrs Marshall selling these at 4s. 6d. and 7s. 6d. each respectively. Each half had a flange around its joint, so that it could be secured against its partner as their respective jellies mingled and set. Today tinned steel chocolate-egg moulds may be used for the original recipes, some of which are quite spectacular, the results looking more like the productions of science fiction than those of the kitchen, as in Mrs Marshall's:

CREAM DE PRINTEMPS[63]

Stage 1: Line each half of the mould with purple-coloured lemon jelly, then small flakes of real gold and silver leaf, and a final lining of jelly.

Stage 2:

2 oz crystallized violets	1 pt / 600 ml milk
2 tbs rosewater	1 pt / 600 ml whipped
2 tbs maraschino liqueur	cream
¾ oz / 20 g leaf gelatin	few drops violet colouring
	a little violet essence

Pound the violets to a smooth paste with the rosewater and maraschino. Melt the gelatin in the milk, keeping it below around 70°C to prevent curdling, mix in the violet mixture, and strain through a fine cloth.

Mix in the remaining ingredients, fill both moulds, set aside, and clamp together just before setting.

(62) ibid.
(63) ibid.

Stage 3: Bake an 8 in./20 cm sponge cake, either in a border mould, or in a cake tin, then hollowing the centre. Place on a dish and sprinkle with maraschino syrup.

Stage 4: Boil 8 oz/225 g cane sugar with ¼ pt/150 ml water to the crack (150°C), dip ten 6 in./15 cm-long pointed strips of angelica and crystallized violets individually into the sugar to form a glaze, laying them on a slightly oiled slab to cool.

Stage 5: Unmould the jelly on to the cake [masked with a little cream] cover with the violets, and stick angelica spears vertically into the cake, point upwards, around the egg.

IMITATION HARD-BOILED EGGS MOULD[64]

Temple & Crook made a mould which looked like a small pyramid of hard-boiled eggs, with one at the top, and the others spaced around beneath it. In use, accompanying hinged yolk-moulds were filled with apricot jam set with isinglass jelly. The egg parts were then filled with clear jelly or blancmange, with the yolks inserted as appropriate. When full, set and unmoulded, the parts of the jelly between the eggs were covered with angelica leaves and pistachios.

SMALL EGG MOULDS, WITH THEIR NESTS

The size of a small hen's egg and constructed like a ballette mould, these moulds were used more for *entrées* with savoury fillings, than for sweet *entremets* (see plate viii). Small nest moulds were made to provide jelly bases in which they might stand. When filled with sweet jellies or gelatin blancmanges, the resulting eggs were often served in a birds-nest mould, 7 in. in diameter by 2¼ in. high, its smooth central bowl being surrounded by a sloping nest modelled to resemble a mass of entwining twigs. This looked best when filled with a clear golden jelly embedding syrup-poached strands of lemon zest. The Benham's catalogue priced the nest moulds at 6s. 9d. each and the accompanying egg moulds at 13s. 6d. the dozen.

(64) Garrett, I 783.

The Victorian macédoine moulds had a fluted domed base rising to a concave-sided cone. Having been turned bottom-up, an internal mould shaped like the top of a pear was inserted, being held in place by three projecting metal straps, secured to the rim of the main mould by means of short pins. When the space between the moulds had been filled with clear jelly and allowed to set, warm water was poured into the inner one and the pins released, so that it could be removed. The hollow it had formed was then filled with layers of different fresh or preserved fruits set in jelly.

RIB MOULDS[65]

Most rib-moulds resemble a cylindrical bundle of twelve dome-topped tubes leaning at a slight angle (fig. 23) . In use, a cylindrical core-mould was first slid inside, enabling each tube to be filled independently, after which the core was removed so that the centre could be filled. The usual combinations included:

> alternate tubes of vanilla and dark chocolate bavarois;
> alternate tubes of pink and white maraschino bavarois;
> alternate tubes of green and white kirsch bavarois;
> alternate tubes of scooped and poached balls of Colville apples, the next of similarly prepared pears coloured pink, and the third of balls preserved greengage [all filled with clear jelly], the centre then filled with mixed fruit and jelly;
> each tube filled with strawberries, filled with clear vanilla jelly, the centre filled with vanilla bavarois, the unmoulded jelly garnished around the base and on top with strawberries glazed by dipping in sugar boiled to the crack (150°C).

(65) Gouffé, 374.

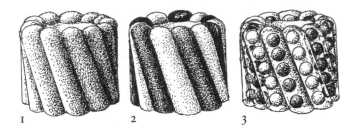

Figure 23. The rib mould was made with a liner so that its individual flutes could be filled with creams of contrasting colours, rows of strawberries, or balls of greengage and pink-stained apple.

SOYER'S ATTELETTE MOULDS[66]

Alexis Soyer, chef to the Reform Club, caterer at the Great Exhibition of 1851, and to many of the soldiers in the Crimea, was the greatest celebrity chef of mid-Victorian England. In the mid-1840s, over a period of ten months, he 'furnished 25,000 dinners, 38 banquets of importance comprising above 70,000 dishes ... and received the visits of fifteen thousand strangers, all too eager to inspect [his] renowned altar of a great apician temple.' At the same time, he wrote his 720-page *Gastronomic Regenerator* designed for the 'Kitchens of the Wealthy'. In its last pages he provided drawings of the jelly moulds he had recently invented. The three tallest were unusual in having small, flat tops to receive his 'new fruit attelettes, one of which, placed at the top of a jelly when turned out, is a very handsome addition'. To make these a silver *attelette*, a skewer with an ornamental gold-plated finial, had pieces of fresh or candied fruits of contrasting colours and shapes threaded onto it, these being enclosed by a cylindrical *attelette* mould. The junction between the skewer and the mould was then sealed with a little flour-and-water dough, and the interior filled with a strong, clear jelly. When this had set, the mould was rapidly dipped into warm water, its locking pin removed, and the mould opened to reveal

(66) Soyer (1847), 518 and last pages.

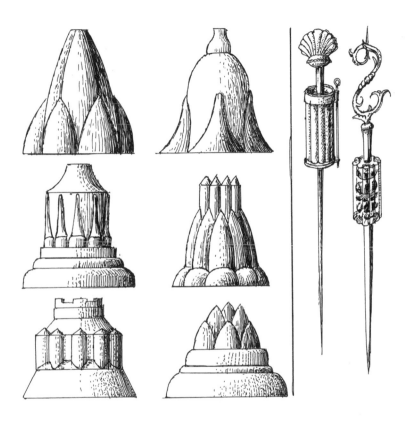

Figure 24. Moulds designed by Alexis Soyer before 1846. Having flat tops, each of these was to be finished with an attelette *of jelly. For these, pieces of fresh or preserved fruits were threaded on to gilt-tipped skewers, encased in special moulds and filled up with clear jelly.*

a cylinder of fruit in jelly ready to be stuck into the top of the moulded jelly to give it an impressive finial.

TINPLATE MOULDS

Unfortunately, most early tinplate moulds have disappeared, either because they eventually rusted, or because they were seen as cheap and disposable by contrast to their expensive tinned-copper superiors. Their forms are now known more from their manufacturers' catalogue illustrations than from surviving specimens. Many were made in and around Birmingham by companies such as J.H. Hopkins & Son at their wholesale tinplate and japanning factory in Granville Street, off Broad Street. Their elaborate pagoda shapes were excellent examples of the tinsmith's craft, being hand-folded, seamed and soldered, only the domed tops being pressings. Most of their other shapes were available in either tin or copper, their price-list showing that no. 64, the 1½-pint 'Wheatsheaf' cost 1s. 8d. each in tin, but more than double that, 3s. 6d., in copper.

As ready-made gelatins encouraged the making of jellies by middle and working-class households, there was a proportionate demand for tinplate moulds, particularly since they released their jellies far better than their ceramic alternatives. The easiest way to make a relatively cheap mould was to shape the top section in high relief under a press, then solder it to another fan-shaped pressing which had been seamed together to form the sides. On 4th February 1899 Messrs W. Morris and L. Wilkinson of 'Beatall' Works, Keighley Road, Burnley took out patent no. 2545 for making jelly-mould seams with the lap or folded joint on the exterior, which therefore made un-moulding much easier. For ordinary moulds, the top pressing was of tinplate, but the same equipment was also used to make tinned copper tops. Companies might produce both types of ware. A.R. Wood & Co's catalogue shows the differences in price between each type:

Figure 25. Tinplate moulds made by J.H. Hopkins & Son at their Granville Street works in Broad Street, Birmingham. Their prices ranged from 3s. 3d. for a 4-pint 'Prince's Feather' mould to 1s. 4d. for a 1-pint 'Acorn'. These rose to 4s. 6d. and 3s. 3d. respectively if supplied in tin-lined copper.

	½ pt	1 pt	1½ pt	2 pt	3pt
Tinned Copper Tops	1s.	1/3d.	1/6d.	1/8d.	2/-d.
Bright " "	1/9	2/-	2/3	2/6	
All Copper	3/6	3/6	4/-	4/6	

The catalogue of Sellman & Hill, established in Wolverhampton in 1880, shows a good selection of such moulds. However, it should be noted that they were obviously using the same pressing dies as most of their contemporaries, these being made by a specialist tool-manufacturer to the trade. This means that it is virtually impossible to attribute any tinplate mould to any particular factory.

The manufacture of tinplate moulds to Victorian patterns continued through into the following century. Harrods' catalogue of 1929 advertised lions, fish, borders and ordinary round shapes at a few shillings each.

The decoration of jellies did not end with their unmoulding onto a dish. *The Book of the Household* of 1862–4 provided the following advice:[67]

> Flowers always strike me as having the prettiest effect, for with them you can contrast the colours so well. Thus on a blamanger place scarlet geraniums or verbenas; on a jelly some white flower, as the white erica, or the small buds of a white rose ... If you can manage nothing else thin slices of lemon placed on each other round a lightly coloured jelly look far better than the bare dish. Even if the cook succeeds in flavouring everything to the "palate of perfection," yet, if the result of her labour is turned on to a dish, and left there without any additions, the appearance of the dinner will be a failure.

In addition to flowers, one of the most scintillating of jelly techniques involved turning a slab of any clear, firm jelly onto a freshly rinsed, wrung and stretched cloth and chopping it into

(67) Landon, 417.

tiny cubes. When placed in a waterproof icing bag fitted with a nozzle, it was then piped as mounds or lines both on and about the main jelly. Here its multiple reflective surfaces gave it the appearance of a crystallized mass of sparkling gems.

Before leaving the topic of jellies in the Victorian era, it is important to provide instructions as to how they should be eaten according to the rules of etiquette and good manners. As an *entremet*, they might be served by a footman who would hold the dish in a folded napkin just by the diner's left elbow, offering the handle ends of the serving spoons at the same time. The diner then turned slightly to the left, and helped him or herself (easier said than done), transferring a portion on to their plate. According to Herman Senn, 'Sweets of an ornamental character ... and other large moulded sweets, may be handed round'[68] in this way. With jellies, this required some skill, even a degree of good luck, to avoid the whole mass sliding into the lap or onto the floor. It was wiser, perhaps, to follow Senn's later advice that 'anything not easily detached and handled should be served on a plate', this being undertaken by a footman, probably having first removed the jelly from the table to a side-table. Once served to the diner, a single fork was the only acceptable way in which to transfer the jelly from the plate to the lips. Chasing a jelly around a plate, or trying to stop it wobbling off the tines to plunge down a low-cut décolletage could again prove a revealing test of social skill and breeding. Mamas were often adept at setting such apparently innocent challenges for potential daughters-in-law.

Such rules were usually strictly enforced, even at the children's parties so fashionable in the upper and middle classes. In her *Manners for Women* of 1897 Mrs Humphry provided one of the most evocative of all descriptions of the place jellies then occupied in our national subconscious:[69]

Creams and jellies should always occupy prominent positions on the table at children's parties. They attract

(68) Senn, 33.
(69) Humphry, 113.

No. 661. No. 662. No. 663. No. 664

No. 665. No. 666. No. 667. No. 668.

No. 669. No. 671. No. 672. No. 673.

3800. Oval.   3100. Oval or Round.   331B. Oval.

A. R. WOOD & Co., DALE END, BIRMINGHAM.

9300. Round.   411. Oval.   701. Oval.

Figure 26. The tinplate moulds made by Sellman & Hill of Wolverhampton from 1880 (top) were priced according to the complexity of their design and their size. Their 'Grapes', No. 663, was supplied in four sizes, 1½ pt. costing 2s. 5d., for example, while the 4-pint version cost 3s. 11d. The other moulds (bottom) come from the pattern book of A.R. Wood & Co. of Dale End, Birmingham.

JELLIES & THEIR MOULDS

SPECIMENS FROM

THE BOOK OF MOULDS,

Containing 68 pages of Illustrations, published by

MARSHALL'S SCHOOL OF COOKERY

And sent POST FREE on application.

TIN MOULDS.

No. 72A.	No. 72B.	No. 72C.
5½ in., 5s.	5¼ in., 5s.	5½ in., 4s. 9d.
No. 72D.	No. 72E.	No. 72F.
5¼ in., 5s.	5½ in., 5s.	5½ in., 5s.
No. 73.	No. 74.	No. 75.
5¼ in., 3s. 9d.	5½ in., 4s.	5½ in., 5s. 6d.
No. 76.	No. 77.	No. 78.
5¼ in., 3s. 9d.	5½ in., 4s.	6 in., 4s. 9d.

Figure 27. Tinplate moulds from Mrs Marshall's Book of Moulds, c. *1891.*

by their prettiness, and, if well made, should be both nourishing and digestible. Jellies especially appeal to the childish imagination by their transparent delicacy of aspect, and it is almost cruel to provide insufficient to go all round. I have seen such longing eyes fixed on the swiftly diminishing, quivering mound as it is handed round, and have known perfectly well that this longing came, not from greediness, but from an innate love of beauty. Hostesses of the Lillyputs! Do have plenty of jelly, amber-clear and rosy red, sparkling like jewels, and saying many beautiful things to the minds of children that you and I used to hear, but have long ago forgotten.

CHAPTER EIGHT

THE TWENTIETH CENTURY & ITS MOULDS

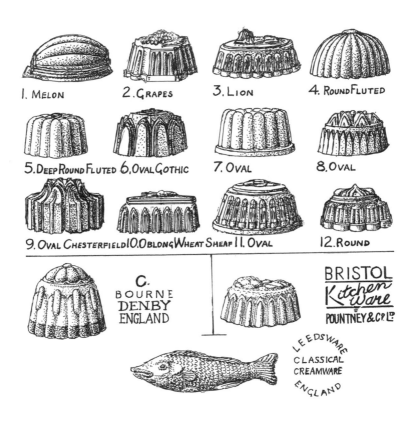

1. Melon 2. Grapes 3. Lion 4. Round Fluted

5. Deep Round Fluted 6. Oval Gothic 7. Oval 8. Oval

9. Oval Chesterfield 10. Oblong Wheat Sheaf 11. Oval 12. Round

C.
BOURNE
DENBY
ENGLAND

BRISTOL
Kitchen
Ware
POUNTNEY & Cº Lº

LEEDSWARE
CLASSICAL
CREAMWARE
ENGLAND

Figure 28. The early twentieth-century catalogue of Pearson & Co. of Chesterfield shows their standard range of twelve stoneware moulds (top). Those made at Joseph Bourne & Sons Denby Pottery from 1912 to the 1930s are attractively glazed in fawn and a rich brown, while those of Pountney & Co. of Bristol in the '30s and '40s are usually in bright yellow and green. The reproduction Leeds creamware fish mould dates from the 1990s.

By 1900 the status of the jelly was changing. In great country houses it still appeared in its most elaborate forms, the pride of the last generation of great domestic chef/cooks, but the world they knew was changing rapidly. Sons and daughters of the nobility, along with many middle-class people, now found it difficult to replace the older generation of resident household servants, since this was no longer a career choice for workers who could earn more and enjoy more freedom in offices and factories. A number of books began to appear, their purpose being to show how families should manage their domestic affairs for and by themselves. Their titles include *A Younger Sons' Cookery Book*, by A Younger Son's Daughter of 1896, *The One Maid Book of Cookery* by A.E. Congreve of 1913 and *Cooking without a Cook* by *Country Life* of 1926.

The first of these manuals states that in the past, 'Jelly-making was naturally looked on as a serious business not to be lightly undertaken ... though, owing to pure and tasteless gelatine being now easily procurable, it has lost its old foundation.'[1] It then goes on to give one of the best descriptions of how to use modern leaf gelatin to make wine, ale and fruit-juice jellies, how to line moulds and decorate them. However, 'excessive or fantastic ornament, or ornament which seems to call special attention to itself, ought always to be avoided.' K. Burrill and A.M. Booth agreed in their *Amateur Cook* of 1905:[2]

> Try not to have too many [sweets], the remains of mushy trifles and half-eaten creams are rather a trial to the spirits and digestions of a small family. Have some good plain jellies in reserve; if they are not wanted they can be

(1) Mallock, 187.
(2) Burrill & Booth, 197, 438–40.

given to a friend who is ill ... or Philomena can take them with some of her pretty flowers to any small hospital that you or she is in the habit of visiting. Never waste jellies; remember there is always some one who will be glad to have them. [However] Jellies seem to present many difficulties, if we judge from the varying results obtained by people who consider themselves fairly good cooks. Jellies stiff as glue, jellies that collapse as they leave the moulds are both unnecessary trials.

There was a growing reaction to late Victorian excess and a demand for greater simplicity in foods in general. Most ordinary Edwardian cookery books give recipes for plain, gelatin-set fruit jellies and creams, along with cornflour blancmanges flavoured with cream, coffee, chocolate, fruit purées and essences.

BANANA CREAM, 1911[3]

5 bananas, peeled   *juice of 2 lemons*
5 oz / 125 g sugar   *4 tsp / 6 leaves gelatin*
½ pt / 300 ml cream whipped to stiffness

Beat the bananas and sugar until smooth, beat in the juice and the gelatin dissolved in a little hot water, fold in the cream, and leave in a mould overnight to set.

ORANGE BLANCMANGE, 1911[4]

3 tbs cornflour   *8 oz / 225 g sugar*
juice of 8 oranges and 2 lemons

Mix the cornflour into ½ pt / 300 ml cold water, add the remaining ingredients and stir while cooking for 10 minutes, then leave overnight in a mould to set.

(3) Selfridge, 172.
(4) ibid., 178.

PRUNE MOULD, 1914[5]

8 oz / 225 g prunes, soaked	*1 oz / 25 g gelatin*
2 oz / 50 g white sugar	*6 tbs claret*
zest of ½ lemon	*¼ pt / 150 ml cream,*
1 in. / 25 mm stick cinnamon	*whipped*
	1 oz / 25 g flaked almonds

Stew the prunes, sugar, zest and cinnamon in ½ pt / 300 ml water until tender, strain the liquid into one bowl, and rub the prunes through a sieve into another. If the stones are present, crack them and add the kernels to the prunes. Sprinkle and stir the gelatin into the cold prune stock and claret, soak for 5 minutes, then warm and stir until dissolved, before mixing thoroughly into the prune purée. Put into a border mould and leave overnight to set. Turn the border on to a dish, fill the centre with the whipped cream and decorate with the almonds, perhaps with glacé cherries and pistachios too.

During the First World War jellies made a quick, cheap and delicious dessert, especially when using the new squares of ready-flavoured fruit jelly, or packet gelatin used with home-grown gooseberries, strawberries or blackberries. When gelatin began to disappear from the grocer's shelves, however, alternatives had to be found. One reader of *Isabell's Home Cookery* magazine wrote in 1918:[6]

'I used to use a great many jelly squares. The children were so fond of jelly, and it made a nice pudding for them, but now I can't get the squares any more. Will you tell me if there is anything to replace them?'

The editor then suggested;

(5) Jack, 442.
(6) Pearson (1918), 223.

WARTIME RECIPES, 1918[7]

1 pt / 600 ml juice made by stewing raw fruit or 1 pt
hot water with either 1 tbs black treacle or 2 tbs jam
or marmalade
2 tbs cornflour

Mix the cornflour with a little cold water, add to the remaining ingredients, stir and cook until thickened, then pour into a mould and leave to set.

A year later, the December edition of the magazine carried a feature on 'Jellies for John and Jane';[8]

'Please, Father Kissmuss' said John before he went to sleep. 'Let's have plenty of jellies tomorrow.' 'Amen' said little Jane. Well, don't you remember when you were a nipper and you went to a party what a quick 'No, thank you,' you said to the bread, and WHAT a 'Yes, please,' to the jellies!

This time gelatin jellies were proposed, made as lemon, orange, coffee, and:

JAM JELLY, 1919[9]

½ lb / 225 g good jam or marmalade juice of ¼ lemon
1 oz / 25 g gelatin a little more sugar if
3 tbs wine required

Melt the jam in 18 fl oz / 500 ml hot water, and strain through muslin. Add the lemon juice, sprinkle and stir in the gelatin, and heat while stirring until hot and dissolved. Stir in the wine and additional sugar, pour into a mould, and leave to set.

(7) ibid., 223.
(8) Pearson (1919), 211.
(9) ibid., 211.

After the War was over, the next twenty years were dominated by great economic and social problems; it was a period of strikes, unemployment and low wages for most of the population, and one of uncertainty and low returns on investments for many of the middle class. People wanted foods which must be cheap, but still put some colour and a hint of pleasure, even luxury into their lives. The foods which best met these criteria were jelly and blancmange. As the demand grew, manufacturers responded by producing more and better packs of pre-prepared ingredients which took only a few minutes to cook in the home. At the Devonshire Works in Birmingham, Alfred Bird & Sons made a popular range of flavoured jelly squares which had only to be dissolved in hot water to produce firm-setting, clear and delicious jellies. In York, Rowntrees produced their first packet jellies in 1923, offering ten flavours: raspberry, lemon, pineapple, blackcurrant, strawberry, lime fruit, vanilla, orange, greengage and cherry. These were transformed into cube jellies in 1932, when their promotion took the form of coupons on each carton which could be collected and exchanged for boxes of chocolates:[10]

Pocket Money and FREE Chocolates
Bob – 'I wish my Dad gave me pocket money to buy boxes of chocs.'
Tom – 'Mine doesn't! I get these by collecting the coupons from Rowntree's Cocoa and Rowntree's Jellies. Get your Mother to buy them if you want free chocs.'

In Brighton, H.J. Green & Co. made both jelly crystals and jelly squares in lemon, orange, raspberry, strawberry, vanilla, pineapple, blackcurrant, wine and tangerine flavours, all 'Beautifully clear and firm. Nothing finer at any price.'[11]
The manufacturers of clear gelatin also rose to the demands of the time by commencing an unprecedented promotion of their products. J. & G. Cox of Gorgie Mills, Edinburgh had

(10) Rowntree (1983), 6, 9.
(11) H.J. Green, 37.

converted from shredded gelatin to powdered gelatin in the opening years of the century, employing Bertha Roberts to write *A Manual of Gelatine Cookery* for use with Cox's Sparkling Gelatine around 1900, further editions of the '20s and '30s being of some ninety pages and illustrated with excellent colour plates. Gelatin also began to be imported from the Dominions, Davis Gelatine coming from factories in Sydney, Australia, and Christchurch, New Zealand. The first edition of *Davis Dainty Dishes* was published in Australia in 1922, the first London edition appearing in 1933. One hundred thousand copies were sold here by 1936. The Charles B. Knox Gelatine Co. of Johnstown, New York State, also started to supply gelatin to England, where copies of the attractive forty-one page *Dainty Desserts for Dainty People: Knox Gelatine* booklet of 1924 are still to be found today. The recipes in these, along with those in other popular cookery books of the period, are really excellent for converting relatively straightforward ingredients into dishes which can satisfy the palate, the eye and the pocket. Here are a few examples:

GINGER JELLY, 1939[12]

whites & crushed shells of 2 eggs	*4 oz / 100 g Demarara sugar*
juice & zest of 1 lemon	*1 tsp vinegar*
2 cloves	*3 fl oz / 90 ml ginger wine*
piece of stick cinnamon	*5 tsp / 7 leaves gelatin*

Whisk the eggs, lemon, cloves, cinnamon, sugar, vinegar and ¾ pt / 450 ml water together over a gentle heat, stop whisking, allow to boil up three times, then set aside for 10 minutes before filtering through a fine cloth. Meanwhile sprinkle the gelatin into the wine, stir, and leave to soak. Mix the jelly and gelatin solutions together, heat and stir without boiling until completely dissolved, then pour into a mould and leave overnight to set.

(12) Cox, 11.

CRANBERRY & APPLE MOULD, 1939[13]

½ lb / 225 g cranberries	1 oz / 25 g gelatin
1 lb / 450 g apples	8 oz / 225 g sugar

Stew the chopped fruits in ¼ pt / 150 ml water until tender and press through a sieve to produce 1 pt / 600 ml of juice. Sprinkle the sugar and gelatin into ¼ pt / 150 ml water, stir and heat gently until dissolved, mix into the fruit juice, stir occasionally until almost set, then pour into a mould and leave overnight to set.

BROWN BREAD CREAM, 1939[14]

2 oz / 50 g grated wholemeal bread	few drops vanilla essence
1 pt / 600 ml milk	1 oz / 25 g gelatin
3 oz / 75 g sugar	½ pt / 300 ml whipping cream

Scald the crumbs with the milk, stir in the sugar, vanilla and the gelatin sprinkled and stirred into ¼ pt / 150 ml water, and leave to cool. When starting to thicken, fold in the whipped cream, pour into a mould, and leave overnight to set.

CARRINGTON MOULD, 1939[15]

1 oz / 25 g gelatin	juice of 1 lemon
small tin peaches, apricots, etc.	½ pt / 300 ml milk
2 tbs sugar	a few drops of vanilla essence & cochineal

Layer 1: Sprinkle two-thirds of the gelatin into ½ pt / 300 ml water and warm until dissolved, add half the sugar, the lemon juice and the juices from the peaches, if necessary making up to 1 pt / 600 ml with more water. Pour a little into a watertight cake tin or charlotte mould, leave to set, arrange the apricot pieces on top, just cover with more jelly and leave to set once more.

(13) ibid., 47.
(14) ibid., 87.
(15) Davis, 33.

Layer 2: Stir the remaining sugar and a few drops of vanilla into the milk, and stir until dissolved. Sprinkle the rest of the gelatin into a little cold water and warm until dissolved. When cool, stir into the milk, pour over the set apricot layer, and leave to set.

Layer 3: Colour the remaining jelly with a little cochineal, pour over the set milk layer, and leave the whole to set overnight before turning out.

CHOCOLATE SURPRISE, 1939[16]

½ oz / 12 g gelatin	a few drops of vanilla
4 oz / 100 g chocolate	essence
1 pt / 600 ml milk	sugar to taste

Warm the gelatin and chocolate in the milk until dissolved, keeping below about 70°C to prevent curdling. Stir in the vanilla and sugar and when ready fill the mould, leave to set, then spoon the surplus from the centre to leave a 1 in. / 25 mm layer all round.

Make a cream with:

¼ oz / 7 g gelatin	½ pt / 300 ml whipping
1½ oz / 35 g sugar	cream
	a few drops vanilla essence

Half whip the cream, sugar and vanilla. Sprinkle the gelatin into 5 tbs / 80 ml water, warm and stir until completely dissolved, and stir lightly into the cream. When about to set, pour into the lined mould, leave until set, then melt the remaining chocolate mixture, and when cool, pour over the cream mixture to completely enclose it. (The mould may be given a preliminary lining of lemon jelly and decorated before the first batch of chocolate mixture is poured in, for a richer effect.)

(16) Cox, 59.

JAMAICA CREAM, 1937[17]

½ oz / 12 g gelatin   2 tbs black treacle
1 pt / 600 ml milk

Sprinkle the gelatin into the milk, stir, then stir in the treacle
and continue stirring over a gentle heat until all is dissolved.
Keep below around 70°C to prevent curdling, pour into a mould
and leave overnight to set.

POACHED EGGS, 1920s–'30s[18]

½ oz / 12 g gelatin   stewed or tinned apricot
¾ pt / 450 ml milk   halves
½ oz / 12 g sugar   a few drops vanilla essence
                      ¼ pt / 150 ml lightly
                      whipped cream

Sprinkle the gelatin into ¼ pt / 150 ml cold water, stir and heat
until completely dissolved and allow to cool. Stir the sugar and
vanilla into the milk, then the gelatin, and pour ¾ in. / 2 cm
deep into a flat dish and leave to set. Cut the milk jelly into
3 in. / 7.5 cm rounds [these may be laid on slices of sponge cake
as 'toast'], place a half apricot 'yolk' on each, and pour over a
little of the cream as extra 'white' of egg.

AN EASTER [EGG] DESSERT, 1924[19]

6 tsp / 9 leaves gelatin   2 tbs sugar
1 pt / 600 ml milk or cream   small pinch of salt
few drops of vanilla essence   6 eggs

Pierce holes in each end of each egg, insert a narrow skewer,
stir the yolk to break it up, then blow out the contents [for
scrambled eggs or other use] and rinse the interior with cold
water. Block the holes in the bottoms of the eggs with a little
cold butter, and stand upright in a dish of flour. Mix the gelatin
with a little of the milk, stir into the remaining milk with the

(17) Heath, 42.
(18) Davis, 21.
(19) Knox, 17.

vanilla, sugar and salt, and stir over a gentle heat until all is dissolved. Keep below about 70°C to prevent curdling. Use a small funnel to fill the eggs with cold but unset jelly, leave to set firmly, then remove the shells to reveal jelly eggs.

They may be served in a 'nest' of chopped orange or lemon jelly. A little chocolate may be added to half the mixture before pouring, to give a few brown eggs too.

VELVET CREAM, 1937[20]

¾ oz / 20 g gelatin *4 oz / 100 g lump sugar*
½ pt / 300 ml sherry *1 pt / 600 ml cream*
2 lemons

Stir the gelatin into the sherry and set aside for 1 hour. Rub the sugar on the lemons to absorb the oils from the zest, and add these to the sherry with their strained juice before stirring over a gentle heat until all is completely dissolved. When nearly cold, stir into the cream, stir gently until about to set, then pour into a mould and leave overnight to set completely.

CARNATIONS IN JELLY, 1937[21]

dark red carnations *any clear pale pink jelly*

Jellies are always *de rigueur* in summertime ... I suggest that the cook should try her hand (especially if she be the mistress also, and an amateur) at those gleaming transparencies wherein a flower or fruit lies imprisoned. It would be a delicate compliment to set before a guest known to be fond of carnations ... a jelly of pink enshrouding a few of these deep-red blossoms, provided that she was sure that the blooms were fresh and absolutely clean.

(20) Heath, 53.
(21) ibid., 39.

Pour ½ in./25 mm jelly into a plain, straight-sided mould, allow to set. Lay in the carnations or roses (or bunch of black grapes embedded in yellow jelly) and build up the jelly in layers until all is fully embedded.

Blancmanges made with cornflour were equally popular in the inter-war years, new recipes being published in Brown & Polson's *Summer Dishes* booklet.

ORANGE SPONGE 1920s–'30s[22]

3 oz/75 g cornflour	*4 oz/100 g caster sugar*
1½ pt/900 ml milk	*2 eggs, separated*
½ oz/12 g butter	*juice & grated zest of 2 oranges*

Mix the cornflour with a little of the milk, stir into the remaining milk with the butter, sugar and beaten yolks, and continue stirring as it boils for 10 minutes. Remove from the heat, fold in the strained juice, the zest, and the stiffly beaten egg-whites before pouring into a mould and leaving to set.

RATAFIA MOULD[23]

3 tbs cornflour	*2 oz/50 g chopped candied citron*
1 pt/600 ml milk	
2 oz/50 g ratafias or macaroons	*4 tbs sherry*
	1 oz/25 g caster sugar

Mix the cornflour with a little of the milk, add to the remaining milk and sugar and boil while stirring for 10 minutes. Meanwhile soak the ratafias and citron in the sherry, then stir into the blancmange, pour into a mould, and leave to set.

(22) Brown & Polson, 14.
(23) ibid., 16.

CREAM PAGLIACCI[24]

'If for some reason the jelly has not set, never mind,
  "On with the Motley, the paint and the powder ..."
make it into this delicious cream. Sprinkle

3 tbs semolina, 3 tbs sugar into 1 pt/600 ml freshly-boiled milk

Cook for 3 minutes, stirring all the time, then pour in
the rebarbative [and unset] jelly, stir well again, pour
into a mould, and this time, it will set, although under
a different name.'

CHRISTMAS PLUM PUDDING JELLY[25]

¾ oz/20 g gelatin	*¼ pt/150 ml raisins*
1½ pts/900 ml milk	*¼ pt/150 ml dates or figs*
1 oz/25 g chocolate or 3 tbs cocoa	*½ pt/300 ml currants or*
½ tsp vanilla essence	*stem ginger*
1 oz/25 g chopped nuts/almonds	*4 oz/100 g sugar*
3 oz/75 g candied peel	*pinch of salt*

Chop all the peel, dates, figs, and ginger and put in a saucepan
with everything but the gelatin, simmer for 5 minutes and
remove from the heat. Sprinkle and stir the gelatin into 5
tbs/75 ml water, heat and stir until completely dissolved, then
thoroughly mix it into the fruit, etc., before pouring into a
pudding mould or bowl and leaving overnight to set.

The increasing popularity of these and other new jelly and
blancmange recipes led to a revival in the production of new
moulds in which to shape them. Up to the outbreak of the
First World War there was an unbroken continuance of ceramic
and metal moulds following the old, established patterns.
Then, particularly in the 1920s, major changes took place with
a flourish of new designs and materials to complement the
colourful recipes of the period.

(24) Mauduit, 109.
(25) Davis (1936), 37.
  See also Cox, 51
  & Knox, 18.

POTTERY MOULDS[26]

Being unmarked, the jelly moulds made in many potteries will always remain anonymous. This section will therefore consider those published in trade catalogues (see fig. 28). Typical of these is that of Pearson & Co. of Chesterfield which shows that all its mid-Victorian designs were still in production in 1914. There was nothing unusual in this, for only a few potteries decided to introduce new lines, and then only in the 1910s '20s and '30s.

JOSEPH BOURNE & SONS LTD.

Established at Denby near Belper, Derbyshire, this company's first distinctive series of jelly moulds was introduced in 1912, continuing into the 1930s.[27] Made in a buff-firing 'leadless glaze stoneware' with a dipped band of red-brown slip around the rim, they usually bear the black printed mark of 'BOURNE / DENBY / ENGLAND'. They followed traditional fluted shapes and sold wholesale for between 8s. 6d. and 14s. the dozen.

BRISTOL KITCHEN WARE

In the 1930s, the old-established pottery of Pountney & Co., Temple Backs, Bristol, introduced jelly moulds with very soft, rounded details covered in apple green and primrose yellow glazes. They have a black transfer-printed mark 'BRISTOL / Kitchen Ware / POUNTNEY & CO. LTD.' and may be dated before 1949, when the works closed. They were sold at 2s. 9d. to 3s. 6d. each.

LEEDSWARE

The eighteenth-century Leeds creamware industry was revived by Leeds City Council in 1983. Within a few years its production was in the private sector, trading under a number of names. That stamped 'LEEDSWARE CLASSICAL CREAMWARE ENGLAND' included reproduction jelly moulds of late-Georgian, but apparently not Leeds, design, including a

(26) The references for the patterns below are taken from Godden, moulds seen by the author, or catalogues at the Beamish Open Air Museum, County Durham.

(27) Kevill-Davis, 32.

well-modelled fish some 10 in./25.5 cm long. Produced in the 1990s, it is press-moulded and has three feet modelled as fluted concave cones with beaded borders.

C.T. MALING & SONS

This major pottery, founded in Newcastle upon Tyne in 1817, manufactured an excellent series of jelly moulds from the 1920s and '30s through to its closure in July 1963. Its catalogue of around 1930 shows fluted and 'Gothic' shapes of earlier traditional form, as well as useful border moulds ideal for blancmanges encircling stewed fruits or whipped cream. Its new designs are among the most interesting and delightful of the period, the most unusual being loosely based on the keep of Newcastle's Norman castle, which also featured on the company's trademark from 1890. One of their abstract designs, No. P, is of particular interest, being one of the few moulds ever made to purposely display the effects of light reflecting off and through clear jelly. It did this by adopting a multi-faceted crystalline form, with buttresses to keep its major planes upright. Rowntrees found it so attractive that they moulded their jellies in it for their 1930s' advertisements.

Most moulds bear a black transfer-printed mark such as 'CETEM WARE/ENGLAND' or 'MALING/MADE IN/ENGLAND' and a code such as 'F. .7', the letter indicating the pattern, and the number its size in inches, anywhere from 3" to 8".

SHELLEY

'Shelley' china and earthenware was first made by Wileman & Co. of Foley Works, Longton, Staffordshire, from around 1911, its jelly moulds already having a fine reputation by 1915. This continued after 1925 when the company changed its name to Shelley Potteries Ltd. and adopted the green transfer-printed mark 'Shelley' in a shield and 'ENGLAND'. The moulds in its 1922 catalogue are very finely made, care being taken to ensure that the exterior shows the pattern just as clearly as the interior,

A. 3".5".6".7". B. 3½".5".6".7".8". C.3½".5".6".7".8". D.3".3½".5".6".7".8"

E.2½".3".3½".5".6".7".8". F.3".5".6".7".8". H.5".6".7".8". J.5".6".7."

K.5".6".7".8". L.5".6".7".8". M.5".6".7." N.5".6".7."

P. 3".5".6".7". R.3". S.5".6".7." T.5".6".7."

SQUARE C. 2¼". CURD MOULD

CETEM WARE
ENGLAND

MALING **F..7**
MADE IN
ENGLAND

Figure 29. Moulds from the 1930s catalogue of C.T. Maling & Sons of Newcastle upon Tyne.

ACANTHUS · ARMADILLO · CRAYFISH · ORNAMENTAL

STAR · RITZ · QUEEN'S · CARLTON (SMALL CREAM CENTRE)

FRENCH · FLUTED BOWL · CECIL (BORDER) · SAVOY (CREAM CENTRE)

CORNWALL 4198 · NATIONAL 4199 · RABBIT 4199A · BUTTERFLY 4202

Figure 30. Shelley moulds of 1922, their exteriors being modelled to show the shape of the finished jellies (above the line). Below the line are shown the new shapes introduced by Spode c. 1902–1910, while at the bottom is one of that company's moulds produced as wall-decorations in 2002.

representing exactly what its jelly or blancmange will look like when turned out. The shapes are all beautifully designed and detailed, some, like the 'Queen's' and 'Ritz', following well-established copper mould patterns. Others are quite new, such as the delightful 'Armadillo', the 'Star' with its reflective flutes and clean lines, and the 'Rabbit', whose neck-bow keeps it upright as the jelly is setting.

The producers of packet jellies used Shelley moulds more than those of any other manufacturer. Symington's featured the 'Star', 'French', 'Queen's' and 'Ornamental', Cox's, the 'Ritz', and Rowntree's, the 'French' and 'Carlton', as may be seen in their respective advertisements.

SPODE

The Spode catalogues show that the company introduced four new shapes between 1902 and 1910, the 'Cornwall', the 'National' with rose, thistle and shamrock, the 'Rabbit' and the 'Butterfly'.

In the spring of 2002 their Blue Room collection produced an oval jelly mould with a triangular flute at each 'corner'. The jellies it produced were among the most plain and undistinguished ever made by an English pottery. The reason for this is that they were not designed for use, but for hanging as wall decorations in kitchens. Attractively transfer-printed in blue, they show one of four patterns, the 'Aster' of c. 1832, 'Lily' of c. 1837, 'Bramble' of c. 1847 and 'Strawberry' from 1852.

GRIMWADES LTD.

The Grimwade brothers started the Winton Pottery at Hanley and Stoke-on-Trent in 1886, becoming a limited company in 1900. They produced a good selection of shapes, the most memorable being a large lion similar to those in Trafalgar Square and introduced about the time of the First World War, and a "BUNNY 1PINT". Most of the moulds bear the transfer-printed mark 'GRIMWADES / STOKE ON TRENT / ENGLAND'.

GLASS MOULDS

Sowerby's continued to make moulds up to 1912. 'Pyrex' heatproof moulded glass moulds were then introduced by Greener & Co., successors to Jobling's of Newcastle upon Tyne just after the First World War. They usually followed traditional round or oval shapes with fluted sides, but also included rabbits and tortoises. Glass moulds were also imported from America and Czechoslovakia.[28] Although attractively clear, and good for blancmanges, jellies stuck firmly within them unless they were properly prepared.

BRANDED MOULDS

A number of companies decided to use the plain outer surfaces of jelly moulds as the most relevant place for their advertisements. These are usually in transfer-print, and include:

COX'S SPARKLING GELATINE / INVALUABLE & INDISPENSABLE / FOR MAKING / JELLIES CREAMS PUDDINGS ETC. / SOLD BY ALL HIGH CLASS GROCERS' for J. & G. Cox Ltd, Gorgie Mills, Edinburgh

'GREEN'S NEWSTYLE JELLIES' for H.J. Green of Brighton's 'Assorted Blancmanges' and 'Jelly Crystals'.

CORN FLOUR BLANC-MANGE
BROWN & POLSON'S
2½ oz (5 table spoonfuls filled level) Corn Flour "Patent" quality.
2 Pints (3 breakfast cups quite full) good sweet milk.
Mix Corn Flour well with a little of the milk.
Heat the rest of the milk to boiling point.
Pour Corn Flour into heated milk stirring well.
Add half a teaspoon of butter.
Boil and stir for 10 minutes (by the clock).

(28) ibid., 58.

BURGESS & LEIGH, Middleport Pottery, BURSLEM.

BLANC MANGE MOULDS.

Figure 31. Earthenware moulds made by Burgess & Leigh around 1889–1920 (top), and by Joseph Unwin & Co. around 1877–1926 (below).

Seamless Tinned Steel Jelly Moulds

No. 170

No. 180

No. 190

No. P2417

No. P2419

No. P2433

No. P2435

No. P2456

No. P2436

No. P2454

No. P2455

No. P2525

No. P2460

No. P2462

No. P2464

No. P2470

No. P2477

No. P2511

No. P2512

No. P2513

No P2514

No. P2517

No. P2518

No. P2520

No. P2966

No. P2969

No. P2971

No. P2977

Figure 32. Tinned steel jelly moulds from the early twentieth-century catalogue of E.T. Everton of Birmingham, most being pressed from a single sheet, and therefore requiring no seams.

JELLIES & THEIR MOULDS

Sugar and flavour, if desired, but served with jam or
marmalade is better.

Pour into this mould, and cool.

Re-heat gently, in mould, if desired, before the fire or
in oven.

Then turn out and serve, cold or hot.

Some of Brown and Polson's moulds have an E.B. monogram
and anchor mark. They cost 1s. each in 1916, but 2s. 6d. in the
1920s.

TINPLATE

Tinplate remained a popular material for jelly moulds, being
cheap, light, and conductive. Due to the relatively hard nature of
the underlying steel, the shapes tended to feature many narrow
flutes to make stamping easier. Usually $5\frac{1}{2}$ to $7\frac{1}{2}$ inches in
diameter, they were made in two qualities, either plain, in which
the protective tin coat was often damaged by the stamping
process, or 're-tinned' after stamping, to leave no exposed steel.
When a plain mould might cost 5s. the dozen, its re-tinned
alternative cost 7s. 6d. One of the main manufactures of the
inter-war years was E.T.E. (E.T. Everton) of Birmingham, who
also manufactured moulds in enamel, aluminium and tinned
copper.

COPPER & TIN MOULDS

Major manufacturers such as Benham's continued to supply top-
quality copper jelly moulds into the 1930s, other companies
producing seamed tinplate moulds, the best having their more
complex top section embossed in tinned copper. The 1912
catalogue of Treliving and Smith, Wholesale Ironmongers,
of 100, Minories, London, provides a good impression of the
shapes of this period.

BORDER MOULDS.

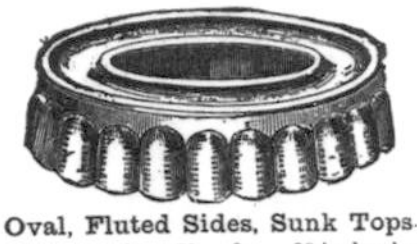

Oval, Fluted Sides, Sunk Tops.

	6½	7½	8	8¾ inches long.
Sizes	0	1	2	3
No. T 55	2/2	2/6	2/10	3/2 each.

Round, Fluted Sides, Sunk Tops.

	5½	6	6½	7 ins. diameter.
Sizes	0	1	2	3
No. T 56	2/2	2/6	2/10	3/2 each.

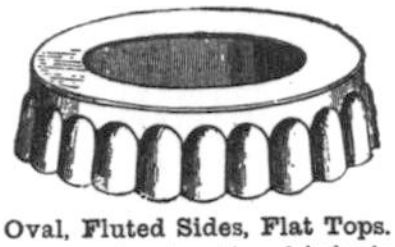

Oval, Fluted Sides, Flat Tops.

	6	7	7½	8 inches long.
Sizes	0	1	2	3
No. T 57	2/2	2/6	2/10	3/2 each.

Round, Fluted Sides, Flat Tops.

	5½	6	6½	7 ins. diameter.
Sizes	0	1	2	3
No. T 58	2/2	2/6	2/10	3/2 each.

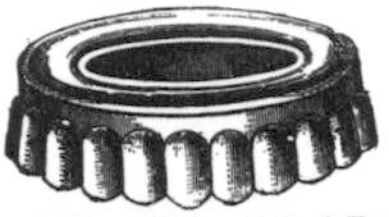

Oval, Fluted Sides, Raised Tops.

	6½	7½	8	8¾ inches long.
Sizes	0	1	2	3
No. T 59	2/2	2/6	2/10	3/2 each.

Round, Fluted Sides, Raised Tops.

	5½	6	6½	7 ins. diameter.
Sizes	0	1	2	3
No. T 60	2/2	2/6	2/10	3/2 each.

Oval, Plain Sides, Flat Tops.

	6	7	7½	8 inches long.
Sizes	0	1	2	3
No. T 63	2/2	2/6	2/10	3/2 each.

Round, Plain Sides. Flat Tops.

	5½	6	6½	7 ins. diameter.
Sizes	0	1	2	3
No. T 64	2/2	2/6	2/10	3/2 each.

Oval, Plain Sides, Sunk Tops.

	6	7	7½	8 inches long.
Sizes	0	1	2	3
No. T 61	2/2	2/6	2/10	3/2 each.

Round, Plain Sides, Sunk Tops.

	5½	6	6½	7 ins. diameter.
Sizes	0	1	2	3
No. T 62	2/2	2/6	2/10	3/2 each.

Oval, Plain Sides. Raised Tops.

	6	7	7½	8 inches long.
Sizes	0	1	2	3
No. T 65	2/2	2/6	2/10	3/2 each.

Round, Plain Sides, Raised Tops.

	5½	6	6½	7 ins. diameter.
Sizes	0	1	2	3
No. T 66	2/2	2/6	2/10	3/2 each.

Oval, Fluted Sides, Fancy Tops.

	5¾	6½	7 inches long.
Sizes	1	2	3
No. T 69	3/4	3/10	4/6 each.

Round, Fluted Sides, Fancy Tops.

	5½	6	6½ ins. diameter.
Sizes	1	2	3
No. T 70	3/4	3/10	4/6 each.

Oval, Fluted Sides, Sovereign Tops.

	6	6½	7½	8½ inches long.
Sizes	00	0	1	2
No. T 67	3/6	4/-	4/8	6/- each.

Round, Fluted Sides, Sovereign Tops.

	5½	6	6½	7½ ins. diameter.
Sizes	00	0	1	2
No. T 68	3/6	4/-	4/8	6/- each.

Oval, Fluted Sides, Fancy Tops.

	7½	8½ inches long.
Sizes	1	2
No. T 71	4/8	6/- each.

BORDER MOULDS.

Oval, Plain Sides, Fancy Tops.

	7	8 inches long.
Sizes	1	2
No. T 72	4/8	6/- each

CAKE OR JELLY MOULDS.

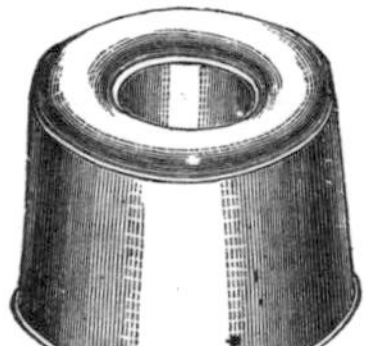

Round, "Timbale."

	4	4½	5	5½	6	6½ inches.
Sizes	1	2	3	4	5	6
No. T 41	2/-	2/4	2/8	3/-	3/4	3/8 each.

"Edinburgh."

	¾	1	1¼	2 pints.
Sizes	1	2	3	4
No. T 39	1/2	1/8	2/-	2/4 each.

Figure 33. Tinned steel jelly moulds (1) from the 1912 catalogue of Treliving & Smith, wholesale ironmongers of London.

DARIOLE CUPS.

Plain, Round.

Sizes 00　0　1　2　3　4

No. T 52　2/1　2/1　2/1　2/2　2/3　2/6 per dozen.

Fluted, Round.

Sizes 00　0　1　2　3　4

No. T 53　2/1　2/1　2/1　2/2　2/3　2/6 per dozen.

Fine Fluted, Round.

Sizes　1　　2　　3　　4

No. T 54　2/1　　2/2　　2/3　　2/6 per dozen.

Plain, Round, Stamped.

Sizes　1　　2　　3

No. 3360　1/9　2/-　2/3 per dozen.

Fluted, Round, Stamped.

Sizes　1　　2　　3

No. 3361　1/9　2/-　2/3 per dozen.

JELLY MOULDS.

Tin, Hand Made.

　　　　　1　　2 pints.

No. 101　..　..　5d.　7d. each.

CARD MOULDS.

Tinned.

No. T 35　Without Cutters　..　3/- each.

Cutters for same, 2/4 per set.

JELLY MOULDS.

Oval, Tinned Tops.

　　　　1　　1½　　2 pints.

Sizes　1　　2　　3

No. T 100　1/0½　1/2　1/3½ each.

Oval, Tinned Tops.

　　　　1　　1½　　2 pints.

Sizes　1　　2　　3

No. T. 20　1/0½　1/2　1/3½ each.

Oval, Tinned Tops.

　　　　1　　1½　　2 pints.

Sizes　1　　2　　3

No. T 21　1/0½　1/2　1/3½ each.

Oval, Tinned Tops.

　　　　1　　1½　　2 pints.

Sizes　1　　2　　3

No. T. 22　1/0½　1/2　1/3½ each.

Oval, Tinned Tops.

　　　　1　　1½　　2 pints.

Sizes　1　　2　　3

No. T 23　1/0½　1/2　1/3½ each.

Oval, Tinned Tops.

　　　　1　　1½　　2 pints.

Sizes　1　　2　　3

No. T 24　1/8　1/10　2/- each.

B2

Figure 34. Tinned steel jelly moulds (2) from the 1912 catalogue of Treliving &
Smith, wholesale ironmongers of London.

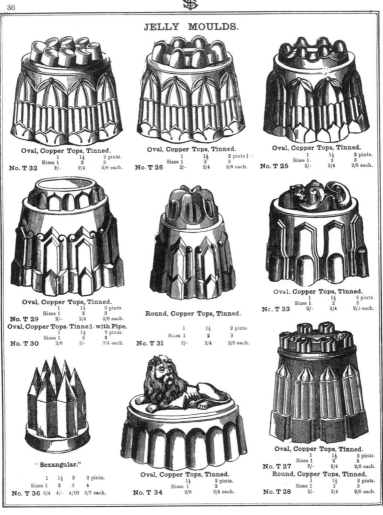

JELLY MOULDS.

Oval, Copper Tops, Tinned.
	1	1½	2 pints.
Sizes	1	2	3
No. T 32	2/-	2/4	2/8 each.

Oval, Copper Tops, Tinned.
	1	1½	2 pints.
Sizes	1	2	3
No. T 26	2/-	2/4	2/8 each.

Oval, Copper Tops, Tinned.
	1	1½	2 pints.
Sizes	1	2	3
No. T 25	2/-	2/4	2/8 each.

Oval, Copper Tops, Tinned.
	1	1½	2 pints.
Sizes	1	2	3
No. T 29	2/-	2/4	2/8 each.

Oval, Copper Tops, Tinned, with Pipe.
	1	1½	2 pints.
Sizes	1	2	3
No. T 30	2/8	3/-	3/4 each.

Round, Copper Tops, Tinned.
	1	1½	2 pints
Sizes	1	2	3
No. T 31	2/-	2/4	2/8 each.

Oval, Copper Tops, Tinned.
	1	1½	2 pints.
Sizes	1	2	3
Nc. T 33	2/-	2/4	2/3 each.

"Sexangular."
	1	1½	2	3 pints.
Sizes	1	2	3	4
No. T 36	3/4	4/-	4/10	5/7 each.

Oval, Copper Tops, Tinned.
		1½	2 pints.
Sizes	1	2	
No. T 34		2/8	3/4 each.

Oval, Copper Tops, Tinned.
	1	1½	2 pints.
Sizes	1	2	3
No. T 27	2/-	2/4	2/8 each.

Round, Copper Tops, Tinned.
	1	1½	2 pints.
Sizes	1	2	3
No. T 28	2/-	2/4	2/8 each.

Figure 35. Tinned steel jelly moulds (3) from the 1912 catalogue of Treliving & Smith, wholesale ironmongers of London.

ENAMELLED STEEL

The replacement of tin by a white ceramic enamel enabled steel moulds to be made with the clean, smooth and hardwearing qualities of pottery. Its only real disadvantages were its relative softness of detail, and its susceptibility to chipping when dropped. Since enamelling was essentially an improved surface treatment for steel, it continued to be made from the same tin-plate stamp-moulds from around 1900 to the 1940s.

ORME, EVANS & CO.

The 1912 catalogue of this company shows the moulds made at its Elgin and Phoenix works in Wolverhampton. Their prices ranged from 9s. a dozen for the simplest one-piece shapes, up to 51s. a dozen for the more complex 'Lion'.

MACFARLANE & ROBINSON LTD.

This company, with works in Glasgow, Wolverhampton and London, made a variety of tureens, pudding and jelly moulds in 'MB' and 'K' brands. Their 1913 catalogue has 4-inch moulds at 10s. 6d. the dozen and 2-pint 'Lions' at 42s. the dozen.

J. & A. BRATT & SONS

Their 1936 catalogue issued from the Clarence Works, Wolver-hampton, shows round 1-pint seamless jelly moulds at 18s. per dozen, up to 3-pint moulds at 30s. the dozen; 1½-pint 'Lions' cost 42s. the dozen.

ALUMINIUM

This light, ductile and highly conductive white metal was first isolated and identified by Sir Humphry Davy around 1812, but it took over a century to enter general domestic use. It was ideal for making jelly moulds, capable of being stamped into tall ornamental shapes without any need for joints or seams. When dipped into warm water, aluminium moulds released their contents with the immediacy and freshness of detail of tinned

Figure 36. These white-enamelled steel moulds were made by Orme, Evans & Co. of Wolverhampton, from their catalogue of 1912 (top), Macfarlane & Robinson of Glasgow and Wolverhampton from their catalogue of 1913 (middle), and J.A. Bratt & Sons of Wolverhampton from their catalogue of 1936 (bottom). Such moulds were sold at around 1s. 6d. each for the pint size and 2s. for the 2-pint size, while the lions, being more difficult to make, cost 3s. 6d. for the 1½ and 2-pint sizes.

JELLIES & THEIR MOULDS

copper, but at a fraction of the cost. Their only disadvantage was that they corroded if left in the damp. For this reason it was essential that they were carefully dried after use, otherwise they became pitted and perforated with small holes. When buying any old aluminium moulds, it is best to hold them up to the light to see if any 'stars' appear. If they do, either plug them with an epoxy resin glue, or smear cold butter over their outer surface and pour in the jelly solution when cold and just at the point of setting.

CLARENCE BRAND
J. & A. Bratt & Sons Ltd. of Dudley Road and Powlett Street, Wolverhampton illustrated 22 of their aluminium moulds in their catalogue of 1932. Of these, two are of particular interest. The first is a large rabbit mould, its front edge having a hinged pair of wire legs which enable it to stand securely while being filled and left to set. Each one has 'PAT. No. 363327/MADE IN ENGLAND' stamped beneath the rim, just under the rabbit's nose. The second is a set of four different individual moulds, six to the pint, packed in a cardboard box marked 'Jellette REGD.' These were later adopted by the Swan brand, when each mould was stamped with a swan within a triangle with 'TRADE MARK' down two of the sides, all within a 'SWAN BRAND/MADE IN ENGLAND' border.

DAVIES' SALOPIAN TIN WORKS
Established in 1866, this factory had extended its products in the 1920s to include stamped satin-finished aluminium jelly moulds. Its catalogue of 1930 shows six shapes, the most remarkable being a copy of the 1863 Alexandra mould, now masquerading as an up-to-date Art Deco design at 12s. 3d. the dozen.

DIAMOND ALUMINIUM WARE
The Diamond Aluminium Ware Co. Ltd. of Witton, Birmingham, made a range of aluminium moulds in the 1930s, including

06
45
55
85

65
95

I
2

3
4
5
7

PAT. STAND. REG^d DESIGN.

6

420/1
420/2

420/3
420/4
420/5
420/6
420/7
420/8

420/11
420/10
420/12

420/9
CLARENCE ALUMINIUM WARE

Figure 37. Aluminium jelly moulds were popular from the 1920s. Those from Davies' Salopian Tin Works catalogue of 1930 (top) cost between 8d. and 1s. 1½d. each, the Alexandra Cross, no. 85, costing 1s ¼d. J. & A. Bratt of Wolverhampton sold their wares as Clarence Brand, these shapes (bottom) coming from their catalogue of 1932. Most cost about 10d. each, but their 'Rabbit', no. 7, along with their 'Tortoise' and 'Swan' cost 1s. 9d. In contrast, their popular boxed sets of six 'Jellette' moulds cost 1s. 4½d.

Figure 38. 'Diamond Aluminium Ware' moulds made by the London Aluminium Co. Ltd. of Westwood Road, Witton, Birmingham, in 1935.

round and oval fluted designs at 9s. the dozen for 1-pint and 12s. the dozen for 2-pint sizes, these costing 18s. and 21s. respectively if fitted with an internal tube. All half-pint moulds cost 6s. the dozen, while their 'Midget' moulds, boxed in sets of 6 assorted shapes ('1 pt fills 6'), were 18s. for the dozen sets. The decline in the use of aluminium jelly moulds after the Second World War is demonstrated by their 1949 catalogue, which includes only one shape, a fluted oval. The products of this factory are easily recognized by their 'DIAMOND' stamp.

LONGLIFF

This company's moulds usually adopt clean-lined Art Deco forms, and bear the stamp '"LONGLIFF" BRAND/BRITISH MADE'.

LUSHETTE

Being designed specifically for use with a single branded product, these midget moulds have

"LUSHETTE" MOULD RD NO. 803019 PINT PACKET MAKES SIX 'LUSHUS' JELLIES OR CREAMS

embossed around their flanges.

The Nutbrown brand of the 1930s produced a variety of kitchen utensils, including jelly moulds. Their most characteristic are small animal moulds, including fishes and rabbits, one of the latter adopting a streamlined Art Deco form. They usually have the stamp "NUTBROWN" or 'A "NUTBROWN" PRODUCT/MADE IN ENGLAND', sometimes accompanied by a registered design number, the fishes bearing 'REG. DES. No. 858202'.

The outbreak of the Second World War in 1939 saw the onset of strict food rationing and the collection of aluminium jelly moulds for recycling into aircraft and other munitions. It was now vitally important to cut down on the consumption of all foods, especially those which had to be imported. Bodies such as the Yorkshire Council for Further Education produced information cards entitled 'LESS SUGAR – BUT STILL SWEET' to hang up in kitchens, these giving instructions on how to save the sugar ration by using treacle or honey, to use more dried fruits, condensed milk and jelly squares, then going on to give appropriate recipes. The Ministry of Food under Lord Woolton introduced one of the most comprehensive and effective programmes of health-related food education ever seen in this or any other country. Though economically produced, its numerous publications were well designed, attractive, easily read and understood, and also gave a wealth of very practical advice. The Kitchen Front was also promoted by the work of demonstrators, including the enthusiastic, energetic and inspirational Marguerite Patten, who showed housewives how to make the best use of their ever-diminishing resources. In addition to the expected semolina and cornflour moulds, the Ministry's leaflets included whips and creams to be served in glasses or dishes:

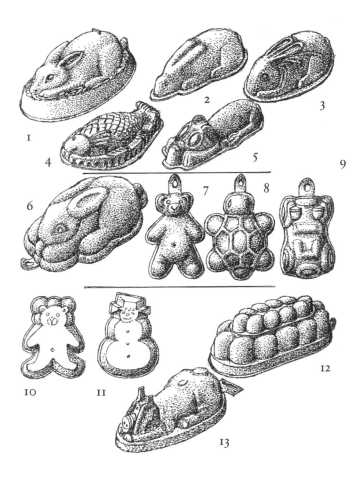

Figure 39. Plastic moulds and aluminium moulds, comprising: (1) a 'Nutbrown' orange plastic rabbit of the 1970s; (2–4) 'Nutbrown' aluminium moulds of the 1930s; (5) an aluminium 'Bonzo Dog' mould; (6–9) a set of brown plastic moulds sold under 'The Working Kitchen' brand in the 1970s; (10–11) white plastic moulds marked 'FOX RUN/HONG KONG', 1990s; (12) a white plastic mould, 2010; (13) a pink plastic pig mould marked 'Kitchen Craft', 2010.

MILK JELLY WHIP[29]

1 pt / 600 ml jelly square or crystals	*¼ pt / 150 ml evaporated milk*

Dissolve the jelly as instructed but in ¾ pt / 450 ml hot water, leave to cool, stir in the milk, and any desired colouring.

FRUIT CREAMS[30]

8 oz / 225 g fruit	*1½ tbs semolina*
½ pt / 300 ml milk	*sugar to taste*

Stew the fruit in as little water as possible. Boil the milk and semolina for 15 minutes, stirring until it thickens, then beat in the fruit, sugar and any desired colouring.

MEXICAN CREAMS[31]

2 tbs dried egg	*pinch of salt*
2 tbs flour	*1 pt / 600 ml moderately*
1–4 tbs cocoa	*strong coffee*
2–4 tbs sugar	*vanilla essence*

Mix the dry ingredients with a little of the coffee, scald with the remaining coffee, simmer for 5 minutes and stir in the vanilla:

Commercial publishers also provided useful recipe books, with the usual run of rhubarb tapiocas, prune moulds, or:

(29) *Making the most of the Fat Ration,* 4.
(30) ibid., 4.
(31) No. 13, 4.

LEMON SAGO[32]

¼ pt / 150 ml sago
2 oz / 50 g sugar

2 tsp golden syrup
1 tsp lemonade crystals
[or juice of a lemon]

Soak the sago in 1 pt / 600 ml water overnight, boil until clear, stir in the remaining ingredients and pour into a mould. Add the grated zest of an orange to the boiling mixture, if available.

Jellies also formed an important part of the diet of babies and young children during the war. Mothers were advised to give portions of the following dishes every week:[33]

9–12 months old	1 gelatin or sago jelly made with fruit juice and sugar.
12–18 months	2 moulds or puddings made with cornflour or Farola.
18–24 months	1 sponge jelly, 1 chocolate blancmange.
2–5 years	1 ground rice pudding, 1 raspberry blancmange.

To make these, a list of approved packet puddings was drawn up, this including Bird's Blanc-Mange, Brown & Polson's Flavoured Cornflour, Chivers Jelly Creams, Creamola Specialities and Viota Jelli-Crest.

After the war simple packet-made jellies still appeared at Sunday teas or as the occasional mid-week dessert, but rarely, if ever, to their rich, decorated late-Victorian, Edwardian and inter-war recipes. They still lay dormant in many sherry trifles, but only reverted to their once-proud glory at children's parties. Children's books such as *Come into the Kitchen* of 1947 explained how a girl could make herself useful by providing an orange, lemon or grapefruit squash jelly for 7 o'clock Sunday supper.[34] *Let's Have a Party* of 1946 preferred to use fresh fruit even if it

(32) Burke, 85.
(33) Cheyne, 6–28..
(34) Gordon & Bliss, 35.

was still hard to find. A few years after this I was being carefully instructed to never accept an offer of fresh fruit when visiting anyone else's home. The rules of hospitality governed that any fruit on display should be offered to a visitor, but the polite visitor realized that to accept would be to deprive the host of a scarce and much-needed food.

MIXED FRUIT JELLY[35]

1 packet jelly, any flavour
1 each, apple, pear, banana

1 small tin pineapple or
peaches
4 oz / 100 g chopped mixed
nuts

Dissolve the jelly in ¾ pt / 450 ml boiling water, stir in the chopped fruit and nuts, pour into a mould, and stir just before setting to distribute the contents evenly.

The same book introduced a strange new form of soured milk which English palates took several decades to accept. It was yoghurt, here mixed with crushed berries and sugar in a form which was to overtake much of the traditional role of jellies, particularly when strongly marketed in the early 1960s.

Lucky children had a mother, grandmother or aunt who could be relied on to make an extra-special jelly for a party. Perhaps she used the surviving aluminium moulds to produce families of blancmange bunnies feasting on green chopped-jelly grass, sometimes with a few well-placed currants to induce naughty giggles from the boys. The first television celebrity chefs developed their imaginative approach with new recipes, as in Fannie and Johnnie Cradock's *Children's Party Cookery with Fanny and Johnnie* of 1959:

(35) Weiss, 61.

Figure 40. Jellies in orange peels. (1) Eliza Acton's orange basket, 1845; (2) Theodore Garrett's orange basket, about 1893; (3) Mrs Leyel and Miss Hartley's Figured Oranges of 1925, carved with 'a ring of little dancing elves'; (4) Fanny Cradock's orange 'clown' of 1959.

CLOWNS[36]

1 pt / 600 ml packet jelly	*2–3 glacé cherries*
3 oranges	*green & red food colour*
8 oz / 225 g almond paste	*12 silver cake bells*

Cut the oranges in half, scoop out the pulp, fill with jelly, and leave to set. Roll out some of the almond paste, cut into 30 leaf-shapes about 2 in. / 5 cm long, arrange each 5 in a daisy pattern, and seal their central points together with a little more of the paste to form a collar. Make 6 balls about ¾ in. / 2 cm diameter to form the clowns' heads, and fix one onto the centre of each collar. Add a small round ball of pink-coloured almond paste

(36) Bon Viveur, 10, 28.

for their noses, and small pieces of glacé cherry to give them eyebrows and turned-up mouths, using the silver balls for their eyes. Colour more of the almond paste pale green, roll into 6 cones, and fit on their heads as hats.

When the jelly has set, set a clown on top of each orange. They may then be stood in a flat dish covered with brown sugar to represent circus sawdust, and the rim decorated with baby chicks if for Easter [N.B. be aware of any problems children might have with nut allergies and silver cake balls].

Other children's jellies featured in the promotional recipe books produced by the packet-jelly manufacturers in the 1960s.

CHOCOLATE BOATS[37]

1 orange and 1 lime or greengage packet jelly
2 oz / 50 g sugar   *1 tbs cocoa*
¼ pt / 150 ml milk
paper, wooden skewers and cream to decorate

Dissolve the orange jelly in ¼ pt / 150 ml very hot water, and set aside. Boil the milk and cocoa together, and when cool mix with the jelly and leave to set ½ in. / 12 mm thick in a baking tin.

Dissolve the other jelly in very hot water and make up to 1 pt / 600 ml with more water, pour into glass fruit dishes and leave to set. Using a hot knife cut boat shapes out of the chocolate jelly, set them on the green jelly 'seas'. Make paper sails for the skewer 'masts', stick in place on the boats, and pipe waves of cream around the bows and seas.

(37) Rowntree (1960s?), 7.

WATER LILIES[38]

1 greengage or lime packet jelly   *1 small tin pears*
¼ pt / 150 ml whipping cream   *glacé cherries & angelica*

Drain the syrup from the pears into a jug, make up to ¾ pt / 450 ml, and heat with the jelly until completely dissolved. Pour into a dish and leave to set. Arrange the pear halves on the jelly, pipe a circle of cream around their hollows, and top each with a glacé cherry. Cut the angelica into thin strips and stick in the jelly to represent clumps of weeds.

From the 1960s and '70s the domestic lives of most people in England began to undergo significant changes. For many, the role of full-time housewife disappeared as women pursued their own careers in the wider world. This created a great demand for pre-prepared foods, one which was met by ever-expanding chains of supermarkets. It was now most convenient to purchase ready-made yoghurts, crème-caramels, rice and jelly in individual plastic pots. If jellies were made in the home, they now tended to be served in bowls, or as part of a trifle. Those who tried to mould the packet jellies found they had real problems, since, apparently following the public demand for soft, dormant jellies, the manufacturers had made them substantially weaker. In a recent trial I found that very few packet jellies could stand vertical when made up to the manufacturer's instructions and unmoulded at normal temperatures. In addition, most modern jelly moulds were unfit for purpose if used without adequate preparation.

PLASTIC MOULDS

Introduced from the 1960s, plastic moulds were inexpensive, clean, smooth and well-defined. Made in bright colours, they sold well; blancmanges, though now rarely made, would turn out of them, but not jelly. The latter often stuck to them and, (38) ibid., 5.

since plastic is a good insulator, it could not give the rapid surface melting of the jelly required for a quick release. For the best results the interiors should be smeared with a thin film of edible oil or butter, and the jelly solution poured in when cold to ensure good separation once set.

Most plastic moulds have no brand-mark, although some of the 1970s onwards have 'NUTBROWN' moulded into them, and some of the 1990s 'FOX RUN/HONG KONG' on bears and snowmen. Some designs follow the traditional round fluted shapes, other are bunny rabbits or pigs, while 'THE WORKING KITCHEN' sold by Timothy White's stores in the 1970s featured teddy bears, tortoises and motor cars.

Over the last thirty years of the twentieth century those who took the trouble to make jellies often did so in earnest, investing their time and the materials necessary to achieve good results. There is no need to reproduce the modern recipes here, for they are readily available in a number of well-illustrated and easily followed books. Perhaps the best are the various editions of Davis Gelatine's *Creative Cookery* and *New Creative Cookery*. Those who wish for more technical guidance and information should also consult books such as Hunter, Tinton and Carey's *Professional Chef level 3 S/NVQ* of 2008.

It is still well worth the effort of making a jelly. No other food can carry flavours and colours so well, can reflect or refract light, or wobble in that distinctive sinuous way which rarely, if ever, fails to raise comment and a smile. It still delights children, and, when properly made, can charm, impress or truly intoxicate all those with more mature tastes. Next time you plan a meal, whether for family and friends, or for someone far more intimate, look through the previous pages, select one of England's great jellies, make it in good time, then enjoy the praise which will surely follow its appearance on the table.

CHAPTER NINE

THE REPERTOIRE

Figure 41. Moulded rice dishes of around 1900: (1) Empress style; (2) à la Condé; (3) Apricots à la Condé; (4) Apricots Créole; (5) Maltese.

Over the last two hundred years the authors of many recipe books written in the Anglo-French culinary tradition have given individual names to each of their particular dishes. These range from basic descriptions such as John Nott's 'Chrystal Jelly' of 1726 and Louis Ude's 'Mosaic Jelly' of the 1820s through to Alexis Soyer's use of French titles for his 'Gelée à la Bacchante', etc., of the 1840s. By the time Mrs A.B. Marshall was publishing her recipes in the 1890s, names such as 'Maltoise à la Chantilly' or 'Apples à la Princesse Maude' had become more usual. By way of contrast, more recent years have seen the appearance of the 'Harry Hedgehog' and 'Fizzy Jelly Sea Monster' jellies.

Any attempt to list and define all the jellies of the past would be a virtually impossible task, and one of little real value, since many never entered the mainstream of English cookery. Those which did, made their way into the all-embracing dictionaries of classical recipes including C. Herman Senn's *Practical Gastronomy and Culinary Dictionary* of 1893, Theodore Garrett's *Encyclopaedia of Practical Cookery* of c. 1893 and Richard Hering's *Dictionary of Classical and Modern Cookery* of 1907, regularly up-dated and first published in English in 1958.

The sweet gelatin and starch-based cold desserts listed in the following pages should certainly prove useful for identifying such dishes in historic menus, and enable them to be recreated. Perhaps just as important, however, is their potential for showing what combinations of flavours, textures, colours and visual effects have proved most successful to generations of fine chefs and cooks. Just browsing through them can suggest many avenues to be either revisited or explored into the future.

APPLES

Angelique: halves of small apples compôte arranged on top of a border of vanilla rice, decorated with strips of angelica and sauced with kirsch syrup.

Condé: apples pared, cored, oven-baked with sugar, lemon juice and butter, arranged on a bed of rice decorated with angelica, glacé cherries, raisins and blanched almonds.

Morgan: scooped out apples filled with a chopped jelly of pineapple and Danziger Goldwasser, the lid replaced, the outside glazed with jelly.

Princess of Wales: jellied apple purée, half coloured pink with cochineal and a little cream, a small quantity of each being chilled, sliced, and cut into one-inch discs. When set in alternate colours in lemon jelly around the inside of a charlotte mould, the interior is filled with alternating layers of the remaining purée.

St Albans: apples sliced and cut into discs of equal size, stewed in syrup, without breaking, and half coloured pink with cochineal, then set in chains or circles around the inside of a charlotte mould with a little clear apple jelly. A smaller mould is then put inside, the space between them filled with more apple jelly and, when set, the smaller mould removed and the space filled with a jelly of lemon-flavoured apple purée mixed with cream and a little apricot marmalade.

APRICOTS

Condé: apricot compôte in a border of cooked rice flavoured with cream and vanilla, decorated with angelica and glacé cherries.

Créole: half apricots on a dome of rice cooked with cream, decorated as *Condé*, and coated with kirsch-flavoured apricot sauce.

Imperial: identical to *Créole*.

Suédoise: poached apricots cut into six segments set around the inside of a charlotte mould using clear apricot jelly, a smaller mould placed inside and the space between them filled with

with more of the jelly. When set, the mould removed and the interior filled with a jelly of apricot purée and cream.

Polish: as *Créole*, but with diced pineapple in the rice and scattered with slivered almonds.

BAVAROIS

Bavarois are jellied custards enriched with whipped cream and flavoured with fruit, nuts, liqueurs, etc.

Adelaide: orange with madeira.

Alexandria: apricot, decorated with Chantilly cream and half-stewed apricots.

de Bananas: vanilla with pulped bananas.

Clermont: vanilla with chestnut purée, decorated with candied chestnuts.

Créole: vanilla with sweet rice and diced pineapple, decorated with Chantilly cream and pineapple slices.

Dalmatian: vanilla with diced sponge and fruits soaked in maraschino.

Diplomate: lined with vanilla, filled with layers of chocolate and strawberry bavarois.

Empress Style: lined with strawberry jelly, the bottom decorated with cherries, filled with vanilla mixed with chopped pistachios.

Figaro: different colours and tastes, cubed and set in clear wine jelly.

Florentine: almond, decorated with kirsch-flavoured cream scattered with chopped pistachios.

Malakoff: vanilla mixed with chopped almonds, currants and sponge fingers soaked in maraschino.

Marie Louise: peach with kirsch.

Marquise Alice: vanilla bavarois mixed with sieved praline and diced finger biscuits soaked in anisette. When turned out, masked with Chantilly cream, decorated with piped lines of redcurrant jelly mottled with the point of a knife, and the base decorated with small triangular Condé cakes.

Mocha: coffee.

My Queen: lined with vanilla, filled with strawberry mixed with kirsch-soaked strawberries, which are also used for decoration.

Nun's Style: lined with chocolate, filled with vanilla.

Pompadour: layers of vanilla and chocolate.

Regina: layers of vanilla and strawberry, decorated with kirsch-soaked strawberries.

Ribbon: lined with wine jelly and filled with layers of different colours and flavours.

Richelieu: lined with jellied prune purée and filled with vanilla.

Spanish: orange decorated with peeled orange segments.

Cuit à la Suisse: lined with wine jelly, filled with a glacé fruit bavarois.

BLANCMANGE

A blancmange is almond milk set with gelatin.

Delmonico: a plain blancmange, or one mixed with cherry jam, stoned cherries and diced angelica.

Dutch: a lemon-juice and sherry jelly poured on egg-yolks and beaten when just removed from the heat.

English: made with milk and cornflour instead of almond milk and gelatin, with further flavouring.

Hazelnut: made with hazelnut milk instead of almond milk.

Parisienne: made with either hazelnut purée or whipped cream and maraschino in the almond milk jelly.

Pistachio: made with half almond milk and half pistachio milk.

Ribbon: different colours and flavours layered in the mould.

Spanish: a jelly of lemon-flavoured cream.

CHARLOTTE

A charlotte is cylindrical mould lined with finger biscuits, sponge cake strips etc., filled with a bavarois, cream or jelly.

Harlequin: sponge cake lining filled with cubes of different bavarois in wine jelly. When turned out, decorate the top with glacé fruit and the cake with chocolate, lemon and green icing.

Imperial Style: lined with maraschino jelly, then wafers filled with vanilla bavarois with diced pears. When turned out garnish with poached pear halves scooped and filled with Chantilly cream, scattered with chopped angelica.

Klondyke: lined with chocolate éclairs, filled with a mixture of Chantilly cream, gelatin and Danziger Goldwasser, decorated with Chantilly cream.

Metternich: lined with sponge fingers, filled with a mixture of Chantilly cream, gelatin and chestnut purée.

Montreuil: lined with sponge fingers and filled with peach purée bavarois with diced raw peach.

Napolitaine: lined with sponge strips, filled with a mixture of Chantilly cream, gelatin, chestnut purée, diced pineapple, candied lemon peel and raisins.

Nordique: lined with strips of Genoise sponge, filled with vanilla bavarois with kümmel and a fruit *salpicon*.

Opéra: lined with wafers, filled with bavarois with puréed glacé chestnuts and a *salpicon* of glacé fruits soaked in maraschino.

Parisienne: lined with strips of Genoese sponge, filled with vanilla bavarois. When turned out the sponge is coated with strained apricot jam and decorated with pink icing.

Pompadour: lined with sponge strips, filled with pineapple bavarois. When turned out decorated with puff-paste half-moons filled alternately with chocolate and vanilla creams.

Renaissance: lined with triangles of sponge cake iced white and pink, filled with vanilla bavarois mixed with a fruit *salpicon*. When turned out top with a round slice of pineapple and decorate with glacé cherries and angelica.

à la Russe: lined with sponge fingers, fill with vanilla (or other) bavarois and Chantilly cream.

Russe à la Princess Royal: Mask the bottom of a charlotte mould with jelly, decorate with fresh or preserved fruits and cover with jelly. When set place a smaller mould inside and fill with layers of red, clear, and Danzig jellies. When set, remove and fill the cavity with noyeau-flavoured bavarois. Turn out and top with a star of angelica and a Princess crown.

CREAM

Chateaubriand: a mould lined with clear jelly stuck with shredded almonds, lined again with jelly and another lining of almonds, the centre filled with noyeau bavarois or cream.

Fairy: a mould lined with maraschino jelly decorated with currants, cherries, blanched almonds etc. Then filled with a lemon and maraschino cream set with gelatin.

Harlequin: cornflour blancmange built up in layers of plain white, apricot juice with yellow colouring, red fruit juice with cochineal, and greengage juice with green colouring.

Italian: egg custard made with gelatin.

Muscovite: egg custard made with gelatin, whipped egg-whites and flavouring beaten in just before putting into the mould.

Nesselrode: vanilla bavarois with chestnut purée, diced glacé cherries, lemon peel and sultanas soaked in Madeira. When turned out covered with chocolate sauce and whipped cream.

Princesse: jelly of cream and isinglass mixed with diced poached pears and preserved cherry halves and flavoured with brandy.

Queen Style: almonds pounded with cream and orange-flower water, mixed with whipped cream, and maraschino, set with gelatin.

Rock: well-boiled rice mashed to a paste, folded into whisked egg-white, sugar, cream, and either rose or almond flavouring, set with gelatin.

Royal: a vanilla egg custard made with gelatin, the whipped whites beaten in while it is still hot.

Spanish: as Italian cream, the gelatin being first dissolved in hot water.

Suédoise: an apple purée, Swedish punch and gelatin jelly, with whipped cream folded in, decorated with vanilla-poached apple quarters and whipped cream.

Velvet: usually a wine jelly into which whipped cream has been folded, but there are other recipes with the same name.

FLUMMERY

A flummery was originally a starch-based jelly made by boiling the liquid squeezed from soaked oatmeal or bran, but most Georgian and Victorian versions are for a form of gelatin jelly. Also:

Chocolate: a semolina and grated chocolate jelly served with *zabaglione* or egg custard sauce.

German Style: semolina cooked with grated lemon-zest, with stiffly beaten egg-white folded in while still hot. Served with fruit syrup.

Nordique: rice cooked to a thick mash, crushed macaroons, diced blanched candied lemon peel and sultanas mixed in, followed by stiffly beaten egg-whites. Served with fruit syrup.

Rhubarb: stewed rhubarb, lemon juice and cinnamon, strained, boiled with cornflour, and stiffly beaten egg-whites folded in. Served with *zabaglione*.

Sour Cherry: purée of sour cherries and ground almonds stewed with rice flour, then stiffly beaten egg-whites folded in. Served with *zabaglione*.

FRUIT LOAF

A fruit loaf or *pain aux fruits* consists of a mould lined with fruit jelly, filled with flavoured egg custard set with gelatin.

George Sand: maraschino jelly lining filled with peach custard.

Parisian: pineapple jelly lining filled with pineapple custard flavoured with orange juice.

Pineapple: pineapple jelly lining filled with a custard containing grated pineapple, lemon juice, white wine and sugared diced pineapple.

Pompadour: anisette jelly filled with layers of maraschino-soaked apricot halves scattered with flaked pistachios, and apricot custard. Decorated with Chantilly cream and glacé chestnuts.

Richelieu: gelatin blancmange lining filled with apricot custard.

Strawberry: gelatin blancmange or strawberry jelly lining filled with strawberry custard.

Victoria: layers of strawberry custard scattered with crushed macaroons, and gelatin blancmange.

JAUNEMANGE

A jaunemange is a yellow jelly made with egg yolks, lemon juice, brandy, raisin wine or sherry set with gelatin.

JELLY

Carmen Sylva: a glass dish or mould with a base layer of strawberry jelly, then vanilla bavarois, strawberries and more strawberry jelly.

Constantine: a pipe-mould of clear jelly layered alternately with dessicated coconut mixed with slivered pistachios, and poached apricots cut into six segments.

Danish: 1 part each of sherry, brandy, and cherry juice, and 1 ½ parts of claret, with lemon juice and zest set with gelatin.

Dantzig: Danziger Goldwasser liqueur and syrup set with gelatin. Some recipes include layers of slivered pistachios.

Earl of Fife: lemon jelly with gold and silver leaf in a pipe mould. When turned out the cavity filled with whipped cream and shredded pistachios.

Fouettée au Jus de Fruits: jellied fruit juices whipped to a froth just before setting.

French: fruits set symmetrically in layers of clear sherry-flavoured jelly.

Fruit, with Maraschino: as French, but with maraschino-flavoured jelly.

Gloucester: equal parts sago, rice, pearl barley and hartshorn shavings gently simmered to a jelly. In use it was dissolved in hot broth, milk or wine as a delicate food for invalids.

Imperial: champagne jelly with cubes of poached pineapple and flaked pistachios.

Italian: clear orange and lemon jelly layered with candied fruits or orange quarters.

Jamaica: rum jelly, encircled by bunches of grapes and with clotted cream poured over when turned out of its mould.

Jubilee: port jelly border mould, the centre filled with Chantilly cream when turned out.

Macédoine of Fruits: clear jelly layered with fresh fruits.

Marbled: whipped jellies of different flavours and colours, mixed lightly and poured immediately into the mould; or small lumps of jelly set together with a little cream or milk jelly.

Mosaic: diamond-shaped slices of jelly and bavarois of different colours set in layers with clear jelly; or slices of gelatin, cream and egg-yolk jelly cut out with tin cutters and set on the base and sides of the mould, line with orange jelly. Continue adding layers of cut out cream jelly and the orange jelly until the mould is full.

Muscovite: a lining of kümmel-flavoured wine jelly filled with a whipped jelly; or any jelly in a cylinder mould frozen just long enough to lightly frost the exterior.

Nordique: kümmel-flavoured jelly.

Normande: wine jelly in a pipe mould layered with thin slices of red and white cooked apples. When turned out the cavity filled with apple purée and cream.

Orange: orange jelly layered with orange segments set in a glass dish.

Panaché: two or three different kinds of jelly set in alternate layers.

Parisian: alternate layers of strawberry jelly and clear wine jelly flavoured with kirsch.

Princess Louise: small pieces of white and pink whipped jellies layered with partly-set lemon jelly in a bowl, poured into the mould just before setting to prevent them from rising to the surface.

Princess Victoria: lemon, coriander and either vanilla or noyeau milk jelly, one-third coloured pink. Put into a rectangular mould one layer of milk jelly, one of pink jelly, one of clear jelly with gold leaf, and finally another of milk jelly. When cold, turn out, cut into slices and use to line the base and sides of a mould, finally filling it with and kind of fruit and jelly.

Ribbon: moulds filled with narrow layers of different jellies.

Royal: pineapple juice, hock and gold-leaf jelly into which small cubes of poached pineapple are stirred just before setting, then poured into champagne glasses.

Russian: any jelly whisked to a froth just before setting.

St Petersburgh: noyeau-flavoured lemon jelly cut into pieces when about to set into which is thrown lumps of pink, whisked lemon jelly.

Sultan's: alternate layers of orange, lemon jelly and pistachio bavarois.

Swedish: wine jelly and diced poached fresh fruit layered in a cylinder mould.

Vanilla: vanilla and kirsch-flavoured jelly in champagne glasses and garnished with Chantilly cream.

Venetian: kirsch-flavoured lemon jelly with a *salpicon* of mixed fruits.

Voltaire: vanilla jelly flavoured with strong coffee and kirsch or cognac.

MAHALEBI

A mahalebi is a rice-flour mould of milk, sugar and rose-water.

ORANGES

Centrale: scooped out, filled with red-coloured orange jelly, and cut into four segments when set.

Charlotte: orange and lemon jelly whipped with egg-whites in a mould lined with orange segments.

Chartreuse: peeled orange segments arranged on a layer of orange jelly in a large charlotte mould and covered with more orange jelly. A smaller mould is placed on top, and the space between the two filled with layers of orange jelly and more orange segments. When the small mould is removed, it is replaced by a cream and orange syrup jelly set with gelatin.

Française: as *Centrale*, or filled with layers of orange jelly alternately clear or stained red with cochineal.

Maltese: scooped out and filled with alternate layers of port wine jelly and vanilla cream jelly, cut into four segments when set, and dressed on rice or vanilla ice-cream.

Sections/Tranches: hollowed out, filled with orange jelly and cut into four segments when set.

PEACHES

Charlotte: a mould lined with fingers of sponge cake filled with layers of chopped peaches soaked in vanilla sugar and rum, and whipped maraschino jelly.

Manuel: peeled, halved, poached in vanilla syrup, embedded in champagne and gold leaf jelly in a dish.

Modern: half-poached, set on vanilla rice mixed with a vanilla cream, decorated with Chantilly cream, scattered with coarse macaroon crumbs, with cold peach sauce served separately.

Montreuil: halved, poached in maraschino syrup, arranged in the centre of a semolina border.

Portuguese: half-poached, set on vanilla rice mixed with diced pineapple, covered with thick apricot sauce and scattered with slivered toasted almonds.

Sahara: a border mould lined with gelatin blancmange filled with half or quartered poached peaches set in raspberry jelly. When turned out the centre filled with Chantilly cream blended with raspberry purée.

Vanderbilt: a border mould lined with champagne jelly, filled with half or quartered poached peaches set in Danziger Goldwasser flavoured jelly. When turned out the centre filled with Chantilly cream.

PEARS

Duchesse: border of maraschino jelly lined with halves of pears, farced with almond custard. When turned out the centre filled with vanilla cream.

Felicia: halves poached, on a bed of Viennese cream, covered with Chantilly cream and scattered with crystallized rose petals.

Florentine: compôte of pears on a bed of semolina flavoured with vanilla, sauced over with apricot marmalade.

Lombardie: stewed in raspberry syrup, arranged on a border of rice, with whipped cream in the centre, and maraschino syrup.

Nelusco: peeled, poached, arranged on vanilla rice and covered with chocolate sauce.

Pailard: poached halves arranged on a pyramid of vanilla rice, covered with vanilla cream, decorated with crystallized violets and angelica, and bordered with vanilla syrup.

PINEAPPLES

Condé: sliced, arranged on a border of cooked rice, decorated with angelica and glacé cherries, served with maraschino syrup.

Creole: poached slices on vanilla rice mixed with diced candied fruit, covered with apricot sauce.

Curtet: mould lined with kirsch flavoured jelly, filled with diced poached pineapple in apricot jelly.

Empress: thin slices arranged on cold vanilla rice mixed with diced candied fruit flavoured with maraschino and covered with raspberry purée.

Georgette: pineapple bavarois mixed with diced poached

pineapple and a *salpicon* of fruit soaked in kirsch and maraschino, packed into a scooped-out pineapple.

Majestic: vanilla bavarois mixed with the mashed pineapple pulp packed into a scooped-out pineapple.

Orleans: slices of pineapple soaked in sugar and kirsch, arranged on cold vanilla rice, decorated with whipped cream, candied cherries and angelica, bordered with kirsch-flavoured apricot sauce.

Savoy: sliced pineapple on cold vanilla rice, half a poached peach on top, covered with strawberry purée and decorated with whipped cream.

Virginia: strawberry bavarois with wild strawberries and diced pineapple packed into a scooped-out pineapple.

PLUMS

Bonne-femme: peeled, stoned plums poached in vanilla syrup in a gelatin flummery border, covered in reduced cooking syrup and sprinkled with slivered almonds.

RASPBERRIES

Erika: a dish half filled with gelatin flummery topped with redcurrant jelly, then raspberries soaked in apricot brandy and sprinkled with slivered almonds.

REDCURRANTS

White Lady: a gelatin blancmange border filled with Chantilly cream mixed with sugared redcurrants.

RICE

Condé: stewed tender in milk and water, then sugar and a little salt stirred in with beaten egg yolks and a little orange-flower water.

Empress: as *Condé*, without the yolks, mixed with a vanilla bavarois. For a border, mix with diced candied fruit soaked in kirsch moulded on top of a layer of raspberry jelly.

Française: boiled Patna rice re-cooked with butter, sugar, milk, macaroons, orange-flower water, candied lemon peel, glacé cherries, muscat raisins and angelica before putting into a mould.

Jackson: parboiled, re-cooked in water and white wine, lemon juice and mixed with a gelatin-thickened *zabaglione*, all layered in a mould with peeled orange segments soaked in kirsch and sugar.

Lord Byron: parboiled, re-cooked in water and white wine flavoured with vanilla, mixed with gelatin-thickened whipped cream and diced pineapple soaked in Grand Marnier, moulded, and served with pineapple syrup.

Maltese: *Condé* rice without yolks mixed with an orange bavarois, in a mould lined with blood-orange jelly, decorated with orange segments.

Nesselrode: *Condé* rice without yolks, flavoured with orange juice and maraschino, mixed with candied orange peel, pineapple and cherries, chestnut purée and gelatin-thickened whipped cream. Mould, and serve with maraschino-flavoured vanilla sauce.

Palermo: Empress rice in a border mould lined with blood-orange jelly, decorated with Chantilly cream and orange segments soaked in Curaçao and sugar.

Princess: parboiled, re-cooked in white wine and water, sugar, vanilla, cinnamon and a pinch of salt, set as a dome in a glass dish, decorated with Chantilly cream, and bordered with thin pineapple slices.

Sarah Bernhardt: a border mould lined with maraschino jelly, scattered with chopped pistachios, filled with *Condé* rice mixed with gelatin-thickened whipped cream, sealed with maraschino jelly, turned out, and the centre filled with Chantilly cream, decorated with wild strawberries.

Singapore: *Condé* rice flavoured with maraschino and mixed with diced pineapple, moulded as a border, turned out and served with maraschino-flavoured apricot sauce.

Swiss: Empress rice without fruit in a mould lined with maraschino-flavoured redcurrant jelly, with redcurrant syrup poured round in the dish.

SEMOLINA

Oriental: semolina cooked with vanilla and milk, mixed with vanilla cream and whipped cream, set in a mould lined with rosewater-flavoured jelly. The dish to hold a pistachio purée and syrup sauce.

STRAWBERRIES

Cappuccino: liqueur-soaked strawberries in a wine jelly border mould, turned out and the centre filled with Chantilly cream.

Charterhouse: as *Cappuccino*, but with maraschino-soaked diced pineapple in the jelly and a fruit *salpicon* in the cream.

Modern: mould lined with champagne jelly, filled with strawberry bavarois, served bordered with maraschino-soaked strawberries.

Suprême: border mould of strawberry bavarois containing kirsch-soaked strawberries, the centre filled with Chantilly cream.

Tivoli: bavarois mixed with strawberry purée in a mould lined with kirsch-flavoured jelly, decorated with diced kirsch jelly.

Wilhelmine: large strawberries scooped out and filled with sweet whipped cream, set in a border mould of orange and kirsch jelly.

TANGERINES

Suédoise: scooped out, filled with tangerine bavarois, the lid replaced, and garnished with leaves of angelica.

BIBLIOGRAPHY

Books are published in London unless otherwise indicated.

A.W., *A Book of Cookrye* (1591)

Acton, E., *Modern Cookery for Private Families* (1845) (1855 ed.)

Austin, T., 'Two Fifteenth Century Cookery Books', *Early English Text Society* O.S. XCI (1881)

Barham, P., *The Science of Cookery* (Berlin, Heidelberg & New York 2001)

Beeton, I., *The Book of Household Management* (1861)

Bell, J., *A Treatise of Confectionery in all its Branches* (Newcastle upon Tyne 1817)

Bon Viveur (Fannie & Johnnie Cradock), *Happy Cooking Children No. 4: Children's Party Cookery with Fanny and Johnnie* (1959)

Bradley, R., *The Country Housewife and Ladies Director* (1736)

Brears, P., *The Gentlewoman's Kitchen* (Wakefield 1984)

——, *Traditional Food in Yorkshire* (Edinburgh 1987),

——, 'Transparent Pleasures, The Story of the Jelly', *Petits Propos Culinaires* 53 (1996) 8-19; *Petits Propos Culinaires* 54 (1996) 25-34

Brown & Polson, *Brown & Polson's Summer Dishes* (Paisley n.d.)

Brown, R., *Puddings, Creams and Jellies* (1900)

Buckton, C.M., *Food and Home Cookery* (Leeds 1879)

Burford, E.J., *Royal St. James's* (1988)

Burke, H., *Wartime Kitchen* (n.d. 1940s)

Burrill, K., & Booth, A.M., *The Amateur Cook* (1908)

Carême, A., *The Royal Parisian Pastrycook and Confectioner* (1834)

Carter, C.J., *The Complete Practical Cook* (1730)

Cheyne, M., *Good Housekeeping's Book of Child Feeding in Wartime* (n.d. 1940s)

Clinton, D. (ed.), *The Court and Kitchen of Elizabeth Cromwell* (1664) (Peterborough 1983)

Congreve, A.E., *The One Maid Book of Cookery* (1913)

Cook, A., *Professed Cookery* (1760 ed.)

Country Life, *Cooking without a Cook* (1926)

Cox, J. & G., *Cox's Manual of Gelatine Cookery* (Edinburgh 1939)

Davidson, A., *The Oxford Companion to Food* (Oxford 1999)

D'Avigdor, E.H., *Dinners & Dishes* (1885)

Davis Gelatine Ltd., *Davis Dainty Dishes* (1936),

——, *Creative Cookery* (Leamington Spa, n.d)

——, *New Creative Cookery* (Leamington Spa, n.d)

Dawson, T., *The Good Huswifes Jewell* (1596)

de Salis, Mrs H.A., *Sweets & Supper Dishes à la Mode* (1888)

Digby, Sir K., *The Closet of Sir Kenelm Digby Opened* (1669) (1997 ed.)

Dods, M., *Cook and Housewife's Manual* (Edinburgh 1829) (1988 ed.)

Eales, M., *Mrs. Mary Eales's Receipts* (1718) (1733 ed.)

Fairclough, M.A., *The Ideal Cookery Book* (1911)

Finchley Manuals of Industry No. 1 *Cookery* (1857)

Francatelli, C.E., *The Modern Cook* (1846) (1855)

——, *A Plain Cookery Book for the Working Classes* (1861)

——, *The Cook's Guide* (1888 ed.)

Furnival, F.J., *Early English Meals & Manners* (1868)

Garrett, T., *The Encyclopaedia of Practical Cookery* (*c.* 1893)

Glasse, H., *The Art of Cookery made Plain and Easy* (1747)

Godden, G.A., *Encyclopaedia of British Pottery & Porcelain Marks* (1964)

Gordon, A. & Bliss, T., *Come into the Kitchen* (1947)

Green, H.J. & Co., *Recipes* (Brighton n.d.)

Gouffé, J., *The Royal Pastry & Confectionery Book* (1874)

Hargreaves, B., *Farmhouse Fare* (1958)

Hasler, C., *The Royal Arms* (1980)

Heath, A., *Good Sweets* (1937)

Hering, R., *Hering's Dictionary of Classical and Modern Cookery* (1958)

Hieatt, C.B., *An Ordinance of Pottage* (1988)

Hieatt, C.B., & Butler, S., *Curye on Inglysch* (Oxford 1985)

Hodgett, G.A.J., *Stere Htt Well* (Adelaide n.d.)

Household Ordinances [*H.O.*], Society of Antiquaries (1790)

Howard, Lady C., *Tasty Tit-Bits and Dishes Dainty* (1892)

Hughes, G.B., 'Sparkling Jelly and its Moulds', *Country Life* (Sept 11, 1969) 628–629

Hughes, T., *Sweetmeat and Jelly Glasses* (1982)

Hunter, G., Tinton, T. & Carey, P., *Professional Chef 3* (2008)

Hyland, P., *The Herculaneum Pottery* (Liverpool 2005)

Jack, F., *Cookery for Every Household* (1914)

Jackson, G.F., *Shropshire Word-Book* (1879)

Jarrin, G., *The Italian Confectioner* (1827 ed.)

Jewry, M., *Warne's Every-Day Cookery* (1821)

Kevill-Davies, S., *Jelly Moulds* (Guildford 1983)

Kidder, E., *Kidder's Receipts of Pastry and Cookery* (1740) (2001 ed.)

Kingston-upon-Hull Museums Bulletin V (Hull 1970)

Knox Gelatine, *Dainty Desserts for Dainty People* (Johnstown NY 1924)

Lamb, P., *Royal Cookery* (1726 ed.)

Landon, J.H., *The Pytchley Book of Refined Cookery* ... (1885) (1889 ed.)

La Varenne, F., *The French Cook* (1653) (2001 ed.)

Leyel, C.F., & Hartley, O., *The Gentle Art of Cookery* (1925, reprinted 1983)

London Printing & Publisher Co., *The Book of the Household* (1862–4)

Lorwin, M., *Dining with William Shakespeare* (New York 1976)

[Mallock, M.M.], *The Younger Sons' Cookery Book*, by a Younger Son's Daughter (1896)

Markham, G., *The English Huswife* (1603)

Marshall, A.B., *Mrs A.B. Marshall's Cookery Book* (1888)

——, *Mrs A.B. Marshall's Larger Book of Extra Recipes* (1891)

Mauduit, Vicomte de, *The Vicomte in the Kitchenette* (1934)

May, R., *The Accomplisht Cook* (1685 ed.)

Montfaucon, Bernard de, *L'Antiquité expliquée et représentée en figures* (Paris, 1722) vol. II

Moxon, E., *English Housewifry Exemplified* (Leeds 1741)

Napier, R., *A Noble Boke off Cookry* (1882)

Nelson, Dale & Co., *Nelson's Home Comforts* (Warwick 1882) (23rd ed. *c.* 1905-10?)

Nichols, J., *The Progresses and Public Processions of Queen Elizabeth* (1788)

Nott, J., *The Cook's Dictionary* (1726)

Oldroyd, W & Sons Ltd., *Quickly Prepared Jelly Dishes* ... (Leeds, n.d.)

Peachey, S. (ed.), *The Good Huswife's Handmaide to the Kitchen* (1588) (Bristol 1992)

Pearson & Co., *Isobell's Home Cookery* (1918–19)

Peckham, A., *The Complete English Cook* (1767)

Pierce, C., *The Household Manager* (1857)

Pinto, E.H., *Treen and other Wooden Bygones* (1969)

Platt, Sir K., *Delightes for Ladies* (1602) (1948 ed.)

Price, R., *The Compleat Cook* (ed. Masson, M., 1974)

Rabisha, W., *The Whole Body of Cookery Dissected* (1661) (2003 ed.)

Raffald, E., *The Experienced English Housekeeper* (Manchester 1769) (1997 ed.)

Rees, A., *The Cyclopaedia or Universal Dictionary* (1819)

Rowntree & Co., *Rowntree's Jelly Recipes* (York n.d.),

——, *Rowntree's Jelly Diamond Jubilee 1923–1983* (York 1983)

Sandford, F., *The history of the Coronation of ... James II* (1687)

Schoonover, D. (ed.), *Ladie Borlase's Receiptes Booke* (Iowa City, 1998)

Selfridge & Co., *The Good Wife's Cook Book* (1911)

Senn, C.H., *Practical Gastronomy and Culinary Dictionary* (1892)

Simpson, J., *Simpson's Cookery* (ed. Brand, H.W., 1834)

Smith, E., *The Compleat Housewife ...* (1727) (1753 ed.)

Soyer, A., *The Gastronomic Regenerator* (1847 ed.)

——, *The Modern Housewife* (1848)

Spurling, H. (ed.), *Elinor Fettiplace's Receipt Book* (1986)

Strutt, J., *Manners, Customs ... of the Inhabitants of England* (1774)

Surflet, R., *Maison Rustique, or the countrie farme* (1616)

Surtees, R., *Jorrock's Jaunts & Jollities* (1838) (1949 ed.)

——, *Plain or Ringlets* (1859) (1957 ed.)

Symington & Co., *Symington's Recipes* (Market Harborough n.d.)

Tibbott, M., *Welsh Fare* (Cardiff 1976)

Ude, L.E., *The French Cook* (1813) (1833 ed.)

Walsh, J.H., *A Manual of Domestic Economy* (1858)

Warner, R., *Antiquitates Culinariae* (1791)

Weiss, C., *Let's have a Party* (Watford 1946)

Wells, R., *Ornamental Confectionery* (1896)

W.M., *The Compleat Cook and Queen's Delight* (1671 ed.)

Woodforde, J., *The Diary of a Country Parson (1755–1802)* (Oxford 1990)

GENERAL INDEX

See also the recipe index below. The Repertoire (chapter 9) has not been indexed and should also be consulted for jelly names. References are to page numbers, references to illustrations are in italics.

Acton, Eliza, 40, 49, 166, *40*
Adams, John, 25
Adams, W., & Son, 155, 165
agar-agar, 38
alginates, 38, 39
almond milk, 22, 60, 61, 69, 80, 81, 111, 121
America, 27, 46, 51, 200
amydon, 39, 62
Argyle, Duke of, 85
Army & Navy Stores, 159
arrowroot, 40, 49
Ash Brothers & Heaton, 155
Aston Hall, Birmingham, 103
Australia, 188
banquets, 66, 68, 73, 74, 78, 79
Barlow, Mr Secretary, 74
Barnes, Surrey, 159
Bath, Somerset, 24
bavarois, 47, 106, 129, 143
Beeton, Isabella, 27, 121, 124, 126, 148
Bell, John, 101, *9*
Belvoir Castle, Rutland, 148, 162
Benham & Froud, later Benham, Herbert & Co., 155, 167, *15–17, 20*
Benham & Sons, 103, 153, 159, *20*
Benningtons, 159
Bermuda, 40
Bick, Joseph, 24
Birch, Capt. Thomas, 86, *4*
Birch & Villiers, 155
Bird, Alfred, & Sons, 30, 126, 187, 215

Blackwell, T.F., 123
blancmange, 22, 24, 29, 37, 38, 40, 42–44, 46, 47, 49, 52, 80, 81, 87, 88, 97, 102, 111, 121, 126, 127, 142, 143, 148, 153, 170, 184, 187, 193, 194, 196, 199, 200, 215, 216, 219
Bourne, J., & Sons., 195, *28*
Bradford, 153
Brande, W.T., 25
Bratt, J.A., & Sons, 207, 209, *36, 37*
brawn, 21, 56, 61
Brazil, 40, 52
Brighton, 126, 187, 200
Bristol Kitchen Ware, 195, *28*
Brown & Polson, 43, 193, 200, 203, 215
Browne, T.B., 123
Buckton, Catherine M., 125, 126
Burnley, 174
cards, playing, 90, *5*
Carême, A., 106, 107, 130, 131, 155
carrageen, 42, 43, 52
cassava, 40, 51
Catherine of Valois, 56
'Cetem' ware, 196
cheeses (bavarois), 113
Cheshire, 48
Chesterfield, 195, *28*
Chiericati, Francesco, 65
Chivers & Co., 30, 126, 215
Christian, King of Denmark, 73
'Clarence' brand, 209, *37*

Clifford, Richard, Bishop of London, 55, *2*
Colmans of Norwich, 43
colourings, 22, 52, 60, 143
confectioners, 104, 111, 125
Cook, Ann, 93, 101
Cookson, Jeffreys & Dixon, 85
Cooper, J.T., 25
Copeland, W.T., & Sons (late Spode), 149, *154*
cornflour, 39, 43, 49, 97, 126, 143, 153, 184, 193, 212, 215
Cornwallis, Lord, 85
Cox, J. & G., 187, 188, 199, 200
Cradock, Fannie and Johnnie, 216, *40*
'Creamola' brand, 215
Crockford's Club, 108
Cromwell, Elizabeth, 79
Crook, A.F., 103, 153
Crosse & Blackwell, 122
curcuna, 40
Czechoslovakia, 200
Davies' Salopian Tin Works, 209, *37*
Dawson, Thomas, 23
Denby Pottery, 195, *38*
Derby, Earl of, 22
Derbyshire, 96, 153, 195
Diamond, Mrs H.M., 21
Diamond Aluminium Ware Co., 209, *38*
Digby, Sir Kenelm, 41
Dods, Meg, 104
Drake, Sir Francis, 50
Dunham Massey, Cheshire, 103
Durham Priory, 24
Edinburgh, 187, 200
Edward VII, King (Prince of Wales), 164, 167

eggs
    moulds of, 93, 170
    nest of, 91, 170
    of jelly, 61, 69, 77–79, *5*
Eitel, 164
Elizabeth I, Queen, 66, 73,
Everton, E.T., 155, 203, *32*
Farola, 44, 215
Farrell, Mr, 123
Fearncombe, Henry, Wolverhampton, 155
Ffarington, Sir Walter, 186
floating islands, 148, *9*
flummery, 24, 90, 91, 92
    bran, 41
    Dutch
    oatmeal, 37, 38, 48
    rice, 48
Fortnum & Mason, 26
Foulis, K., 89, *5*
'Fox Run' brand, 220
Francatelli, Charles Elmé, 43, 123, 130, 137, 155, 165
fruit, dried, 82, 212
Garrett, Theodore Francis, 45, 46, 143, 164, 223, *40*
George I, King, 85
George IV, King (Prince Regent), 106
Glasgow, 44, 207
Goodall & Backhouse, 126
Gouffé, Jules, 127, 128
Green, H.J., & Co., 126, 187
Greener & Co., 200
Grimwade Ltd., 199
ground rice, see rice, ground,
Hanley, Staffs., 102, 199
Harewood House, Yorks., 13, 103, 104, 162
Harington, Sir John, 74

Harrods, Knightsbridge, 155, 159, 176
Hartley, Olga, *40*
Hartley, William P., & Co., 30
Henry, IV, King, 55
Henry, V, King, 55
Henry, VI, King, 56
Henry, VIII, King, 65
Hertford, Earl of, 66
Hong Kong, 220
Hopkins, J.H., & Son, 174, *25*
Howard, Lady Constance, 47
Hull, 102
Humphry, Mrs, 177
Irish moss, 42
isinglass, 15, 23–28, 66, 68, 69, 98, 106, 108, 109, 121, 127, 170
    patent, 25–27, 29, 120, 127, *1*
    Russian, 25–27
ivory, 15, 34, 37, 38, 46, 74
Jack, Florence, 41
James I, King, 73
James II, King, 24
Jarrin, Guglielmo A., 104, 109
'Jellette' brand, 209, *37*
jellies, see recipe index,
Joan of Navarre, 55
Jobling & Co., 200
Johnson & Davey, 155
Johnstown, N.Y., 188
Jones Bros., 159
Jonson, Ben, 73
'K' brand, 207
kanten, 38
Kelsay, J.F., 86
Kepp & Co., 159
Kingston upon Hull, see Hull
Knox, Charles B., & Co., 188
Lamb, Patrick, 24, 80, 81
Lancashire, 48, 86, 96

Langdale's colourings, 126, 143
Lankester, Edwin, 43
La Varenne, François Pierre de, 45
leaches, 62, 66, 68, 77, 78, 80, 5
Leale, A.F., 159, *18, 19*
Leeds, Yorks., 28, 125, 126, 195, *28*
Liverpool, 102
locust bean gum, 47, 52
London, 25–27, 46, 51, 55, 66, 85, 101, 123, 142, 153, 155, 159, 162, 164, 165, 188, 203, 207, *10*
'Longliff' brand, 211
'Lushette' brand, 211
Macfarlane & Robinson Ltd., 207, *36*
maizine, 171
Maling, C.T., & Sons, 196, *29*
Manchester, 24, 103, 125
manna, 47
Marshall, Mrs. A.B., 44, 142, 143, 159, 166, 167, 169, *20, 21, 27*
Marshall, James, 44, 49
Marshall's Crème de Riz, 49
Mauduit, Vicomte de, 194
May, Robert, 74, 78, *3*
Minton, 149, *11, 12, 13*
Montfaucon, Bernard de, 97
Morris & Wilkinson, 174
moulds, makers
    Adams, W., & Son, 155, 165
    Ash Bros & Heaton, 155
    Benham, Herbert, & Co. (formerly Benham & Froud), 155, 159, 166, 167, 170, 203, *15–17, 20*
    Benham & Sons, Wigmore Street, 103, 153, 166, *20*
    Bourne, Joseph, & Sons , 195, *28*
    Bratt, J. & A., & Sons, 207, 209, *36, 37*

moulds, makers *cont.*

Bristol Kitchen Ware (Pountney & Co.), 195, *28*
'Cetem' ware, 196, *29*
'Clarence' brand, 209, *37*
Copeland (W.T. Copeland & Sons; Copeland [late Spode]), 149, *14*
Davies' Salopian Tin Works, 209, *37*
Denby Pottery (Joseph Bourne & Sons), 195, *28*
Diamond Aluminum Ware, 209, 211, *38*
'E.B.' mark, 203
Eccleshill potteries, 153
Everton, E.T. ('E.T.E.' mark), 155, 203, *32*
Fearncombe, Henry, 155
Greener & Co., 200
Grimwades Ltd., 199
Herculaneum Pottery, 102
Humber Bank Pottery, 102
Hopkins, J.H., & Son, 174
'Jellette' moulds (J. & A. Bratt), 209, *37*
Johnson & Davey, 155
Jones Bros., 159
'K' brand (Macfarlane & Robinson), 207
Leale, A.F., 159, *18, 19*
'Longliff' brand, 211
'Lushette' brand, 211
Macfarlane & Robinson, 207, *36*
Maling, C.T., & Sons, 196, *29*
'M.B.' brand (Macfarlane & Robinson), 207
Minton, 149, *11–13*
Neale, James, 102

moulds, makers *cont.*
'Nutbrown' brand, 212, 220, *39*
Orme, Evans & Co., 207, *36*
Pearson & Co., 195, *28*
Pountney & Co. (Bristol Kitchen Ware), 195, *28*
Pyrex, 200
Sellman & Hill, 176, *10, 26*
Shelley Potteries Ltd. (Wileman & Co.), 196, 199, *30*
Smith & Matthews (late Eitel), 164
Spode, 101, 149, 199, *30*
'Swan' brand, 209
Temple & Crook, 153, 164, 170
Temple & Reynolds, 153, 165
Villiers & Wilkes (previously Birch & Villiers), 155
Wedgwood, 92, 96, 99, 102, 148, 149
Wood, A.R., & Co., 174, *26*

moulds, materials
aluminium, 32, 207–213, *37–39*
copper, 32, 103, 109, 153–174, 176, 199, 203, *15–25*
earthenware, 96–102, 148–153, 195–199, *7, 11–13, 29–31*
enamelled steel, 203, 207, *36*
glass, 32, 80, 81, 85, 86, 92, 123, 132, 200, *4*
plastic, 32, 220, *39*
stoneware, 92, 93, 124, 153, 195, *28*
tinplate, 32, 104, 166, 174, 176, 203, *25–27, 32–35*
wood, 77, 92

moulds, names of designs
acanthus, *30*

moulds, names of designs *cont.*

acorn, *14, 25*
Albert, *31*
Alexandra cross, 164, 209, *21, 22, 37*
anemones, 97
armadillo, 199, *30*
asparagus, 164, *22*
attelette, 172, *24*
ballette, 165, 170, *22*
Belgrave, 155, 165, 166, *22*
Bonzo Dog, *39*
Brunswick star, 166, *21, 22*
bunny, 199, 220
butterfly, 199, *30*
car, 220
Carlton, 199, *30*
Cecil, *30*
charlotte, 142, *14*
Chesterfield, *28*
chicken, 93, 149, *14*
conch, *14*
Cornwall, 199, *30*
core moulds, 99, *8*
crayfish, 97, *30*
dolphin, *14*
dome, *14, 31*
doric, *14*
Edinburgh, *33*
egg, 61, 69, 77, 78, 90, 91, 93, 155, 169, 170, *6, 22*
filbert, *14*
fish, 93, 95, 96, 148, 176, 196, 212, *6, 9, 28*
fluted, 92, 96, 99, 101, 102, 149, 166, 171, 195, 196, 199, 200, 203, 211, 220, *28, 30, 31, 33, 34*
French, 199, *30*
fruit, 91, 92, 99, 142, 165, 171, 172, *14, 25*

moulds, names of designs *cont.*

game, *14*
gothic, 196, *28*
grape, 96, *14, 25, 26, 28*
heart, 93
hedgehog, 93, 223
hen, 93, 149, *14*
hollow-centre, 149, *14*
holly, *25*
imperial crown cushion, 169, *22*
Khiva, *14*
lion, 97, 148, 176, 199, 207, *28, 36*
macédoine, 104, 111, 129, 171, *9, 22*
melon, 93, 96, *6, 14, 28*
Minton, *31*
moon, 93, *6*
national, 199, *30*
new gothic, *14*
new pine, *14*
old gothic, *14*
ornamental, 199, *30*
oval, *28, 33–35*
pagoda, 174, *25*
pig, 220, *39*
plum, *14*
pineapple, 96, *14, 25*
pine cone, *14*
pipe-and-pine, *14*
pipe-and-star, *14*
prince's feather, *25*
pyramid, 92, 99, 101, 149, *14, 25*
Queen's, 199, *30*
rabbit, 199, 200, 209, 212, 220, *30, 37, 39*
rib, 171, *23*
Ritz, 199, *30*

moulds, names of designs *cont.*
  rose & thistle, 102, 199, *31*
  round, 165, *28, 31*
  Sandringham, *14*
  Savoy, *30*
  scallop shell, 78, 92, 93, *3*
  sexangular, *35*
  shamrock, 102, 199, *7*
  shell, 77, 92, 93, 97, *14*
  Solomon's temple, 98, *7*
  star, 92, 93, 199, *6, 7, 14, 30*
  step, *14*
  steeple, 101, 149, *14*
  strawberry, 199, *14*
  sun, 93, *6*
  sunflower, 97
  swan, 93, 148, *9, 37*
  teddy bear, 220, *39*
  tortoise, *37, 39*
  Turk's cap, 92, *7, 14*
  well, *31*
  wheatsheaf, 97, 174, *28*
  vine, vineleaf, 96, *14*
Moxon, Elizabeth, 85
Neale, James, 102
Nelson, G., Dale & Co., 28
Neville, George, Archbishop of
  York, 56
Newcastle upon Tyne, 85, 93, 101,
  196, 200
New Zealand, 188
Norwich, 43
Nott, John, 41, 223
'Nutbrown' brand, 212, 220
oatmeal, 37, 38, 47, 48
Odessa, Russia, 47
Oldroyd, W., & Sons, 28
Oswald's Jelly House, 85
oranges, *Frontispiece, 40*
Orme, Evans & Co., 207, *36*

Orpwood, Joseph, 148
Paisley, 43
paps, Spanish, 81
Parker & Sons, 125
Patten, Marguerite, 212
Pearce Duff & Co., 30
Pearson & Co., 195, *28*
Peckham, Ann, 91, *5*
Perrins & Barnitt, 51
Petworth House, Sussex, 103
Pontefract, Earl of, 85
Poole, John, 103
Pountney & Co., 195, *28*
Pyrex, 200
Rabisha, William, 45, *3*
Raffald, Elizabeth, 24, 86, 91, 93,
  98, 104, *6, 9*
Reform Club, 155, 172
rice, 48, *41*
  flour, 49, 62, 81, 106
  ground, 43, 49, 126, 215
  mange, 49
Richard II, King, 22, 55
'Rizene' brand, 49
Roberts, Bertha, 188
Rogers, Joseph, & Co., 46
Russell, John, 55
Rutland, Duke of, 148
sago, 50, 215
St Kitts, 40
St Vincent, 40
Salford, Lancs., 24
salop, 40
Salopian Tin Works, 209, *37*
Sanine, Mr, 47
Scarborough, 101
Sefton, Earl of, 108
semolina, 47, 50, 51, 126, 212
Senn, Charles Herman, 177
Sheffield, Yorks., 46

Shelley Potteries Ltd., 196, 199, *30*
Sidney, Manduell, & Wells, pharmacists, 27
Smith & Matthews (late Eitel), 164
Smith, J. & J., Ridgeway, J., and Hipswell, J., 102
Smith, Captain John , 46, 51
Sowerby & Co., 200
Soyer, Alexis, 120, 128, 129, 172, 223, *24*
spinach, eggs & bacon, *5*
Spode, 199, *30*
Staffordshire, 92, 96, 102, 196
Surflet, Richard, 39
Surtees, Robert, 123, 148
Swinborne, George Philbrick, 25, 26, 27, 120
Symington, W., & Co., 30, 199
tacca starch, 40
Tahiti arrowroot, 40
tapioca, 40, 51, 52
Taganrog, Russia, 47
tarts, 76, 85, *3*
Temple Newsam House, Leeds, 103
Temple & Crook, 153, 164, 170

Temple & Reynolds, 153, 165
Theobalds House, Herts., *73*
Thevenot, Louis, 164
Tomlin's Jelly House, 85
Ude, Louis Eustache, 108, 112, 115, 123, 128, 223, *9*
Vickers, William, Manchester, 103
Vickers Isinglass, 26, 27
Viota Jelli-Crest, 215
Wales, 37
Warwick, 28
Wedgwood, J., & Co., 92, 96, 99, 102, 103, 148, 149, *7*, *8*
Whitaker, Mary, 24
Wileman & Co., 196
Williams, James, & Sons, 159
Winton Pottery, 199
Witton, Birmingham, 209
Wolverhampton, W. Midlands, 155, 176, 207, 209
Wood, A.R., & Co., 174, *26*
Wood, Ralph, 92, *7*
Woodforde, Rev. John, 101
Worden, Lancs., 86
'Working Kitchen' brand, 220, *39*
York, 89, 187
Yorkshire, 48, 96, 153

RECIPE INDEX

The Repertoire (chapter 9) has not been indexed and should also be consulted for jelly names.

agar-agar jelly, 38
almond milk, 60
  a fish pond, 95
  a green melon in flummery, 96
  gilded fish in jelly, 95
  hen and chickens in jelly, 95
  parted jelly, 60
  Solomon's temple, 98
  vyaunde leche, 61
  see also leach
[amber] crystal jelly, 67
amydon jelly, 39
apples
  à la Princesse Maude, 141
  apple jelly the Regent's way, 107
  apple, cranberry and apple mould, 189
  bavarois de riz aux pommes, 145
apricots, poached eggs, 191
arrowroot shape, 41

banana cream, 184
barley-sugar cream, 113
Bavarian creams, iced, 114
bavarois de riz aux pommes, 145
bavaroise, pineapple, 135
biscuit jelly, 41
blancmange
  a Roman pavement, 147
  edgings for, 147
  orange, 184
  oranges à la Bellevue, 131

blancmange cont.
  orange sponge, 193
  Patrick Lamb's, 81
  rice, 50
  sponge, 143
  see also leach
boats, chocolate, 218
border of rice à la Parisienne, 145
brandy
  claret and brandy jelly, 137
  Danish jelly, 136
bread jelly, 42
brown bread cream, 189

caramel cream, 113
cards, Anne Peckham's playing, 90
carnations in jelly, 192
carrageen mould, 43
Carrington mould, 189
Celestina strawberry cream, 130
Champagne, gelée de fleurs d'orange au vin de, 130
Chantilly, maltoise à la, 138
checker'd jelly, or leach, 89
cheeses
  fruit, 114
  infused,
cherry brandy
  a Roman pavement, 147
  Danish jelly, 136
  jelly, 136
cherry jelly, 110
chicken and pork meat jelly, 59

chocolate
 boats, 218
 cream, 113
 cream, *maltoise à la Chantilly*, 138
 custard, *timbale à la Versailles*, 139
 surprise, 190
Christmas plum pudding jelly, 194
claret jelly, 68
claret and brandy jelly, 137
clowns, 217
coffee cream, 113
coffee jelly, 111
coloured jellies, 74
consumption, an excellent recipe for the, 82
cornflour jelly, orange, 144
cornflour mould, 44
cranberry and apple mould, 189
cranberry jelly, 134
cream(s)
 an Easter [egg] dessert, 191
 banana, 184
 barley-sugar, 113
 brown bread, 189
 caramel, 113
 Celestina strawberry, 130
 chocolate, 113
 coffee, 113
 de printemps, 169
 fruit, 214
 ginger, 135
 iced Bavarian, 114
 Jamaica, 191
 jellies *en surprise*, 132
 lemon, 113
 maltoise à la Chantilly, 138
 marbled, 115

cream(s) *cont.*
 Mexican, 214
 mosaic, 116
 moulded, Ude's, 112
 orange, 113
 orange-flower, 113
 Pagliacci, 194
 panachée jelly, 133
 pineapple bavaroise, 135
 piramidis, Queen Henrietta Maria's, 77
 pistachio, 129
 tangerine, 135
 tea, 113
 vanilla, 113
 velvet, 192
crème à la genet, 113
custard, *timbale à la Versailles*, 139

Danish jelly, 136
Danziger Goldwasser, jelly *à la Victoria*, 131
Dutch flummery, 122

Easter [egg] dessert, 191
eggs
 an Easter [egg] dessert, 191
 in Lent, 69
 jelly, 78
 jelly eggs, 61
 to make a nest of, 91
 white jelly, 78

fish jelly, 20, 58
fish pond, 95
floating island, 105
flummery, 48
 a green melon in, 96
 Dutch, 122
 ground rice, 146

flummery *cont.*
    to make a nest of eggs, 91
    see also leach,
fruit, dried
    an excellent recipe for the consumption, 82
    Christmas plum pudding jelly, 194
    rice *à la Française*, 144
    transparent pudding, 87
fruit, mixed, jelly, 216
fruit, tinned, Carrington mould, 189
fruit cheeses, 114
fruit creams, 214

gâteau de rhubarbe, gooseberries or red or white currants, 134
gelatin moulded jelly, from cubes, 30
gelée de fleurs d'orange au vin de Champagne, 130
gilded fish in jelly, 95
ginger cream, 135
ginger jelly, 188
gooseberries, *gâteau de*, 134
grape jelly, 110
great dish of jelly, 78
green melon in flummery, 96
ground rice
    flummery, 146
    Spanish paps, 82

hartshorn jelly, 45
hen and chickens in jelly, 95
hippocras, jelly, 65
hominy mould, 46

iced Bavarian creams, 114
infused cheeses, 114

isinglass milk jelly, 23

jam jelly, 186
Jamaica cream, 191
Jarrin's clear jelly stock, 110
jellies
    en surprise, 132
    marbled, 115
    mosaic, 116
    of [pork & chicken] meat, 59
jelly
    à la royale, strawberries in, 167
    à la Victoria, 131
    carnations in, 192
    clear, 110
    Danish, 136
    eggs, 61
    hippocras, 65
    great dish of, 78
    mosaic, 140
    Mrs Elizabeth Cromwell's excellent, 79
    of flesh, 57
    on fish days, 58
    Patrick Lamb's, 81
    whisked (lemon sponge), 122

laid tart of jelly, 76
leach
    a white, 68
    checker'd, 89
    great dish of jelly, 78
    in the French fashion, 79
    of almonds, 69
    strawberry, 62
lemon
    à la Bellevue, 131
    cream, 113
    jelly, 110

lemon *cont.*

lemon jelly quarters, 75
maltoise à la Chantilly, 138
sago, 215
St James's Coffee House jelly,
86
sponge, 122
wine, orange or lemon jellies,
75

macédoine jelly, 104
maltoise à la Chantilly, 138
maraschino, cranberry jelly, 134
marbled creams, 115
marbled jellies, 115
marsala jelly, 137
meat jelly, 20, 57, 59
melon, green, in flummery, 96
Mexican creams, 214
milk jelly whip, 214
mixed fruit jelly, 216
moon and stars in jelly, 93
mosaic creams, 116
mosaic jellies, 116, 140
mould
    Carrington, 189
    chocolate, 190
    cranberry and apple, 189
    prune, 185
    ratafia, 193
    wartime (1918), 186
moulded creams, Ude's, 112
moulded jelly, 30-34
Mrs Elizabeth Cromwell's
    excellent jelly, 79
mulberry jelly, 67

oatmeal flummery, 48
orange
    à la Bellevue, 131

orange *cont.*

& lemon jelly quarters, 75
blancmange, 184
clowns, 217
cornflour jelly, 144
cream, 113
sponge, 193
orange-flower cream, 113
orange-flower water
and Champagne jelly, 130
jelly, 110

Pagliacci cream, 194
panachée jelly, 133
paps, Spanish, 82
Parisienne, border of rice *à la*, 145
parted jelly, 60
Patrick Lamb's blancmange, 81
Patrick Lamb's jelly, 80
pears, water lilies, 219
pig's feet jelly, 21, 57
pineapple bavaroise, 135
piramidis cream, Queen Henrietta
    Maria's, 77
pistachio cream, 129
playing card leach, 90
plum pudding jelly, Christmas,
194
poached eggs, 191
pork and chicken meat jelly, 59
pork rind jelly stock, 127
Princesse Maude, apples *à la*, 141
printemps, cream *de*, 169
prune mould, 185
pudding, transparent, 87

Queen Henrietta Maria's piramidis
    cream, 77

raspberry jelly, 67

ratafia mould, 193
redcurrant jelly, 110
redcurrants, *gâteau de*, 134
rhubarbe, gâteau de, 134
rhubarb and sago mould, 50
ribbon jelly, 89
rice
    à la Française, 144
    bavarois de riz aux pommes, 145
    border of rice *à la Parisienne*,
    145
    mould, 49, 50, *41*
rice, ground
    flummery, 146
    Spanish paps, 82
Robert May's coloured jellies, 74
Roman pavement, 147
roses, jelly of, 106
rosewater, Venus's clear jelly, 110
rum jelly, 111

sago
    lemon, 215
    rhubarb and sago mould, 50
semolina
    cream Pagliacci, 194
    mould, 51
sherry
    a Roman pavement, 147
    Mrs Elizabeth Cromwell's
    excellent jelly, 79
    velvet cream, 192
silver or golden web, 87
Solomon's temple, 98
Spanish paps, 82
spices
    [amber] crystal jelly, 67
    excellent recipe for the
    consumption, 82
spinach, eggs & bacon jelly, 90

sponge
    blancmange, 143
    lemon, 122
    orange, 193
St James's Coffee House jelly, 86
strawberry
    Celestina strawberry cream,
    130
    jelly, 108, 110
    in jelly *à la royale*, 167
    leach, 62
    strawberry, mulberry or
    raspberry jelly, 67
    timbale à la Versailles, 139
sugar, silver or golden web, 87

tangerine
    cream, 135
    maltoise à la Chantilly, 138
tapioca jelly, 52
tart, laid, of jelly, 76
tea cream, 113
tea jelly, 111
timbale *à la Versailles*, 139
to make a jelly, 57
transparent pudding, 87
treacle, Jamaica cream, 191

Ude's moulded creams, 112

vanilla
    cream, 113
    custard, mosaic jelly, 140
    custard, *timbale à la Versailles*,
    139
    jelly, 111
velvet cream, 192
Venus's clear jelly, 110
Versailles, *timbale à la*, 139
vyaunde leche, 61

wartime mould (1918), 186
water lilies, 219
whip, milk jelly, 214
whisked jellies, 111
whisked jelly (lemon sponge),
    122
white currants
    gâteau de, 134
    jelly, 110
white jelly eggs, 78
white leach, 68

wine
    claret jelly, 68
    Danish jelly, 136
    great dish of jelly, 78
    jelly hippocras, 65
    orange or lemon jellies, 75
    Patrick Lamb's Jelly, 80
    Robert May's coloured jellies,
        74
    to make a next of eggs, 91
    transparent pudding, 87
    vyaunde leche, 61